Parmenides, Plato, and the Semantics of Not-Being

Parmenides, Plato, and the Semantics of Not-Being

Francis Jeffry Pelletier

The University of Chicago Press
Chicago and London

FRANCIS JEFFRY PELLETIER is professor of philosophy and comput-
ing science at the University of Alberta, Canada. He is co-editor of
the journal *Linguistics and Philosophy,* and is the author of seven
books, including *New Essays on Plato.*

The University of Chicago Press, Chicago 60637
The University of Chicago Press, Ltd., London
© 1990 by The University of Chicago
All rights reserved. Published 1990
Printed in the United States of America
99 98 97 96 95 94 93 92 91 90   5 4 3 2 1

Chapter three contains a slightly revised version of "On Reading
'Incompatibility' in Plato's *Sophist,*" *Dialogue* 14, no. 1 (March
1975): 143–46, reprinted with the permission of the editor of *Dialogue.* An earlier version of chapter four appeared as "Plato on
Not-Being: Some Interpretations of the συμπλοκὴ εἰδῶν (259E) and
Their Relation to Parmenides' Problem," *Midwest Studies in Philosophy* 8 (1983): 35–65. Reprinted with the permission of the University of Minnesota Press.

⊗The paper used in this publication meets the minimum
requirements of the American National Standard for Information
Sciences—Permanence of Paper for Printed Library Materials,
ANSI Z39.48–1984.

Library of Congress Cataloging in Publication Data

Pelletier, Francis Jeffry, 1944–
    Parmenides, Plato, and the semantics of not-being / Francis Jeffry
Pelletier.
        p.   cm.
    Includes bibliographical references.
    1. Parmenides—Contributions in concept of non-being.   2. Plato—
Contributions in concept of non-being.   3. Nothing (Philosophy)
4. Negation (Logic)   5. Semantics.   I. Title.
B187.N66P45   1990   89-27650
184—dc20   CIP
ISBN 0-226-65390-0 (alk. paper)

For the women in my life: Betty, Cathy, Sophie

Contents

This book has been "in the works" for longer than I care to remember. My first interests in Ancient Greek Philosophy were kindled by Sandra Peterson, Montgomery Furth, and Frank Lewis in the late 1960's when I was a graduate student at UCLA. I wrote a paper on Plato's *Sophist* as an answer to Parmenides, and received extensive comments from Peterson on it. A few more attempts at rewriting, now under the guidance of both Peterson and Lewis, generated what might be called an ancestor of chapters 2 and 4. The demands of a new job in 1971 forced me to lay the manuscript aside, and in any case my immediate academic interests were drawn to linguistics. In 1975–76 I took a study leave at the University of Texas, and got back to writing on Plato due to the encouragement of Alexander Mourelatos. Most of chapters 1, 2, 3, and 4 were done at this time. Correspondence with Frank Lewis and Julius Moravcsik forced me to alter many of the positions I had taken in this version, and Lewis showed me some unpublished manuscripts of his own on the topic which in turn deeply influenced my thinking about the whole topic. This latter led to a draft of the present chapter 5, which in turn underwent careful scrutiny by Alan Code, Richard Bosley, Roger Shiner, Mohan Matthen, and Susan Haley. They convinced me that much more needed to be done, and (discouraged) I set the manuscript aside—and in any case I had become more interested in Computer Science. A time release grant from the University of Alberta in 1980 plus a Social Sciences and Humanities Research Council Grant in 1981 made it possible for me to return to my manuscript. Another entire draft was written of chapter 4, and the SSHRC Grant allowed me to hire Joanne Freed, research assistant extraordinaire, to investigate more carefully the topics discussed in chapter 5. But once again the manuscript was set aside, until my Study Leave of 1987–88 which was spent at Australia National University. I wish to thank Frank Jackson (Philosophy, RSSS) and Zorba McRobbie (Automated Reasoning Project, RSSS) for their hospitality and for providing a pleasant opportunity to work on the manuscript. Sincere thanks are due also to Frances Redrup for typing services there. I should also point out that detailed comments, especially on the issues of chapter 5, were provided me by Roger Shiner and Frank Lewis. Their constant probing caused many revisions, and I believe the result is much better for it. Thanks also again to Mohan Matthen for many general discussions concerning Parmenides and Plato.

Versions of portions of this book have been read at: University of Alberta, University of Texas, Australia National University, University of Western Australia, and University of Rochester. Thanks are extended to the audiences at these universities, and also to the anonymous reviewers for University of Chicago Press who made many valuable suggestions.

As the title indicates, this is a book about Plato's response to Parmenides, as put forward in Plato's dialogue, the *Sophist*. But it would be a mistake to think that the difficulties raised by Parmenides and Plato's response are merely of antiquarian interest, for many of the same problems emerge in modern discussions of predication and (especially) of mental representation of natural-language statements. The intricacies and difficulties involved in giving a coherent account of Plato's position will be familiar to scholars in the field of ancient Greek philosophy, as will be the general philosophic difficulty to which Plato is responding—the Parmenidean problem of not-being.

This introduction is written to show to philosophers interested more in natural-language understanding and knowledge-representation than in ancient philosophy that the issues being grappled with by Plato remain crucial to these modern enterprises, and to show classical philosophers that many of the interpretive choices they face have modern analogues in the choices that researchers in cognitive science make in giving an adequate account of the relations that must hold among language, the mind, and reality.

Parmenides challenges what might be called the "naive semantics of natural language." If, as this naive semantics holds, a sentence describes an event or state of affairs that occurs in the world, and is true when and only when that event occurs or state of affairs obtains, then, says Parmenides, there are certain sentences that cannot be true (on the grounds that they refute themselves). A particularly clear example of this—but by no means the only one, according to Parmenides—is afforded by "negative existentials": sentences such as 'Silas Marner does not exist'. If this sentence is true, then there is no Silas Marner, no state of affairs at all in which Silas Marner takes part, and therefore not the one allegedly described by the sentence. Parmenides generalizes this argument against naive semantics mercilessly (in the manner detailed in chapter

2), showing that it yields the conclusion that naive semantics can admit at most one true sentence (i.e., that all true sentences mean the same). Plato, I claim, recognized this consequence and set out to replace naive semantics as applied to ordinary language.

How can we modify naive semantics to make it immune to this argument? One answer, the undergraduate student answer, is that 'Silas Marner' denotes not a real entity "out there" but a certain mental item—an "idea." But surely that does not by itself answer the puzzle raised by negative existentials, Parmenides would say; for the idea of Silas Marner *does* exist and hence this cannot be what the original sentence was saying. Another answer, the graduate student answer, is to say that, ontologically speaking, there are more things than those which exist. This Meinongian-style answer might usurp the word 'subsist' for all the things that are—some of which exist and others of which do not. Then 'exists' becomes a predicate true of some of the items that subsist and false of other items. The history of philosophy has not been kind to this view, even when it is fully dressed with a model theory a la Parsons (1980) or Routley (1980). Parmenides, it seems clear, will have none of this: an item exists or it doesn't. If it does, then the negative existential is false; if it doesn't, then it is not there to be talked about—one can't even say it's not there to be talked about.

Plato's reactions are perhaps less clear. He does not seem to think that there might be two conflicting sources of intuition, the intuition that the use of a name presupposes the existence of a referent, and the intuition that 'existence' is not a predicate. Rather, like Parmenides, he locates the difficulty in the use of negation, and seems to believe that there is one analysis of negation that will simultaneously show what is wrong with the naive-semantics treatment of negative existentials and also of the other negative sentences that Parmenides believes naive semantics will yield self-refuting claims about—such as simple copulative negations (Plato's example is 'Theaetetus does not fly'), negative universal claims ('No man files'), and negative identity statements ('Motion is not Rest'). Chapter 2 lays out the Parmenidean argument which concludes that all these types of negation are self-refuting in the same way that negative existentials are. This in turn yields the overall consequence that any meaningful statement means the same as any other. At the end of chapter 4 I consider the question of whether Plato's general analysis of negation really carries over to negative existentials, and some further remarks about this are made at the end of chapter 5.

It seems obvious that any "realist" semantics program—any program that identifies meaning with "things that exist" or with "things constructed out of things that exist"—will have problems with negative existential statements. This holds equally of those who employ a first-order logic as a semantic language and semantically interpret this with first-order models (e.g., classical natural language understanding systems in artificial intelligence, or philosophers of two generations ago), those who employ intensional logic as a semantic language and semantically interpret this in a possible world setting (Montague Grammarians, for example), and those who allegedly eschew a semantic language but would rather try to interpret ordinary language in terms of events or situations "in the world" (e.g., situation semantics, at least of the classical variety adumbrated in Barwise and Perry 1983). The moral seems to be that one must adopt a Meinongian semantics or admit to the inability to treat negative existentials.

Parmenides and Plato would take this failure to be indicative of the more general disease of failing to understand negation. And without going into the details of the Parmenidean argument here, I will just say that if no satisfactory account of negation can be given, the rest of the argument (to the conclusion that all meaningful sentences mean the same thing) follows immediately. Thus, our semanticists must find some acceptable account of negation.

Now, modern theorists think they *can* understand negation—at least in contexts other than negative existentials. But do their theories really answer the Parmenidean argument against naive semantics? They claim such things as: a sentence like 'Theaetetus is not flying' might be given the representation $\sim Ft$, which is interpreted by saying that it is true (in a model) if and only if $[t] \notin [F]$ in the model. According to Parmenides and Plato, this is no advance in understanding; the 'not' of *not flying* has become merely *is not an element of*. Is there or is there not, they ask, an event or state of affairs of Theaetetus' flying (or, of Theaetetus' being an element of the class of flying things)? If there is, then the sentence was false, not true; if there isn't, then there is no "item of reality" corresponding to it. And so, just as with the negative existentials, the sentence refutes itself.

"Perhaps," you might be saying to yourself, "there *is* an event occurring in reality corresponding to our sentence: the event of Theaetetus' not flying." The positing of such "negative events" as primitives—not definable or reducible to positive events—has not been popular in the history of philosophy. For one thing (as Plato notes in the *Sophist*), numerical concepts do not apply to them. We cannot speak of *one* thing which is not, or of *many* things which are not, for we have no criterion of identity for what does not exist. All things and groups of things that exist are either singular or plural, but negative events are neither. The question of how many nonoccurring earthquakes are in Edmonton right now, or of whether the nonoccurring earthquake in Edmonton right now is the same or different from the nonoccurring earthquake in Calgary yesterday, simply has no answer. Reality, or so it is said, is determinate—but you cannot determine what something is merely by saying what it is not.[1] The upshot of this, according to Parmenides and Plato, is that we cannot content ourselves with trying to give the meaning of negative sentences by invoking negative events which do not specify what reality is like. I'm quite sure that they would say the same for a representation like: e_1: = <at l: flying, Theaetetus; no>, unless there were some further analysis of e_1 in terms of "positive" events.[2]

Since the "realist" semantic strategy fails to account for negative sentences, perhaps we should look at an alternative. A "representationalist semantics" would try to identify the meaning of a natural-language sentence with some mental structure. Just which structure is a matter of theory: "informational structure" for Jackendoff (1983; 1987), "mental models" for Johnson-Laird (1983), "idealized cognitive models" for Lakoff (1987), "mental spaces" for Fauconnier (1985), "mentalese" for J. A. Fodor (1983; 1987), "conceptual structure" for Schank (1975), to list only a few of the proposals in the literature. The underlying thought here is that a natural-language sentence will get represented as, or translated into, some mental item. In some of these theories, the mental item is itself a sentence (of another language), while in other theories it is a "frame" or "conceptual structure," et cetera. I will not here remark on the realist critique (of D. Lewis 1972) that such translation into "mentalese" is not real semantics (since it does not yield truth conditions), for the theories under consideration deny that such a "language-world link" should be accorded any particular primacy in understanding. Instead, I wish to focus on a Parmenidean/Platonic critique of such an outlook.

---

1. For further remarks about negative events and negative states of affairs, see Gale (1975).

2. Even Barwise and Perry admit that their account of negation only works for VP-negation, not S-negation. J. D. Fodor (1985) remarks that even this seems the wrong way to look at it: she believes that they are unable to handle negation in the presence of quantifiers.

Now, Plato is a semantic realist; indeed, he is a Platonic realist. Still, the method he pursues in trying to answer the Parmenidean objection to naive semantics can be viewed with representational-semantics glasses. Indeed, except for his insistence upon a final "linkup with the world," his method is isomorphic to semantic representationalism. Plato's method is to construct a "philosopher's language" with which to describe reality. This philosopher's language is to meet two conditions of adequacy (as we would say): on the one hand, it is to describe correctly a mental state occasioned by any use of a sentence of the language, and on the other hand it is to correctly describe reality. For Parmenides and Plato, there are not two separate conditions here; they believe that "what is and what is thought are one and the same," as Parmenides puts it. So, they think we can use considerations from either the mental or the ontological realm to aid us in the construction of the philosopher's language. The idea is that natural language is misleading in various regards: it embodies shorthand abbreviations and other *façons de parler*, and we are misled into incorrect ontological and mental suppositions on this basis. We therefore need a translation procedure from ordinary-language statements into the philosopher's language. As Plato sees it, the philosopher's language will obey naive semantics; all the puzzles discovered by Parmenides are due to his attempt to apply naive semantics to ordinary language rather than to the (ontologically and mentally correct) philosopher's language.

Put this way, Plato's philosopher's language strongly resembles a language for mental representation, as found in various modern mental-representationalists—except for the claim that reality exactly mirrors cognition. This way of looking at it means that those interested in constructing some mental language (or other format for describing mental representations) ought to take seriously the difficulties—especially the "logical" difficulties—that Plato finds to infect attempts to construct such a language. As remarked above, the occasion for Plato's construction of his language was Parmenides' critique of negation. It is therefore quite astonishing that modern representationalists pay no attention to these difficulties concerning negation.

Plato calls the referents of predicates "forms," which are entities that exist in reality and are directly apprehended by a mind. But we could dispense with this and just identify forms with a mental item of the sort representationalists advocate. Plato also uses the phrase *participates in* to describe the relation between an object and a form, when the object exemplifies the property named by the form. In a mental-representationalist version, we might call this relation "IS-A." Plato's position is that two things need to be done: give a general account of the possible relationships among the forms, and give an account of the particular relationship that confers meaning to negative sentences. In chapters 4 and 5, I call these "giving a backdrop theory" and "giving a correspondence theory," respectively. From the representationalist viewpoint these become the requirements (a) of specifying what concepts and relationships among them are necessary in order to begin having a mental language adequate for representing natural language, and (b) of explicating the specific relationship among these concepts that corresponds to a negative sentence of natural language.

With regard to the "backdrop," Plato proposes that there is a form denoted by most (but not all) predicates. (Some predicates, those that do not "carve nature at its joints," do not denote a form. Presumably they instead designate a certain interaction among forms. Plato's example is 'barbarian,' which means "not Greek.") Our representationalist presumably will also take this direction: there are certain simple concepts that are the meanings of some predicates, while other predicates designate a certain interaction among, or conglomeration of, the more simple concepts. Plato believes that certain forms, the "greatest kinds," will play a crucial role in explaining the organization of reality. Representationalists presumably think the same about certain fundamental concepts. Plato picks out the forms Sameness, Difference, Being, Motion (= Change), and Rest; and the first task, as he sees it, is to convince ourselves that these must be different forms. A representationalist might likewise pick these (and possibly others) as central concepts; and would be well-advised to provide a demonstration that they really are different concepts. (That is, demonstrate that the mental language can represent the alleged facts that they are distinct.) Note that this is not a trivial task: the concepts of Sameness, Difference, and Being are each true of the same things—namely everything. Everything has being; is the same as something; is different from something. Representationalists tend to assume that they can invent concepts at will, and that the mere giving of different names confers distinctness upon concepts. It would behoove them, I should think, to find some criterion according to which they could guarantee that the alleged concepts are distinct. As we have seen, it cannot be anything concerning what instances they have, whether one takes these instances to be "in reality" or "in the mind."

Many representationalists invoke the relation IS-A to hold among concepts. 'Fido is a dog' and 'A dog is mammal' get represented as 'Ref(fido) IS-A Ref(dog)' and 'Ref(dog) IS-A Ref(mammal).'[3] As many people have noted, these IS-A hierarchies in fact confuse two relationships: "being an instance of" and "being a subset of" (or "being included in"). In Plato's philosopher's language, these two relationships are differentially marked, or so I argue in chapter 5. Representationalists would do well to mark them differently also: 'A dog is a mammal' is a statement that entails facts about individual dogs, while 'Dog is a concept' makes no such entailment. In Plato's realist theory, all forms are at rest (= unchanging); therefore 'Motion is at rest' is true. But he also believes there to be a sense of this sentence akin to the representationalist's IS-A reading, which would say that instances of motion are at rest—and that the sentence in this sense is false. He therefore posits different relationships corresponding to the copula, and gives them different grammatical structure. Sentences like 'Fido is a dog' and 'Dog is a form (concept)' express the same copular relationship; and this is different from that expressed by 'A dog is a mammal'. The latter relationship is transitive, as the IS-A relationship is in most representationalist theories; the former relationship is correctly described as not transitive. Plato also thinks there is another relationship that should also be grammatically marked, "overlaps with," used to represent sentences like 'Dogs are pets' (= 'among the pets, there are some dogs'). Plato says that language becomes possible through the interweaving of forms, meaning that these different types of relationships among the forms is what makes possible our statements about reality. Similarly, a representationalist ought to hold that language becomes possible through the interweaving of concepts, and mean that his theory has sufficient structure so that all the different types of predication can be represented. So far as I am aware, no representationalist has even attempted to do this.

Representationalists would do well to consider these foundational issues in the construction of a "language of the mind." But it is not only these foundational issues with which Plato is concerned; he takes his overall task to be giving an account of negation so as to avoid Parmenides' objections. He realizes that he must find a specific "part of reality" that corresponds to a negative sentence. The discussion of the underlying foundation, the "backdrop," is geared to providing the necessary basis for this "correspondence portion" of his theory. Likewise, repre-

---

3. 'Ref (Φ)' denotes whatever mental structure corresponds to Φ.

sentationalists might try to use their "foundations" to try to overcome the Parmenidean objection that in their mental language any meaningful representation is the same as any other (or represents the very same thing).

It seems plain to Plato that if a sentence explicitly denies that an event takes place (e.g., as "Theaetetus does not fly" so denies), and if the language being used to say this is logically/ontologically/conceptually perfect, then there will be a logical/ontological/conceptual problem. From the realist perspective, since there is no such event, the sentence (perfectly mirroring reality) cannot be true. From the representationalist perspective, we need to show how the representation of this event differs from that of an event which does occur (e.g., "Theaetetus is sitting"). One way, of course, would be to posit a mental negation operator, NEG, and claim that the sentence is to be represented as NEG(Ref(Φ)), where 'Ref(Φ)' is the representation of "Theaetetus flies." But as Plato saw clearly, such a move is not a solution to the problem, but merely a redescription of it. What is wanted is an explication of NEG, not its miraculous invocation. Without such an explication there is no real answer to Parmenides' difficulties.[4]

On the whole, representationalists have not had much to say about negation other than to assume miraculous invocation of NEG. One of the few to say anything is Lakoff (1987, pp. 133–34), who points to three ways negation interact with "idealized cognitive models" (ICMs):

> There are three kinds of relationship possible between a negative and a cognitive model:
>   1. The negative is "outside" the cognitive model and functions to reject the ICM as being an inappropriate way to understand the situation.
>   2. The negative is "outside" the cognitive model, accepts the ICM as an appropriate way to understand the situation, and denies the truth of the foregrounded conditions of the ICM.
>   3. The negative is "inside" the ICM.
>
> A case like *Sam didn't spare me a trip to New York, he deprived me of one* has a use of the negative in 1. . . . A case like *Sam didn't spare me a trip to New York, he forced me to go* has the use

---

4. And in any case there is a special problem for such a representationalist in that there will be no account of the difference between "believing a negative" and "not believing a positive."

of the negative in 2. . . . Cases where the negative is inside
the cognitive model are often marked linguistically with prefixes like *dis-*, *un-*, and *in-*.

Much of this is quite evocative of some method of analyzing different
uses of negations; but none of it seems to touch on the question "What
is negation?" What is meant by rejecting the ICM? It seems to me that
representationalists ought to focus on the foundational issue of deter-
mining what *one* meaning of negation is, before going on to distinguish
among various uses of negation.

In chapter 4 I canvass a number of different positions one might take
on how a simple negative statement ought to be translated into the philosopher's language. All of these positions can be translated into a representationalist idiom. For example, Plato considers that there might be
"negative forms," so that 'Theaetetus is not flying' would be represented
as "Theaetetus partakes of the form Not-Flying." Plato's perception of
the ontological implausibility of such an analysis ought to be followed
by representationalists: they should find it implausible to analyze such
a sentence as 'Ref(theaetetus) IS-A Ref(not-flier)'. It is just psychologically implausible to assume that there are separate concepts for every
negated concept, concepts that are not in some way "constructions" out
of the positive concept, but are rather primitive and unanalyzable mental items.

A variety of other ways might suggest themselves as a representation
that is plausible to assign to a simple negation. For example, a nonidentity statement might seem to call for a special concept Non-Identity. Presumably this concept is not "constructed from" a concept of Identity
plus a general NEG concept, for, as we have seen, the mere addition of
NEG does not answer the puzzle. Instead, we are trying to build up an
analysis of negation—and one of our building blocks will be the (simple)
concept of Non-Identity. Plato in fact has such a form: Difference. In one
of the very few representationalist works to discuss the ingredients required for a representational language, Johnson-Laird (1983, p. 425)
adopts such a concept:

> A *monadic* model represents assertions about individuals,
> their properties, and identities between them. It consists of
> three components:
>
> i. a finite number of tokens representing individual entities and
>   properties.

ii. two binary relations, identity ($=$) and non-identity ($\neq$), either of which may hold between any pair of individual tokens from two different sets to indicate that the corresponding individuals are, or are not, identical. Non-identity is the negation of the identity relation.

iii. a special notational device . . . indicating that it is uncertain whether there are any entities of a particular sort.

This is all to the credit and good sense of Johnson-Laird. Unfortunately, he does not employ this in his account of copular negation. Instead he says (1983, pp. 423–24):

> Negation can be accommodated by a one-place relation associated with a model, or a component of a model; the relation is treated by the procedures for interpreting models as signifying that the model, or the component of the model, does not correspond to the relevant state of affairs. Thus, if a token is negated, the entity that it represents does not exist; and if a relation is negated, the corresponding entities are not in that relation.

One relation in the mental model here is the IS-A relation. Johnson-Laird's negation relation allows us to negate the IS-A relation, yielding such mental structures as 'Ref(theaetetus) NEG(IS-A) Ref(flying)'. This hardly seems an advance, and one might compare the objections I raise in chapter 4 to schema V there, in which NEG(IS-A) is called "the negative counterpart of relational being." ("Relational being" is the name given to 'IS-A' in Moravcik's interpretation of Plato.)

Given that Johnson-Laird had Non-Identity at his disposal, he could have analyzed a copular negation of the form 'a is not F' in any of the following ways:

(1)   For some concept G, Ref(a) IS-A G and G NON-ID Ref(F).
(2)   For every concept G, if Ref(a) IS-A G then G NON-ID Ref(F).
(3)   For every concept b, if b IS-A F then Ref(a) NON-ID b.

These have each been proposed as being Plato's account of the analysis of negation. (Respectively, they are schemata VII, VIII, and XII of chapter 4.) But as an adequate account of negation they seem to each fall short. For example, (1) would make contradictions true: if *a* is both an *F* and an *H*, then we have both of '*a* is an *F*' and '*a* is not an *F*' (since Ref(H) NON-ID REF(F)). Analysis (2) has the shortcoming of making verification unending, since to know that '*a* is not an *F*' is true we would have to check all the positive properties that *a* has. (3) has the shortcoming that it assumes the well-definedness of every class; in order to know that *a* is not an *F* we must first find the class of *F*'s. But the assumption that there always is such a class is contradictory.

Clearly an adequate representation language (or philosopher's language) must do better than this. Plato was no dummy, I claim, and his solution to the simple copular negations (schema X of chapter 4) is easily generalized to other types of negation—such as negative general sentences ('No man flies') by clever use of the backdrop relations. The final account of Plato's correspondence is detailed at the end of chapter 5. I would urge those interested in constructing an adequate language of mental representation to take seriously Plato's philosopher's language as a reasonable candidate. At least, it avoids Parmenides' objection to naive semantics, and it avoids the generalization of this objection applicable to representationalist languages. Furthermore, the components of the account—the "greatest kinds" and the relations among them—are all psychologically plausible.

One of the marks of a truly great thinker is that, even when one finds an underlying assumption to be incorrect or even wrong-headed, one finds that the background motivation and the steps toward a final solution of a problem can be adapted by those who reject the underlying assumption. Here, one might reject the Platonic posit of an ontologically independent "world of forms," and yet find that the same problems that adhere to the positing of such a world likewise adhere to theories that do not posit it. And many of the steps toward a solution will have to be adopted in any replacement theory. One might be even more radical and deny the realist conception of semantics as relating language and the world. Yet one will find the same difficulties in constructing a representationalist replacement that Plato found in trying to account for a realist semantics.

Perhaps cognitive science, as well as philosophy, is a series of footnotes to Plato.

ONE

Methodological Preliminaries

Philosophers who specialize in an area of the history of philosophy habitually approach the object of their study with one of three attitudes. Some would say, "The history of philosophy is explanation and textual critique." Others would say, "The history of philosophy is history with a special subject matter." And still other would say, "The history of philosophy is philosophy of a special kind."

The first approach, which I shall call the literal approach, views its tasks as exegetical in a very narrow sense. The historian of philosophy has as his job the explication of the thought of the historical figure, or of a portion of his thought (e.g., a particular piece of text), as it is manifested in the extant writings available to us. Writings exhibiting this attitude tend to be rather like sophisticated book reports in which the thought of the philosopher under consideration is explained in terms more familiar to our modern ears. The controlling question of such an approach is: *What did the object of our study actually say?*

The second approach, which I shall call the historical approach, views its task as the placement of the object of study in his proper historical perspective. The historian of philosophy has as his job the discerning of major trends and subtrends in "the history of ideas," and the showing of ways a historical figure fit into a trend or changed it. Writings instantiating this approach tend to treat (what are usually considered) innovative philosophers as basically unintelligible, since they constitute an initiation of a new historical process, and therefore inhabit an incoherent, transitional stage in the overall trends (see Ayers, 1975, p. 27: "History of philosophy is a department of history"). The controlling question of such an approach is: *What was the orthodoxy of the time and in what ways did the object of our study challenge it?*

The third approach, which I shall call the eternal-questions approach, views the possible philosophical motives, mistakes, and insights as the same at all times. The historian of philosophy has as his task the reformulation of the (archaic) language used by the historical figure in such a way that it is recognizable as the statement and attempted "solution" to a problem which will (naturally) be of contemporary interest. Writings manifesting this approach are particularly common these days; so much so that it is almost the orthodox approach to the history of philosophy. And given the modern predilection for finding interest almost exclusively in questions of logic (construed broadly) and language, writings instantiating this third approach find historical figures worrying about problems of meaning, denotation, negation, naming, and so forth. The controlling question of this third approach is: *To what modern questions could the object of our study be reasonably taken to be addressing himself?*

With such divergent attitudes on the proper techniques for pursuing history of philosophy, I hope I may be excused for considering these approaches in a little more detail, with one eye to showing where each is right and where each is wrong, and with the other eye to drawing the best from each.

The problem with the historical approach is that it gives us no starting point. How can we place a figure in his "historical context," so as to evaluate his contribution to the evolving history of ideas, or claim justifiably that he was a "transitional figure," without first having a firm grasp on precisely what his predecessors meant in their writings? In order to evaluate a philosopher's influence on the then-prevailing trend in philosophy, we need to know what that trend was. And in order to do this, we need some interpretive bedrock; we need to know by some method other than the historical approach what was going on at the time, for the historical approach is merely a temporary restraining action. Sooner or later we will need other types of reasons to justify a belief that one historical process is going on rather than another; and this the historical method by itself cannot supply.

One way to supply the information missing from the historical approach is to assume the eternal-questions approach. We may assume that the philosopher under study is interested in such-and-such a problem and immediately look for what might reasonably be taken as his answer to this presumed problem; or we may combine this approach with the historical approach, apply it to a predecessor, and look to our philosopher for his response. The problems with this method are obvious. Without further checks, there is no guarantee that the problem summarily assigned to our philosopher is the one he is in fact interested in. Furthermore, even if we are right in assigning it to a predecessor, it may very well be the case that our philosopher did not see the matter the same way. His answer to the problem might be due entirely to a misunderstanding of what the problem is. In any case, it is hard to believe that the thought of a philosopher can be discerned solely by what interests us or his predecessors, without reference to what the philosopher actually said. We obviously need some more basic method of obtaining evidence so that we can judge whether the philosopher *really* is considering the problem we think he is (or wish him to be). This information the eternal-questions approach cannot supply.

So the literal approach would seem to be the only one that can be reasonably maintained. Yet there are problems with this approach too. It is often assumed that there is little if any serious problem in discerning the meaning of an author's words. That is, some philosophers, classicists, and historians seem to believe that an author's *own* meaning (or at least what he said) lies somewhere on the surface, and that extensive excavation of his thought, cultural milieu, and philosophical preconceptions is unnecessary to determine it. In particular, such historians of philosophy are wont to decry what they view as the modern tendency of finding logic and conceptual analysis in ancient authors instead of the crude cosmological speculations they are truly espousing.

To some, it might at first seem plausible to take this literal approach in its entirety; however, there are many problems. Let us first consider a problem that especially bedevils the history of ancient philosophy: the Greek language and the condition of the texts. All workers in the field will admit to the difficulties attending the fact of the texts having been copied over and over by (sometimes) incompetent hands. Nevertheless, some scholars feel that their knowledge of ancient Greek allows them to make statements such as: "Aristotle just couldn't have meant *this*! The Greek language just cannot support such a meaning!" or "Such-and-such in Greek would normally be taken to mean so-and-so," or "Such-and-so is not possible Greek." Perhaps some of these claims are justified, but it must always be borne in mind that there have been no native speakers of classical Greek for over two millennia, and linguists have for years warned us that even gross linguistic judgments are often made incorrectly by non-native speakers, however fluent they may be. Even worse are the judgments made by non-native speakers who have never come into contact with native speakers. By the time we come to the rather subtle judgments called for to support philosophical disputes over an author's intended meaning, present-day scholars of Greek are in no position at all to make such judgments.

In any case, what a philosopher *said* is only an indirect guide to what he *meant*. And clearly this is what is of interest in the history of philosophy. There are various reasons for a divergence between what is said and what is meant. In Plato, for example, the medium of a dialogue imposes certain literary constraints: an author will not state obvious and boring premises of an argument, and the techniques of irony and dialectic often leave intended things unsaid and said things unintended. In the case of Aristotle, we might conjecture that various obvious claims were left out of his lecture notes. It is at least part of the job of the historian of philosophy to ferret out these omitted claims. And this leads to an incredible multiplicity of ways to understand our author. A cursory survey of the writings about any historical figure will show that some other constraints need be added.

This brings us to the central issue of how we can get at the author's meaning, given all the obstacles mentioned above. Obviously we have to start somewhere, and two places suggest themselves. We might first have some (contemporary) problem in mind and find something suggestive as we are reading our historical author. Or we might be reading our author and find that something he says suggests to us a problem (which may or may not be of contemporary interest). In either case the bedrock is something said by our author which, for one reason or another, strikes a responsive chord in us. Thereafter it is our job to discover whether any assurance exists that the author *really* had that problem in mind. One way to find out is to look at other things he said. But this, unfortunately, seems to lead us back to where we started: for how can we determine whether these other things are even addressed to the same problem? And even if, for some reason, we do decide that these new remarks are so addressed, what should we do then? How should we understand all these remarks together? Suppose they sound like an incorrect answer to what we conceive to be the problem, or like unnecessary premises in its statement. Are we then to say that our figure was talking about that problem but was confused? Or should we rather think he had some other problem in mind?

Similar difficulties attend to viewing the author's problem as an attempt to answer a predecessor. Suppose we decide he is so addressing his remarks—he may even say he is. We still need to know what the predecessor's puzzle is, or at least what our author thought it was. And that again leads us back to the original difficulty: what, exactly, does our author take to be a resolution of a puzzle, in general? Matters are even more complicated when the author does not tell us he is going to rebut this particular predecessor. Consider for example Locke's *Two Treatises on Government*. Just because *we* would have wanted to rebut the only influential political tract in existence at the time (Hobbes' *Leviathan*) if we had written such an essay then, this is no assurance that *Locke* undertook the task. In fact he almost certainly did not.[1] With Locke, being relatively a modern, there are some ways to help decide such matters (or at least make very educated guesses); with the ancients we are in no such posi-

---

1. For further discussion of this matter see Dunn (1971).

tion. *We* might have written against Parmenides if *we* had been Anaxagoras, Empedocles or the atomists; but there is no evidence that *they* actually did, other than the feeling of ours that we would have done so, and the fact that some of what they said can be seen as (imperfect) answers to what we think Parmenides might have meant. Not very good evidence indeed!

Many of these conflicting pressures in doing history of philosophy lead to the disease of precursoritis—a driving zeal to make certain figures in the history of philosophy (namely, those figures our modern commentator has studied for so long) become suddenly respectable by having them espouse modern doctrines. Usually these symptoms of precursoritis are present: (1) our commentator finds startling new evidence that the historical figure has been "misinterpreted for ages and falsely accused of holding such-and-so doctrine by almost everyone"; (2) the inability of our commentator to account for how all other commentators, both the modern and those contemporary with the figure, have read our author in some opposed manner (other than the condescending "Until recently, X's logical acumen outstripped that of his commentators"); (3) the overreliance by our commentator on unjustified quotations, taken both out of context and from areas of the text other than where the specific issue is being discussed (e.g., supporting a commentary on Plato's *Sophist* by quoting the *Symposium* or *Lysis;* supporting a reading of Locke on qualities by quoting the *Treatises on Government* or Book III of the *Essay;* or explaining Russell's views on logical atomism by quoting *Principles of Mathematics*); (4) the commentator does not take sufficient material into account from other areas of the work of the author in question (as for example, clever interpretations according to which Aristotle holds a doctrine of sortal predicates, Aquinas is an atheist, or Wittgenstein a dualist)[2]; (5) our commentator overemphasizes similarities and dissimilarities between our author and other authors or between our author and certain schools of thought ("Locke is an empiricist and so must believe such-and-such"); (6) our commentator has an overabundance of 'admittedly X says conflicting things about this' or 'not everything X says about this squares well with my account', and not then going on to say why the particular quotations selected are the ones to be taken seriously.

I wish to invoke some principles that will help select some reasonably

2. The Wittgenstein example is from Woozley's introduction to his edition of Locke's *Essay* (Woozley 1964, p. 35 n); the Aquinas example is from Ayers (1975, p. 3). Both Woozley and Ayers are using the examples to make the same point I am making.

small number from all the possible understandings of the historical figure on a given problem, attempting to assign them an order of preference. Some may find this unsatisfactory, since it recognizes an indeterminancy of interpretation—that there is no guaranteed-to-be-true interpretation (or any absolutely impossible interpretation) but only a range of more and more plausible interpretations. But I hope that the preceding comments have made the alternative, absolutist position less attractive, and made the indeterminacy position seem plausible.

In all these principles, principles I call *generosity of interpretation*, it must be kept in mind that they have a *ceteris paribus* clause: they can all be overridden by other principles.

1. The problem attributed must be interesting to us; if not, there must be some independent way to explain why it was interesting to our author.
2. The problem attributed must plausibly be understood from what is said. Not all premises of an argument (e.g.) must be stated, but if any crucial one is missing, reasons for its absence must be adduced.
3. If an argument is attributed to an author, it should be relevant. That is, it should further an already-started train of thought or, if directed against some other position, it should have the effect of showing that a crucial argument for that position is invalid or unsound.
4. If an argument is attributed to an author, it should be valid (missing premises to be supplied).
5. Anything supplied for an author (as described in statement 4) should be plausible to us; if not, reasons should be given for supposing the author found it to be plausible.
6. If an argument with a (to us) unacceptable conclusion is attributed to an author, fault should be found with the missing premises (as supplied in accordance with statements 4 and 5), and an explanation given as to why the author omitted them, and why he believed them, even though they are false.
7. If an author gives an argument, a reconstruction of the argument must make use of all stated premises.[3]
8. What is attributed to an author in one part of his writings should not overtly conflict with his other pronouncements, unless other

3. This condition would rule out, for example, a reconstruction of Plato's third-man argument, in which two of the four premises contradict, and hence the conclusion follows from them alone. A better reconstruction would not have this feature. Of course, there might be independent reasons for thinking that Plato believed the contradictory statements; but that can't be what he had in mind when presenting the argument.

convincing evidence can be adduced to show he changed his mind.

Lest these principles take us too far along the track of making our object of study an anachronism, let us add this as a corrective.

9.   Precursoritis (and its symptoms) are to be avoided.

I hope, in the essay which follows, to have violated none of these principles of generosity of interpretation and not to have evinced symptoms of precursoritis. And I hope to have picked out the most plausible interpretation of the central portion of Plato's *Sophist*.[4]

4. For further reflections on the methodology of history of philosophy, one should consult Frede's excellent work (1987). Although I disagree with some of Frede's views, there is much in this work that repays careful reading. Frede is, after all, one of the premier historians of ancient philosophy, and his views on the art of history of philosophy are bound to be of interest. For a somewhat different view of the subject, forcefully presented, see Ayers (1975).

T W O

Parmenides' Problem

□

The most intriguing of all the things said in the *Sophist*, in my opinion, is this remark at 259E5–6: "Any discourse we can have owes its existence to the interweaving of the forms with one another."[1] I take this to be the central conclusion of the *Sophist* as a whole.

What is this interweaving? Why is it important to discourse? What argument against the possibility of discourse could Plato ever have had in mind that this interweaving of forms is supposed to solve? And how does it solve whatever problem Plato finds? These are the central questions which any interpretation of the *Sophist* must answer.

It is not easy to answer these questions simply on a reading of the *Sophist*. For example, Plato has only used the term συμπλοκή twice prior to this conclusion, and neither of these contexts are explanatory as to its meaning (or even to giving a straightforward example).[2]

> STRANGER: Then that which we call a likeness, while not really being, really is?
>
> THEAETETUS: It does seem that not being is interwoven with being in some such way. (240B–C)
>
> STRANGER: Certain later muses of Ionia and Sicily perceived that it was safer to interweave the two accounts, and say that being is both one and many. (242D–E)

Neither of the two times συμπλοκή is used after 259E supplies us with an adequate understanding either, for in these cases interweaving is a relation that holds between kinds of words, not among the forms.[3]

---

1. διὰ γὰρ τὴν ἀλλήλων τῶν εἰδῶν ουμπλοκὴν ὁ λόγος γέγονεν ἡμῖν.

2. In the main, the translations from the *Sophist* follow Cornford (1935), although I have on various occasions, especially in the more technical discussion of chapter 5, departed from his version. With respect to the present text, there are some textual problems with the Stranger's speech at 240B7, but none with Theaetetus', where συμπλοκή occurs: Θεα: Κινδυνεύει τοιαύτην τινὰ πεπλέχθαι συμπλοκὴν τὸ μὴ ὂν τῷ ὄντι, . . . (240C1).

3. I translate ῥήματα as "verbs" and ὀνόματα as "names" (perhaps unjustifiably). The point, in any case, is that they aren't forms (εἴδη), and that is all I'm arguing for here. In the second quote, the referent of the subject is ambiguous. It could be the person making the statement 'A man learns' or it could be the statement itself. The point will rise again in discussion of Bluck in chap. 4, below.

ΞΕ: τότε δ' ἥρμοσεν τε καὶ λόγος ἐγένετο εὐθὺς ἡ πρώτη συμπλοκή, . . . (262C6)

ΞΕ: καὶ οὐκ ὀνομάζει μόνον ἀλλά τι περαίνει, συμπλέκων τὰ ῥήματα τοῖς ὀνόμασι. (262D3–4)

There is also a use of συμπλέξαντες at 268C5 in what appears to be an idiom ("wrap up the whole story from beginning to end"). Variants of συμπλοκή can be found in the following places, none of which are a weaving together of εἴδη. I detect seven clearly nontechnical

STRANGER: Once you do this [combine "verbs" with "names"], they fit together and their minimal interweaving is a statement, . . . (262C7)

STRANGER: . . . it [the statement; or, *he* the maker of the statement] does not merely name, but rather gets somewhere by interweaving "verbs" with "names." (262D5)

About the only thing that is clear is that Plato is in some way or other talking about Parmenides in this dialogue. There are various places where Plato explicitly says that Parmenides is the opponent, but one of the most important ones for my purposes is 258C–D:

STRANGER: . . . in our disobeying Parmenides, we have gone further than the limit set by his prohibition. . . . In proceeding along in our search, we have shown him things which he forbade us even to examine. . . . He says, you know, "Never shall this be proved: that not-being is; Nay, keep your thoughts from this way of inquiry." . . . Whereas we have not merely pointed out that what is not, is; but also we have shown what the character of not being is.

With this statement immediately before the passage at 259E, it seems to me entirely reasonable to conclude that Plato took himself to be refuting a Parmenidean argument to the effect that discourse is not possible, and that this argument turned on "not-being." And it also seems clear that Plato's refutation of the argument depended upon having forms interweave with one another. That Plato thought this is, I believe, also borne out by *Parmenides* 135B–C where these words are put (significantly, it seems to me) in the mouth of the character Parmenides:

PARMENIDES: If a man refuses to admit that the forms of things are, . . . he will completely destroy the significance of all discourse.[4]

---

meanings: *Polit.* 305E, 306A, 311B, where the art of fitting human arts together is being discussed; *Sym.* 191A, 191C, 192A, *Laws* 833A, *Epistle VI* 323B, where the talk is of people embracing; *Sym.* 202E, about the combining of the human with the divine; *Tim.* 80C, 83D, about the interaction of physical principles; *Laws* 935C, a description of being in the grips of a habit. Besides the occurrences in the *Sophist,* the following might reasonably be taken as technical uses: *Polit.* 278B, a combination of letters to form words; *Theaet.* 202B, combining names to form a description; *Rep.* 533C, the combining of premises to form a conclusion.

4. While we don't here have mention of συμπλοκή, the sentiment is remarkably similar to 259E. It is rather as if Plato in the *Parmenides* recognized the problem posed by Parmenides, but couldn't yet see how to solve it (except, of course, that somehow the forms will

So it might seem reasonable to turn to Parmenides in order to find the argument Plato was so concerned to refute but which we cannot easily identify in the *Sophist*. Unfortunately, the Parmenidean fragments are themselves very opaque, indeed perhaps more so than the *Sophist*, and have been given a number of interpretations. But we are not quite back where we started, for we know (by the principles of generosity of interpretation) that we should favor an interpretation of Parmenides that attributes to him some argument with the conclusion that meaningful discourse is impossible, and an interpretation of Plato that will show a weakness in this argument. So, ideally what we should do is line up all interpretations of Parmenides that attribute to him such an argument, line up all interpretations of Plato that show him to be refuting some such argument, and then try to pair up argument and rebuttal in the appropriate way. Finding such a pair would lend enormous weight to the plausibility of the interpretations of *both* Parmenides and Plato; if more than one such pair can be found, others of the principles of generosity of interpretation need to be invoked to decide which is the better interpretation pair (or perhaps a wider "historical context" should be called upon for help).

So, as I see the task before us, it is (1) to ferret out all the textually possible interpretations of Parmenides, (2) to consider only those interpretations which accord him an appropriate sort of argument (to the conclusion that meaningful discourse is not possible), (3) to line up all interpretations of Plato which accord to him an attempt to answer an argument of this type,[5] (4) to rule out those which attribute to Plato a "bad" solution (whether they be bad because they don't show the Parmenidean argument to be invalid or bad for other philosophic reasons), (5) to subtract all those interpretations of Plato which textual evidence from other areas seems to contradict, and (6a) of those interpretations left, to rank them in order of plausibility, (6b) if there are no interpretations left, relax the restrictions on a "bad" solution (according to (4)), but justify why Plato didn't see that it was bad.

---

help); while in the *Sophist* he thinks he has solved it. The similarity of the sentiments can charitably be interpreted as intentional on Plato's part: more evidence that he was thinking about some particular argument of Parmenides' which would take away all significant discourse.

5. Even those interpretations of Plato which claim to be attributing this motive to him cannot always legitimately be so taken. In chapter 4 I call these sorts of interpretations "nonstarters."

Now, I am not going to carry out (1) fully; in fact, I am just going to give one interpretation of Parmenides (but it is an interpretation which satisfies (2)). I hope that this essay will lead others who wish to give interpretations of either Plato or Parmenides to show how their understanding of the one fits—or can be understood as fitting—with the other; for it is only in this way, I believe, that an adequate understanding of either will be reached.

PARMENIDES' DIALECTICAL ARGUMENT

"We have witnessed," says Mourelatos (1979, p. 3), "in the 'sixties and 'seventies, in English language scholarship, that rarest of phenomena in the study of ancient philosophy, the emergence of a consensus." This interpretation is so agreed upon that "one may even speak of a standard Anglo-American interpretation of Parmenides." Mourelatos here is somewhat overstating the case, for there remain substantive interpretive differences among the holders of this standard Anglo-American view. Still, it *is* true that these views have a single upshot, and that many of the steps along the way to this conclusion are the same in the different interpreters. So I hope to present this "standard interpretation" as a plank that is likely to fit into an overall interpretation of both Parmenides and the *Sophist*. If the two mesh well, then this "standard interpretation" receives yet more support, and conversely, the present strength of the interpretation would support the account of the *Sophist*.

The standard interpretation of Parmenides focuses on "negative predication" and "false statements," attributing to Parmenides certain principles which he treats as premises to an argument that concludes with the impossibility of meaningful discourse. The further ontological conclusions for which Parmenides is infamous are then taken to be corollaries of this basic conclusion. The fundamental idea, then, of the standard interpretation, is to treat the Parmenidean notion of "not-being" as a description (or ontological correlate) of negative sentences or negative predication.

The particular version of the standard interpretation that I will develop is due to Furth (1968). This is, according to Mourelatos, one of the paradigms of the standard. I shall not myself attempt to justify the attribution of Furth's version (or indeed of any of the standard interpretations) to Parmenides—for such discussion, see Furth's article (1968) or Mourelatos (1979).

As presented in Furth (1968), Parmenides' argument is dialectical in nature. It imagines someone trying to present an *ontology:* a complete account of those things which this person believes to exist and those things he believes not to exist. Our ontologist is, unfortunately for him, giving this presentation in the company of Parmenides; and at various times Parmenides makes certain objections to the ontology. In the end, our ontologist is forced to admit that there is but one thing, and but one thing can be said of it. After presenting the dialectic, we are to go back and pick out the underlying premises that were used by Parmenides in the dialectic. When this is done, we can present a number of different versions of "the underlying argument of Parmenides." As I mentioned, the goal here is to emphasize this argument's affinities with the hidden argument in the *Sophist,* and so we wish to discern the conclusion that meaningful discourse is not possible.

Dialectically, our ontologist is seen as presenting two lists: the Beings and the Nonbeings. In the first list go those items he believes to exist. Now, it doesn't matter whether our ontologist is correct in this, for Parmenides is concerned rather to show that *any* such lists are contradictory or incoherent. Let us imagine, then, that on the Beings list we have such items as Socrates, Zeus, atoms, The Void, cows, Socrates' having a snub nose, atoms being smaller than cows, . . . Now our ontologist starts to list Nonbeings: Pegasus, Centaurs, Apeiron, Socrates' being handsome, cows being smaller than Socrates, . . . At any stage of hearing the second list, Parmenides is imagined to retort somewhat as follows: "Pegasus? You said 'Pegasus' goes on the Nonbeing list, so according to you there is no such item. So, then, what are you talking about when you try to use the name? Nothing, obviously, so it is not meaningful to use that name at all!" (We will ignore the "change the subject" rejoinders to this, such as: "It's the *idea of Pegasus* which gives it meaning." For Parmenides would merely reply, "Very well, if you think the idea of Pegasus is a being, put it on the Beings list. What I want to know is whether there is any *Pegasus.* If so, it's on the wrong list; but if not, then you are speaking of nothing, and speaking unintelligibly.") Similar remarks are made about such purported nonbeings as *Socrates' being handsome.* If the ontologist is correct, then there is no such fact, state-of-affairs, or event as the sentence purports to name or describe; thus it is talking about nothing, i.e., it is meaningless. (Once again Parmenides will dismiss "changes of subject," as for instance, this one: Socrates exists and handsomeness exists—that's what I'm talking about. Clearly Parmenides would say that Socrates and handsomeness then should go on the Beings list, but would demand to know what item it is that is claimed *not* to exist. That item, whatever it is, the item expressed by saying for instance that Socrates is not handsome, cannot be named or described since, by hypothesis, it does not exist.)

Thus we have, as an intermediate conclusion, that the ontologist cannot construct a list of Nonbeings. Also note that an item's being on such a list would correctly be described by some negative sentence. If the item were a name like 'Pegasus,' for example, the related sentence would be "Pegasus does not exist." If the item were a general term like 'centaurs', the related sentence would be "Centaurs do not exist." If the item were a complex nominal like "Socrates' being handsome," then the related sentence might be either of "Socrates' handsomeness does not exist" or (perhaps more naturally in English) "Socrates is not handsome." These related sentences would all be meaningless. So the first part of the Parmenidean critique shows that one cannot construct a list of Nonbeings, and that consequently, negative sentences (either negative existentials or negative predications) cannot be uttered meaningfully.

The second part of Parmenides' critique returns to the list of Beings, making the claim that the ontologist is forced to admit that there is no difference among any items found on the list. For if there were a difference, say, between Socrates and Zeus, then some true sentence—for example, "Socrates is not Zeus" or "Socrates is human and Zeus is not human" or "Socrates is human and Zeus is a god"—would have to describe the difference. However, we have just seen that "Socrates is not Zeus" is meaningless, and we notice that "Socrates is human and Zeus is not human" contains a meaningless part; hence, these will not do. So far as the third sentence goes, Parmenides will claim that the two parts are repetitions of each other. To show otherwise would involve having to show either that Socrates and Zeus are different (the beginning of an infinite regress) or that humans and gods are different (which starts the entire procedure over again). Thus there is, really and underneath the apparent multiplicity of names, only one existing object. Since all items on the list of beings are the same, concludes Parmenides, we should perhaps just use the name ἐόν ("it is").

As remarked above, from this fundamental conclusion, we can arrive at the further Parmenidean conclusions involving change, motion, coming-to-be, destruction, and so forth. For, with any of these concepts, if such an event were to take place then some negative sentence would be true, such as "This thing once was small but now isn't," or "This object now is here but used not to be here," and the like. There are, by the above argument, each meaningless—yet their truth is a precondition for there being such events in the world.

PARMENIDES' UNDERLYING ARGUMENT

Now, what does the dialectical argument presented above presuppose as premises? And also to the point, does it implicitly rely on a confusion of the 'is' of existence and the 'is' of predication? I will first present a set of premises making use of this distinction, and show that the argument (in its dialectical form) can still be generated. This is a *regimentation* of the dialectical reconstruction that was given by Furth.[6] And having this regimentation make the distinction between "types of 'is'" makes the argument sound better to our modern ears than not making it. In any case, Parmenides has sometimes been accused of presenting an argument vitiated precisely because of a failure to make this distinction.[7] (Together with this last claim is the related claim that Plato's solution to whatever Parmenides' argument is, was to make this distinction). Since, as I shall show, there is an interpretation of Parmenides which makes his argument valid no matter how carefully we distinguish between the predicative 'is' and the existential 'is', it follows (by the principles of generosity of interpretation) that making such a distinction cannot be Plato's solution. After this first presentation of the argument, I shall conflate the senses, show what the argument would look like then, and indicate why I think Plato wasn't at all concerned to make this distinction.

A good regimentation of the dialectical Parmenidean argument presented above seems to me to go like this:

1. For any declarative sentence, either it is true or its negation is true, but not both.
2a. The meaning of a sentence is the fact to which it refers.
  b. The meaning of a singular term (or a predicate) is the object(s) to which it refers.
3. Whatever ("really") is, can meaningfully be stated by true sentences.
4. There are no "negative facts."
∴5. All true, meaningful sentences mean the same thing.

---

6. This is not to say that Furth would entirely approve of my version of the argument. Note 14 of this chapter indicates some differences.

7. E.g., Kirk and Raven (1957), p. 270. This claim appears to be withdrawn in Kirk, et al. (1983), p. 246.

As I said before, I shall not give textual justification for attributing to Parmenides these claims as premises, but I do want to say something about my use of 'negative fact' in premise (4). What I have in mind by 'negative fact' is perhaps best illustrated by example: if it is true that John is not a cat, then (someone might argue—e.g., Bertrand Russell in *Logical Atomism*) there is a fact or state of affairs that exists in the world that makes this true, namely John's not being a cat. I take Parmenides to be denying this. Another (equally unilluminating) way of putting this is that the only facts in the world (i.e., the only things that happen) are things that really happen, and not things that do not happen (like negative facts). I suppose that a better way of putting this would be to say, if one has an ontology of facts, the proper way to describe the ontology is by a list of true statements which includes only those of the form $\ulcorner \alpha$ is $\Phi \urcorner$ or $\ulcorner \alpha$ is a $\Phi \urcorner$, and none of the form $\ulcorner \alpha$ is not $\Phi \urcorner$ or $\ulcorner \alpha$ is not a $\Phi \urcorner$.[8] The preceding discussion of negative facts may seem to have an undesirably modern ring to it, one that makes it unlikely that Parmenides could even have considered the doctrine denied by (4). After explaining how the argument runs from (1)–(4), our conclusion, I shall "fuse" the notions of 'is' involved in the argument and try to show why Parmenides might not need (4) at all.

From these premises we should obtain a denial of Plato's claim, that is, we should deduce the claim that we cannot have any meaningful discourse. Otherwise one might suggest that this was not the problem that

8. A word is perhaps in order about my use of quotation marks. Single quotes form names of the phrase inside, or are used for quotes within quotes. Double quotes are used for direct quotation and as "scare quotes." Corner (or quasi) quotes (that is $\ulcorner$ and $\urcorner$) are employed more or less along the lines of Quine (1951), namely, in connection with expressions of the object language, but in situations in which not all constituents of the expressions are definitely specified. Roughly speaking, the convention is this. If $\Phi_1, \Phi_2, \ldots,$ are designatory expressions of the metalanguage (say, names of German expressions or variables referring to German expressions) then the expression $\ulcorner \Phi_1, \Phi_2, \ldots, \urcorner$ is to designate the concatenation of the expressions to which $\Phi_1, \Phi_2, \ldots,$ refer. If, however, any of $\Phi_1, \Phi_2, \ldots,$ are not designatory expressions of the metalanguage but rather individual words or phrases of the object language, we first replace such words by their quotation names. For instance, if ϕ is an expression of German, then $\ulcorner$ schlafen $\Phi \urcorner = \ulcorner$ 'schlafen'$\Phi \urcorner =$ the result of writing 'schlafen' following by Φ; $\ulcorner$ schlafen $\urcorner = \ulcorner$ 'schlafen' $\urcorner =$ 'schlafen'; and $\ulcorner$ es regnet $\urcorner = \ulcorner$ 'es' 'regnet' $\urcorner =$ the result of writing 'es' followed by 'regnet' = 'es regnet'. Greek letters serve as metalinguistic variables, that is, they take object-language expressions as values (e.g., German, Greek, or English). Normally, alphabetically late Greek letters are reserved for taking general terms as values, and alphabetically early Greek letters take either singular terms or general terms as values. I sometimes use 'A' and 'B' as metalinguistic variables ranging over meanings expressed in the object language, and 'S', 'S_2', etc., as metalinguistic variables ranging over sentences.

Plato was trying to solve, and our discussion would be irrelevant as to which of the many commentators on Plato were correct. I take it that it is a sufficient condition for the impossibility of meaningful discourse that every true sentence should have the same meaning. That is to say, given *any* two sentences, either (a) they both are meaningless, (b) one is meaningless and not the other, or (c) they have the same meaning. If this latter is the conclusion of Parmenides' argument, then it really is an argument for the impossibility of meaningful discourse.

Now for the dialectical arguments using these premises. Suppose some person utters a sentence of the form ⌜α does not exist⌝ or ⌜α's do not exist⌝. By premise (1) either such a sentence is true or its negation is true, but not both. Consider the case where it is true: if the sentence is true, α refers to nothing and thus by premise (2b) α is meaningless; so the sentence containing α would be meaningless. So either it is false (in which case ⌜α does exist⌝ is true), or it is meaningless.) Suppose on the other hand the person utters a sentence of the form ⌜α is not Φ⌝. By premise (1), either it is true or its negation is true. Take the case where it is true. By premise (2a), the meaning of this sentence is the fact (or state of affairs) to which it refers, namely, that what α indicates does not have the property Φ indicates. But according to premise (4), there exists no such fact; hence the statement either is not true (and so ⌜α is Φ⌝ is true), or it has no meaning. In any case no sentence of the forms ⌜α is not Φ⌝ or ⌜α's do not exist⌝ or ⌜α does not exist⌝ can be true. Furthermore, this is not merely somehow a fault of our language; premise (3) assures us that if a situation is real (i.e., if in "the world" something actually happens) then *some* true sentence will describe it. But no true sentence describes such purported events. So there are ontological implications for all this also (namely the ontological implications that Parmenides draws concerning monism, as indicated above).

Continuing the dialectical argument, we now assume that the person in question realizes that he can utter no true sentence of the form ⌜α is not Φ⌝ or ⌜α('s) does (do) not exist⌝. Consider sentences of the form ⌜α exists⌝ and ⌜β exists⌝. Do these sentences have distinct meanings when α ≠ β? Well, if they do, there must be some difference in meaning between α and β (since the rest of the sentences are identical). It is, by premise (3), a necessary condition of there being a difference in meaning between α and β, that there be some true sentence which describes the difference. One such sentence might be ⌜α does not mean the same as β⌝. But we have already ruled out sentences of this form as either not being true or as not being meaningful. Hence, sentences of this form will not do to describe the difference in meaning between α and β. Another sentence might be, ⌜α and β have different meanings⌝; but if this is true there must be a true sentence which describes the difference (premise (3)). Since we have ruled out ⌜α does not mean the same as β⌝, we must find some other sentence. Possibly one would want to say ⌜α means A while β means B⌝. But *saying* this is not sufficient, since that does not *describe* the difference. Parmenides would just say to such a sentence "So what?" and the only replies to this are (a) ⌜α and β have different meanings⌝ is true, or (b) ⌜what A applies to is not what B applies to⌝ is true. Now, (a) cannot be a sufficient reply, for that introduces the precise problem it is supposed to answer, and (b), as we have seen, is either not true or it is meaningless. Hence there is no true sentence which describes the difference in meaning between α and β in the sentences ⌜α exists⌝ and ⌜β exists⌝. And so the two sentences have the same meaning (via premise (3)). Since these sentences were chosen at random, we can generalize to the conclusion that given any number of sentences of the form ⌜α exists⌝ they have the same meaning if they have any meaning at all and are true.

Now consider any two sentences ⌜α is Φ⌝ and ⌜β is Ψ⌝. Do these have different meanings? If we hold some compositionality principle like "the meaning of a complex expression depends only on the meanings of its constituent expressions" (plus the "mode of combination"), there must either be a difference in meaning between α and β, or between Φ and Ψ (or both), since the rest of the sentences are identical. But there is no such difference, since (as shown above) there is no true sentence that can describe the difference; and premise (3) says that if ever there is any difference, *some* true sentence will describe it. However, some (very stubborn) person might insist that even though there is no difference between the meanings of α and β or between those of Φ and Ψ, there still is a difference between that of ⌜α is Ψ⌝ and ⌜β is Ψ⌝, thus denying the above-mentioned compositionality principle. But if there is such a difference, some true sentence will describe it (still premise (3)). Following the pattern of the preceding argument, one cannot say "⌜α is Φ⌝ does not mean the same as ⌜β is Ψ⌝." And if one were to try to say "⌜α is Φ⌝ means A whereas ⌜β is Ψ⌝ means B," this will not help either, since it would imply that either (a) ⌜α is Φ⌝ differs in meaning from ⌜β is Ψ⌝, (b) A differs in meaning from B, or (c) even though ⌜α is Φ⌝ means the same as ⌜β is Φ⌝, and even though A means the same as B, there is still a difference in meaning between "⌜α is Φ⌝ means A" and "⌜β is Ψ⌝ means B." Now, (a) is just what we are trying to prove, so we cannot noncircularly affirm that; (b) implies (via premise (3)) that some true sentence will describe the difference in meaning between A and B—and either this has been shown impossible as above, or it reduces to the present problem; and (c), besides being merely the second step of an infinite regress, has the peculiarity of implying just what Parmenides wants—that ⌜α is Φ⌝ means the same as ⌜β is Ψ⌝. Thus every meaningful sentence of the form ⌜α is Φ⌝ means the same as any other meaningful sentence of that form, if they are true.

The next step is to show that true sentences of the form ⌜β is Φ⌝ mean the same as true sentences of the form ⌜α exists⌝, since we have shown that, within each of these two categories, all sentences mean the same, if they mean anything. As in the case of the arguments *within* each of these two types of statement, premise (3) is used to generate the claim that if there be a difference in meaning between statements, then there must be a true statement that describes the difference. But the only statement that describes this difference is equivalent to "⌜α exists⌝ does not mean the same as ⌜β is Φ⌝," and this type of statement has already been shown to be either meaningless or false. Hence there is no difference in meaning. If we now make the simplifying assumption that all sentences can be transformed (with no change in meaning) to one of these two types,[9] we arrive at the conclusion that every true sentence means the same as any other.[10] This was stated before to be a sufficient condition for the impossibility of meaningful discourse. Thus it is shown that the problem posed here by Parmenides stands a chance of being the one Plato was concerned to refute, a statement of his conclusion being at 259E5–6.

More Versions of Parmenides' Argument: "Fused" senses of 'is'

The above arguments were "dialectical" in the sense of showing an opponent, step-by-step, where his assumptions led him and allowing the opponent to try out various evasions along the way. But the argument can also be given without the use of a dialectic. Such a proof from these

9. It certainly would seem reasonable to Parmenides and Plato to say this. After all, even Aristotle did not recognize that polyadic predicates cannot be reduced to monadic ones.

10. What about false statements? So far as the above argument goes, there was no need to consider them; for premise (3) always enjoined us to find true statements, and not being able to do so was what generated the conclusion that all true, meaningful statements mean the same. However, as we will see in the next section (and also when we discuss Plato's Parmenidean arguments in chapter 3), there is a natural bridge from the impossibility of true negative sentences to the impossibility of false positive sentences. To put the point into a Platonic idiom, both true negative sentences and false sentences attempt "to speak of what is not."

same four premises can be generated as a reductio; this proof is perhaps less faithful to the actual argumentation found in Parmenides, but perhaps not. In any case it does show rather clearly the overall structure of the argument.[11]

(i)   If meaningful discourse is possible, then at least two true sentences have distinct meanings, say the sentences are S_1 and S_2.

(ii) S_1 and S_2 have distinct meanings if and only if there is a true and meaningful sentence, S_3, which claims that S_1 and S_2 have different meanings. (by premise (3))

(iii) S_3 is true if and only if $\ulcorner S_1$ does not mean the same as $S_2 \urcorner$ is true.

(iv) $\ulcorner S_1$ does not mean the same as $S_2 \urcorner$ is either false or meaningless. (by premises (1), (2a), (4).

(v) S_3 is not true. (by iii and iv).

(vi) S_1 and S_2 do not have distinct meanings. (by i and v)

(vii)   Meaningful discourse is impossible. (by i and vi)

As I mentioned above, the reconstruction of the Parmenidean argument which uses premise (1)–(4) perhaps does not accurately represent the real Parmenides. For, this reconstruction (in particular, the (a) and (b) parts of premise (2)) makes it appear as if Parmenides made a distinction between the "existential 'is' " and the "predicative 'is'." This is something I do not believe Parmenides to have done; instead, I put forth the reconstruction of (1)–(4) to show that even if the distinction is made, a Parmenidean conclusion is still derivable. Let us see how we might go about giving a reconstruction akin to (1)–(4) which does not make the distinction.

It has been noted by many writers that ἔστιν is used by Greek philosophers down to (and probably including) Plato in a way that we would call ambiguous between at least these two senses and the "veridical 'is' " (= "is the case").[12] The preceding versions of the Parmenidean argument show that the unacceptable Eleatic conclusion is not due to a fail-

11. This argument ought to be compared also to the one in Gödel (1944), n. 5, where it is used to explain why Russell held the doctrine of "incomplete symbols" with reference to his theory of definite descriptions. Gödel claims that if definite descriptions were to denote what they describe, then (given certain assumptions very like our (1)–(4)), all proper definite descriptions would denote and describe the same thing.

12. The most thorough study is by Kahn (1973). Kahn also finds other uses of ἔστιν: the 'is' is identity, the 'is' of being possible, the 'is' of being alive. Kahn, however, would demur from my presenting Parmenides as using a veridical sense of 'is'. The account to be given here of the fused sense of 'is', and of how it makes (what we would call) predicative statements appear to have the force of an existential statement, has also been argued for in

ure to distinguish these different senses of ἔστιν; but I think it nonetheless instructive to see what the argument would look like if it employed this undifferentiated, "fused" sense of ἔστιν. The "fused" sense of ἔστιν is supposed to encompass the sense of 'is' which means "exists," the sense in which it introduces a predicative expression (i.e., as a copula), and a sense which means "is true." What English word shall we use for this "fused" sense of ἔστιν? One possibility is simply to use "is," relying on an implicit ambiguity of the English "is." Here we would say 'Theaetetus is' and 'Sitting Theaetetus is' for the ordinary 'Theaetetus exists' or 'Theaetetus is sitting'. Alternatively we might use 'exists' for the "fused" sense; in this case we would say 'Theaetetus exists' and 'Sitting Theaetetus exists'. I suggest instead that we use the English expression 'is the case'. Here we use 'Theaetetus is the case' and 'Sitting Theatetus is the case' for the ordinary 'Theaetetus exists' and 'Theaetetus is sitting'. None of these expressions has quite the right syntax—but then, it has often been noted that Parmenides' use of ἔον also seems syntactically suspect.

(1'). Every declarative sentence either is the case or its negation is the case, but not both.
(2'). The meaning of any linguistic item is: what is the case with reference to it.
(3'). What is the case, can be stated by what is the case.

Note that (1') remains very similar to (1); and that stating (3') this way makes it look even more tautological than (3). A (4') is absent for a reason I shall discuss shortly. (2') introduces the expression 'with reference to it', a very broad covering term which functions as a way of picking out that part of "what is the case" described by whatever the relevant linguistic item is.[13] Thus Theaetetus' sitting (or maybe: (the) sitting Theaetetus) is "what is the case" with reference to 'Theaetetus' sitting'. This shows why a (4') is not needed: given that Theaetetus is not flying, there is no Theatetus' flying (or, no flying Theaetetus) to be the case. So if Theaetetus is not flying, then the flying Theaetetus is not the case; and

---

Matthen (1983) as a way to understand Aristotle. He calls such items as *the sitting Theaetetus* a "predicative complex," a term I shall occasionally use below. On the question of whether Plato distinguished an 'is' of identity from all the others, see Lewis (1975).

13. One might note that Plato uses similar constructions, e.g., at 255A9, and 263B10, among other places.

hence by (2') the sentence 'Theaetetus is not flying' has no meaning.[14] Generally speaking, the move to the fused 'is' makes both predicative and existential sentences appear to take the same form, namely, the form we associate with the existential sentences. 'Cows exist' and 'Cows are large' both take the form 'X's are the case', a form that perhaps looks more like 'X exists' than it does like 'X is Y': 'Cows are the case' and 'Large cows are the case'.[15] It is probably for this reason that some commentators think Parmenides guilty of error solely due to the lack of distinction.[16] But as I've shown above, the argument can be made to work no matter how carefully the distinction is made; therefore, Plato is going to have to do something more than just make an "existential/predicative distinction" if he wants to dissolve Parmenides' problem. In the ensuing chapters, I shall show why I think Plato never even tried to make the distinction—he thinks there is another route that will legitimately get around Parmenides' problem.

14. This is not the line Furth (1968) seems to take. He presents the argument by distinguishing the predicative and existential 'is', and in this case the move made here in the text does not seem to go through correctly; for we would need to rule out the (more plausible sounding case of the) possibility of negative facts to take care of the predicative 'is'. That is, the move to the "predicative complex" makes negation operate more like a negative existential than a predicate negation. Just as negative existentials make it clear that if they are true then there can be no object for the subject to denote, so too does the predicative complex (a nominal phrase) when joined to an "is not the case" demand that there be no such item to be designated. But if we sharply distinguish predications from this more existential-sounding alternative, then it seems to some philosophers that there *can* exist a fact which makes it true. It's a negative fact. The present version of the argument, using the fused 'is,' operates differently. It "reduces" what we would call the predicative cases to what we would call an existential case. And the existential cases are automatically ruled out: if X doesn't exist, it doesn't exist. With predicative cases, when these are taken as indicating facts, the nonexistence of the fact F does not seem automatically to rule out the existence of the fact not-F. The conclusion to be gained from this is: either (a) the reasoning presented in these last few sentences about the distinction between predicative complexes and predications is invalid and we never really needed premise (4) in the original argument, or (b) the present use of a fused 'is', together with the notion of "is the case with reference to" in premise (2) hides an illegitimate ruling-out of some genuine ontological possibility, and thus a premise (4') is needed even in the case of the fused 'is'. I will not take a position on this, but will rather understand Parmenides' argument to be the one which does in fact distinguish existentials from predications.

15. I hope that this explanation of the "fused sense of ἔστιν" and its role in Parmenides' argument goes some way towards answering Barnes's (1982, p. 611 n. 22) complaint that Furth (1968) "does not explain the difference between fusion and confusion." The fusion here is in no way confused.

16. Kirk and Raven (1957), p. 270; see also Cornford (1935).

Plato's Problems

In this and the following chapters, I shall refer to the argument given in chapter 2, especially the version given in (1)–(4), as "Parmenides' Problem." In the present chapter we shall see that Parmenides' Problem can reasonably be taken to be what Plato is addressing his remarks to in the middle portions of the *Sophist*. So I shall be motivating my contention that the Platonic discussion between 237 and 264 can justifiably be taken as an exposition and rebuttal of Parmenides' Problem. It should be borne in mind, however, that (in accordance with the preliminary discussion of chapter 2) I would *not* say that this is the only possible reading of the *Sophist*. I merely wish to put my contention high on the scale of "likely interpretations of the point of the *Sophist*," and then rely on the fact that the interpretation of Parmenides is high on the scale of "likely interpretations of Parmenides" to drive home the superiority of this pair of interpretations.

Ideally, of course, I would like to be able to show that Plato had in mind precisely Parmenides' Problem as presented in chapter 2; it would also make our exegetical task easier if he were to say that such-and-so is what is wrong with the Parmenidean argument. Unfortunately he is quite vague as to the precise Parmenidean argument he has in mind, and as to what precisely he thinks is wrong with it. But he does tell us what we have to do in order to refute Parmenides (241D): We must "put to the question the pronouncement of Father Parmenides and establish by force that what is not, in some way is, and conversely and what is, in a way is not." And by 259B it has been claimed that these two doctrines had been established (it is allegedly explained between 258C–259B).

But the question still remains: what evidence can be brought to bear on the claim that Plato had what I call Parmenides' Problem specifically in mind? It is tempting, but I think illegitimate, to say simply that Plato's intended audience would know exactly the argument meant from the fact that Plato mentioned Parmenides. It would be much more satisfying to be able to show that Plato recognized that each of the premises of Parmenides' Problem somehow is involved in whatever he took to be the Parmenidean argument. This would give us some concrete warrant for believing Plato to be attempting to refute specifically what I have called Parmenides' Problem. I think quite compelling evidence can be found, (a) both in the *Sophist* 237–241 and in the overall structure of the *Sophist*, and (b) also in pronouncements Plato makes elsewhere about Parmenides and the general view he takes about the proper way to discover "what is." We start, however, with some discussions from outside the *Sophist*.

Parmenidean Arguments in Plato

Parmenides' Problem, as presented in chapter 2, has obvious affinities with another argument, the Problem of Falsity, an argument to the conclusion that false statement is not possible. For one thing, it seems that if Φ is false, then ⌜not-Φ⌝ would be true; but Parmenides' Problem shows inter alia that ⌜not-Φ⌝ can never be true, so therefore no sentence can be false. Furthermore, focusing our attention on the version of Parmenides' Problem using the fused sense of 'is' (premises (1')–(3')), we can see rather clearly the intuition behind the denial of the meaningfulness of false statement. If one takes speaking to be "spearing the object with the spoken word,"[1] and if the spoken words are false—i.e., if they are constructed improperly for hitting anything—then speech employing false sentences will be impossibly misguided. Similarly, if the sentences contain a negation—i.e., if they are so constructed as to be suited only to hit what is not there to be hit—speech will again be impossible. There is, finally, the fact about Greek semantics that 'what is not' (ὀυκ ἔστιν; μὴ ὄν) is indiscriminate in meaning between "what does not exist" and "what is false," in precisely the same way that 'what is' (the fused notion) is indiscriminate between "what exists" and "what is true."

Plato has earlier (prior to the *Sophist*) used this kind of argument. I hasten to add that, as opposed to Cherniss (1957, p. 341), I do not believe that the doctrines, "solutions," and general strategies or motivations behind these arguments to be the same as that in the *Sophist*. Rather, I use these as illustrations (a) of the fact that Plato was aware of *some* problems with false belief, and (b) of the continuing presence of some of the Parmenidean assumptions. I give here four examples. The first, from the *Republic* is not explicitly about *false* belief and the difficulties surrounding it, but rather a related puzzle having to do with the identification of the objects of knowledge with "what is." Thus, if knowledge is of what is, and belief is different from knowledge in respect of the objects of each, then belief must be of what is not. But can this happen? (In other places, where *false* belief has "what is not" as its object, Plato will use similar arguments. But here, *all* belief has "what is not" as its object.)

---

1. As Furth (1968) puts it. See his discussion, p. 265 n; and the discussion in Kahn (1970).

Republic V:478B6–C2

> SOCRATES: Does one believe that which is not? Or is it impossible even to believe that which is not? Think about this. Does not the man who believes direct his belief to something? Or is it possible to believe but believe nothing?
>
> GLAUCON: Impossible.
>
> SOCRATES: But the man who believes, believes some one thing?
>
> GLAUCON: Yes.
>
> SOCRATES: But surely that which is not, is not correctly called one, but rather, nothing.
>
> GLAUCON: Quite so.

The next example is from the early dialogue, *Euthydemus*.[2] Here we are given, as a requirement on speaking, that one speaks of one of the things that are—but then that amounts to speaking truthfully. (The passage continues with Ctesippus trying to claim that false speech is speaking of things that are, but not as they obtain. The discussion of this option seems to lead nowhere.)

Euthydemus 283E7–284D7

> "Why Ctesippus," said Euthydemus, "does it seem to you that one can speak falsely?"
>
> "By Zeus, yes," he said, "unless I am mad."
>
> "In speaking of the thing one's statement is about, or not in speaking of it?"
>
> "In speaking of it," he said.
>
> "Then if he is speaking of that, he is speaking of no other amongst the things that are except that of which he is speaking?"
>
> "How could he be speaking of anything else?" said Ctesippus.
>
> "And that of which he speaks is *one* of the things that are, apart from the others?"
>
> "Certainly."
>
> "Then he who speaks of that," he said, "is speaking of that which is?"
>
> "Yes."

2. My thanks to Russ Dancy for pointing this out to me. The *Euthydemus* translation is his; the *Republic* translation follows Grube; the *Cratylus* translation is Jowett's; and the *Theaetetus* translation is Cornford's.

"But yet he who speaks of that which is and things that are speaks truth; so that Dionysodorus, if he is speaking things that are, is speaking truths, and speaks in no way falsely about you."

"Yes," he said, "but he who says these things [accusations made against Ctesippus] does not speak of the things that are, Euthydemus."

And Euthydemus said, "But the things that are not of course are not?"

"They are not."

"And isn't is so that the things that are not are nowhere things that are?"

"Nowhere are they so."

"Then is there any way that anyone can do anything about these things, the things that are not, so that anyone could make them be when they are nowhere?"

"It doesn't seem so to me," said Ctesippus.

"Well then, do orators, when they speak in public, do nothing?"

"They do something," he said.

"Then if they speak is they do and act?"

"Yes."

"Therefore to speak is to do and act?"

He agreed.

"Therefore," he said, "no one speaks of the things that are not—for he would be acting on something; but you have agreed that no one can act on that which is not—so on your account no one speaks falsehoods. But rather, if Dionysodorus speaks, he speaks truths and things that are."

The last two passages are from *Cratylus* 429D–430A and *Theaetetus* 188D–189B.

Cratylus 429D–430A

SOCRATES: Are you maintaining that falsehood is impossible? For if this is your meaning I should answer that there have been plenty of liars in all ages.

CRATYLUS: Why, Socrates, how can a man say that which is not—say something and yet say nothing? For is not falsehood saying the thing which is not?

SOCRATES: Your argument, friend, is too subtle for a man of my age. But I should like to know whether you are one of those philosophers who think that falsehood may be spoken but not said?

CRATYLUS: Neither spoken nor said.

SOCRATES: Nor uttered nor addressed? For example, if a person, saluting you in a foreign country, were to take your hand and say, Hail, Athenian stranger, Hermogenes, son of Smicrion—these words, whether spoken, said, uttered, or addressed, would have no application to you but only to our friend Hermogenes, or perhaps to nobody at all?

CRATYLUS: In my opinion, Socrates, the speaker would only be talking nonsense.

SOCRATES: Well, but that will be quite enough for me, if you will tell me whether the nonsense would be true or false, or partly true and partly false, which is all that I want to know.

CRATYLUS: I should say that he would be putting himself in motion to no purpose, and that his words would be an unmeaning sound like the noise of hammering at a brazen pot.

Theaetetus 188D–189B

SOCRATES: May it not simply be that one who thinks what is not about anything cannot but be thinking what is false, whatever his state of mind may be in other respects?

THEAETETUS: There is some likelihood in that, Socrates.

SOCRATES: Then what shall we say, Theatetus, if we are asked: 'But is what you describe possible for anyone? Can any man think what is not, either about something that is or absolutely?' I suppose we must answer to that: 'Yes, when he believes something and what he believes is not true.' Or what are we to say?

THEAETETUS: We must say that.

SOCRATES: Then is the same sort of thing possible in any other case?

THEAETETUS: What sort of thing?

SOCRATES: That a man should see something, and yet what he sees should be nothing.

THEAETETUS: No. How could that be?

SOCRATES: Yet surely if what he sees is something, it must be a thing that is; or do you suppose that "something" can be reckoned among things that have no being at all?

THEAETETUS: No, I don't.

SOCRATES: Then if he sees something, he sees a thing that is.

THEAETETUS: Evidently.

SOCRATES: And if he hears a thing, he hears something and hears a thing that is.

THEAETETUS: Yes.

SOCRATES: And if he touches a thing, he touches something, and if something, then a thing that is.

THEAETETUS: That also is true.

SOCRATES: And if he thinks, he thinks something, doesn't he?

THEAETETUS: Necessarily.

SOCRATES: And when he thinks something, he thinks a thing that is?

THEAETETUS: I agree.

SOCRATES: So to think what is not is to think nothing.

THEAETETUS: Clearly.

SOCRATES: But surely to think nothing is the same as not to think at all.

THEAETETUS: That seems plain.

SOCRATES: If so, it is impossible to think what is not, either about anything that is, or absolutely.

THEAETETUS: Evidently.

SOCRATES: Then thinking falsely must be something different from thinking what is not.

Note that all these passages exhibit the close connection I've pointed to between Parmenides' Problem and the Problem of Falsity. In the *Cratylus* we see both an argument about the impossibility of saying something and yet saying nothing (= what is false) and also an argument about how it would be meaningless, "an unnaming sound." Note also that they (Cratylus and Socrates) do not object to calling a name or phrase true (or false), nor does Theaetetus. This suggests that Plato doesn't (and generally the ancient Greeks don't—at least until Aristotle's *De Interpretatione*—in particular Parmenides doesn't) sharply distinguish among (a) having a denotation (a concept appropriate to names and other singular terms), (b) being true of something (a concept appropriate to predicates and open formulae), and (c) being true (a concept appropriate to sentences). Presumably there will be a similar lack of distinction among (d) not having a denotation, (e) not being true of anything, and (f) being false. And the fact that falsity gives rise to "an unnaming sound" suggests that (a)–(c) are identified with meaningfulness, while (d)–(f) are identified with meaninglessness.

As we shall see, the failure to distinguish sharply these concepts both leads to various difficulties in Plato and also strongly influences his

thoughts on what a philosophically correct language will look like. In all
these passages we find the form of argument "to X meaningfully is to X
of something that is": in the *Republic,* this argument is applied to believing; in the *Euthydemus,* it is applied to speaking; in the *Cratylus* it is applied to saying; and in the *Theaetetus,* it is applied to thinking.

PLATO'S VERSION OF PARMENIDES: 237–241

In the *Sophist* we also have a series of Parmenidean arguments presented
by the Eleatic Stranger. I shall here give the five that occur between 237
and 241. In these arguments we can see at work the problems engen-
dered by the failure to distinguish sharply the concepts mentioned
above.

The first of the five arguments occurs at 237B7–E7. In outline, it can be
put (1) To say anything, one must either speak in the singular (τι), the
dual (τινε), or the plural (τινες). (2) What is not, cannot be in either the
singular, the dual, or the plural (i.e., what-is-not is neither one, two, or
many). Therefore, to speak of what is not is to say nothing whatsoever.

In his commentary on this argument, Cornford (p. 205) correctly remarks that "the phrase λέγειν τι is used in two ways. (1) 'to speak of
something' that your words refer to; and (2) 'to express a meaning' or
say something significant as opposed to 'saying nothing' or 'talking nonsense' (οὐδὲν λέγειν)." This would seem to indicate that the argument is
invalid due to some equivocation in premise (1)'s use of "speak in" (in
"one must either speak in the singular, . . .") between "saying something" (= speaking meaningfully) and "speaking of" (= referring to
in). Indeed, this is precisely the analysis given it by Wiggins (1970, p.
271) and Owen (1970, p. 241),[3] and as such it might be given the title
"the argument from idiom." But, Cornford continues,

> the ambiguity does not vitiate the argument. We are here tak-
> ing 'what is not' as equivalent to 'the totally unreal', 'absolute
> nonentity' and to that only. The suggestion is that, when I
> utter the sounds 'what is not', those sounds are meaningless
> noises: there is nothing whatever for them to refer to, and I
> have no meaning before my mind which I can hope to convey.
> How can I talk significantly or think of what has no sort of
> being at all?

Cornford has been widely criticized for this (admittedly peculiar-sound-
ing) "defense" of Plato (e.g., in Owen 1970), but given the discussion in

3. Although Owen also thinks the argument serves another purpose, see p. 244.2

the preceding section of this chapter, he is clearly correct. For, so long as the distinctions (d)–(f) of that section are not recognized, one will inevitably identify "speaking of nothing" and "not speaking meaningfully." (Of course, this is putting the Greek train of thought in reverse; it rather goes this way: οὐδὲν λέγειν has one sense, so there is no such distinction as that of meaning from denotation. From this point of view the argument would be called "the no distinction in sense" argument). That is to say, the "two ways" distinguished by Cornford of "using" the phrase λέγειν τι are merely different usages, that is, different occasions on which one could apply the (univocal) term. One does not say that the English term *person* is ambiguous merely because one can "use it to talk about" both men and women. A Greek would say that λέγειν τι similarly can be "used to talk about" speaking meaningfully and speaking of an existing object. The argument being offered by the Stranger—the "no difference in sense" argument—tries to show that, because of the peculiarities of one of the "uses" the other "use" must share this peculiarity. That is, both "uses" are illegitimate.

The argument from 238A1–C11 tries to establish that sentences that have 'what is not' as their express subject are meaningless. A sentence with the subject 'things which are not' implicitly attributes plurality to what does not exist, while a sentence with the subject 'that which is not' implicitly attributes unity to what does not exist. It follows that what is not cannot have *any* attributes, since it cannot be one or many of anything. It therefore eludes any attempt to refer to it. As Plato puts it,

> STRANGER: You see how it goes, then. Not-being itself can neither be spoken of, uttered, nor thought of; it is unthinkable, unutterable, unspeakable, and undescribable.[4]

Once again we see the easy transition made from the impossibility of describing it (nothing is *true* of it) to the impossibility of referring to it (nothing *denotes* it) to the impossibility of speaking meaningfully about it (it is *unutterable*). It seems clear here that Plato is (a) attributing these arguments to Parmenides (indeed, 237A8–9 is a source for Parmenides' Frag. 7), and (b) attributing to Parmenides the view expressed in our premise (2) of Parmenides' Problem.

The third argument, 238D1–239C8, points out that if the conclusion to the previous arguments were correct, those arguments cannot be mean-

---

4. ΞΕ. Συννοεῖς οὖν ὡς οὔτε φθέγξασθαι δυνατὸν ὀρθῶς οὔτ' εἰπεῖν οὔτε διανοηθῆναι τὸ μὴ ὄν αὐτὸ καθ' αὑτό, ἀλλ' ἔστιν ἀδιανόητόν τε καὶ ἄρρητον καὶ ἄφθεγκτον καὶ ἄλογον; (238Ψ9–10).

ingfully formulated (since they use τὸ μὴ ὄν in their very statement). Indeed, this is precisely one of the reactions one has to Parmenides' Problem (for discussion, see Furth 1968, 269–70), perhaps yielding further support for the contention that Plato was explicitly concerned with Parmenides' Problem in the form presented in chapter 2.

The fourth and fifth arguments apply the conclusions of the first three to specific cases, showing thereby that much (all?) of our ordinary talk involves the contradictions/incoherencies which had already been brought out in the abstract by the first three arguments.[5] The fourth argument, 239C9–240C6, asks one to consider how a semblance of image of X differs from X itself. The answer supplied is that X is real or true (ἀληθινόν), but the semblance is not. Since "not true" is the opposite of "true;" it follows that the semblance is the opposite of real. That is to say, it does not exist (240B7–8). But surely it is what it is: a semblance, that is, a real unreal. So although images don't really have being, they really are beings. As Theaetetus remarks to this, "It does seem that not being is interwoven with being in some such funny way, and that's most perplexing." 'Perplexing' here is an understatement, for at 237C7 it has already been remarked that "this much at any rate is clear: 'what is not' cannot in any way be applied to what is."[6]

The fifth argument (240C7–241B3) is another instance of the false belief argument. False belief is believing the opposite of what is, believing that which is not. So false belief is thinking that what is not, is (and vice versa). But any such analysis of false belief has to mention what is not as though it had being, has to attribute being to not being, which has already been agreed by Theaetetus and the Stranger to be "most impossible."

The last two arguments drive home the point that the Parmenidean arguments are not mere linguistic curios, but wreak havoc with much of our ordinary discourse. If the arguments cannot be defeated, then indeed we will be unable to talk, we will have "completely destroyed the significance of any discourse."

From our vantage point we tend to diagnose Parmenides' Problem and Plato's problems as a failure to distinguish sharply "denotes," "satisfies," "is true of," "is true," and "is meaningful." Yet we should be wary

---

5. Again note the parallel to Parmenides' Problem. The abstract, general argument for the impossibility of meaningful discourse is given (Parmenides' Problem proper), and then various applications of it are made (e.g., that change, becoming, growth, etc., are impossible).

6. ΞΕ. ’Αλλ’ οὖν τοῦτό γε δῆλον, ὅτι τῶν ὄντων ἐπί ⟨τι⟩ τὸ μὴ ὄν οὐκ οἰστέον.

of any such facile analysis, for the mere making of these distinctions will not automatically rid us of puzzles similar to the Parmenidean ones. As I mentioned earlier, the puzzle raised its head anew in the logical atomists' discussions earlier this century about the existence of "negative facts." And one need only consider works on "negative existentials" to convince oneself that the problem is still with us.[7] More than just the distinction needs to be made; Parmenides' and Plato's problems resist a speedy solution from the "make a distinction" quadrant just as they resist a speedy solution from the "distinguish the 'is' of existence from the 'is' of predication" quadrant.

We should perhaps, therefore, turn to how Plato sees the issue.

PRELIMINARIES TO SOLVING PARMENIDES' PROBLEM: 241–249

How is Plato to solve Parmenides' Problem? At 242C the Stranger remarks that Parmenides and all the others who have given a precise account of what is, have spoken carelessly. He carries on with a series of arguments against hem which go something like this: Suppose someone were to say that only two things existed—e.g., the Hot and the Cold. Now, he says, consider what they would be forced to admit about sentences like 'The Hot is' (exists, is real). Either 'is' means the same as 'The Hot' (in which case 'The Cold is' would mean the same as 'The Cold is the Hot', which is absurd), or it means something different. If different, it either means the same as 'the Cold' (which gives rise to the same absurdity), or it means some third thing, in which case there are three things which exist.

I do not propose to delve deeply into these arguments between 242 and 248, except to point out various presuppositions they all have in common, which presuppositions will lay out a framework within which Plato proposes to give a solution to Parmenides' Problem. We might note first, however, that Plato apparently intends these arguments to apply equally against his earlier self of the *Phaedo* and *Republic* (the "Friends of the Forms" of 248), although, as I shall argue in the next section, the "Friends of the Forms" makes for a broader category than just the earlier Plato. It is as if Plato had discovered that not only are there various internal incoherencies in the early theory of forms (of the sort already shown in the *Parmenides*) but also that his theory is subject to a kind of *external* critique to the effect that it has not been stated in a way precise enough

7. See, for example, Cartwright (1960), Hintikka (1966), Wekler (1970), Redman (1973), Donnellan (1974), to name just a few. See also the wide literature on "free logics;" and for a somewhat different vantage point on the problem of not-being, see Gale (1975).

to allow determination of what entities it is committed to and what relations hold among them. In the earlier theory, the Forms are posited as separate (χωρίς), and it is claimed that while particulars exist only in virtue of the Forms, the Forms exist "just by themselves." Now, this is not the place to discuss the Platonic idea of separation, but it is at least worthwhile to see that in the early theory, part of the function of the Forms is to explain why a sensible particular has the properties it does, explain how change amid sensibles is possible, and so on. The crucial feature of such accounts is that the existence, distinctness, properties, features, explanatoriness, et cetera, of the Forms are taken for granted, and these are then used for the explanation of the similar qualities manifested in sensible particulars. It seems not to have occurred to the earlier Plato to try to explain the existence, distinctness, properties, features, explanatoriness, et cetera, of the Forms themselves (compare Aristotle *Meta.* 990a34–b8, 1078b32–1079a4). What Plato finally discovered (and expresses through the mouthpiece of Parmenides) is that he needed to put names of Forms in the subject position of such questions as "Why is Φ thus-and-so?" Once one tries to draw out in detail the implications of questions of that type, the antimonies generated will convince anyone that nothing of significance can be significantly asserted about the Forms. The reason is because the theory has neglected to explain what the logical structure of statements with Form-names in subject position is.[8] Here in the *Sophist* that defect is to be remedied.

One of the presuppositions of the arguments of 242–248 is what might be called "the naming principle": a word names what it means (or vice versa). This principle has, of course, been tacitly assumed in many of the earlier dialogues, as whenever the "one over many" principle is invoked, or when an object is said to have the property F because it partakes in the-F-itself. But its employment here is much more direct: "if 'is' means something different from 'the Hot' and from 'the Cold', then there are three things which exist." It is this naming principle which lies behind the modern view that Plato's theory of forms is actually a theory of meaning—that every general term in the language names some Form which is its meaning.[9]

This portion of the text also apparently indicates that Plato thinks that

8. For a more extended discussion of this view, see Stough (1976) and Vlastos (1973).

9. This is not, as we shall see, quite Plato's view. It is only the general terms in the philosopher's language which have this property of naming some Form which is its meaning. In colloquial language, there are such terms as 'barbarian' which do not name any form (contra Frede [1967], p. 41). I argue this more, below.

the proper solution of Parmenides' Problem will be to "speak carefully" by means of a "philosopher's language"—a language which mirrors reality exactly. Such a language will, as we would say, wear its ontological commitments on its sleeve: it is to be obvious from an inspection of the language what objects exist, whether two purported objects differ, what truth consists of, and so forth.[10] It seems to be Plato's view, although it is not mentioned in this portion of the *Sophist*, that the proper solution to Parmenides' Problem will be to show that in the philosopher's language there are no purely negative statements—that the apparent use of 'not' and the like in ordinary language is some kind of "abbreviation" or "shorthand" for a more complex statement without negation in the philosopher's language. And finally, as we shall see, the puzzles about Being and not-Being are to be explained away as a kind of interweaving among the Forms—those entities which are named by the general terms of the philosopher's language.

THE GOD-SCHOOLS: *SOPHIST* 249D9–257A12

I think that the "indeterminancy of interpretation" thesis espoused in chapter 1 and reiterated in the beginnings of chapters 2 and 3 preclude giving a definite, hard-and-fast statement of what Plato is up to here in the central area of the *Sophist* (249–264). I further think that many authors have gone wrong in trying to take the literal approach and "lay bare" Plato's meaning by working their way, line by line, through this section. For example, I do not think that one can be assured he has had an adequate understanding of (say) the case against the "late learners" of 251A until he has understood the explanation of not-being (255E–259B); nor can one understand the explanation of not-being without first understanding the case against those who think all things blend (252D–E); the latter is not to be understood until the explanation of being has been made (253–255); but being and not-being go hand-in-hand so far as their explanations go. It is because of my view that all these parts are interrelated, and not to be independently understood, that I wished to break out of the interpretive circle by examining first the sections on the impossibility of not-being (237–241) and the difficulties with being (241–248) first. But, as I mentioned at that time, there is simply not sufficient

10. The properties a language must have in order to be a philosopher's language are not so clear as I have been making out. For discussion, see the Introduction of Rorty (1967) and Kaplan (1972), esp. pp. 234ff. The term 'philosopher's language' is suggested by Ackrill's remarks in his (1957) p. 208ff., and was explicitly used by Frank Lewis in his unpublished (1974). See also Vlastos (1973).

information presented in those sections to determine uniquely what problem Plato thinks he must solve. We therefore backtracked to Parmenides to find a problem to which Plato feels he will provide an answer. The "indeterminacy of interpretation" arises once again with Parmenides, of course, but perhaps we can use a temporary interpretation of one of Plato and Parmenides rather as a stepping stone on which to stand as we alter our view of the other. And then use this altered view as a further stepping stone to readjust our view of the first.

With this in mind, let us begin with a cursory reading of 249–255—a reading that hits the highlights and ignores the details, and one that we shall be prepared to relinquish as our understanding of the Parmenides/ Plato interaction grows—in order to give us a place from which to start.

At 246 Plato distinguishes "gods" from "giants" as philosophical opponents, and undertakes to examine what, according to the gods, the structure of reality must be like. The "giants" are those who believe "being belongs only to that which can be held and offer resistance to touch"; and it is taken to be a distinguishing mark of the gods that they believe in "forms," which are objects of thought and are non-material.[11] It does not follow that the gods are necessarily to be identified with the Forms of Plato's earlier self—only that to believe in the classical Platonic Forms is one possible way to be a god. This possibly explains why Plato uses the term γένη rather than the more Platonic εἴδη for his later examples: he wants to emphasize the fact that his discussion applies to all the god-schools. However, it is true that he uses εἴδη also—as in stating his conclusion at 259E. One therefore wants to ask, what is the relationship between εἴδη here and as it is used in the earlier theory? I claim that it is no more than this: the conclusions reached here apply to *any* god-school. Plato's is one such school. Of course, the different schools might also add further claims, so long as they are not inconsistent with those reached here. Thus, for example, Plato might distinguish his school from others by insisting that his forms are paradigms; and other schools might disagree. But so long as nothing in the *Sophist* speaks to one side or the other on this issue, there is no general prohibition that must be followed. On the other hand (as we shall shortly see), there *is* a general prohibition against the view that every form must exemplify exactly one property, and exhibit that property to the fullest extent,[12] for Plato makes

---

11. νοητὰ ἄττα καὶ ἀσώματα ἔιδη βιαζόμενοι τὴν ἀληθινὴν οὐσίαν εἶναι.

12. A claim that might be attributed to Plato's earlier theory, although it must also be admitted that the evidence for it is somewhat sparse and controvertible to many other things he says.

it a condition of any form-theory that the forms each be able to manifest various properties.

Ketchum (1978), and Teloh (1981) claim that in this section Plato only uses "predication of kinds" and not "predication involving Forms;" and they deny that these "kinds" are Platonic forms. In one sense this seems right to me: Plato is not *merely* presenting a challenge to the classical theory of forms, but to a much wider group of theories. And he will try to vindicate at least some of these theories. But it is incorrect to say he is not at *all* concerned with the classical theory. Ketchum and Teloh are at pains to make Plato in the *Sophist* consider such "kind predications" as *Whales are mammals*, and go from there to the claim that, since these cannot adequately be represented in his classical theory, Plato cannot here be considering the classical theory—that not only did he give it up, but it is no longer even a theory to be considered. I agree that Plato did give up many details of the classical theory, but I disagree that he has forgotten it and is starting afresh in a new theory of "kinds." For, the classical theory *is* a theory of "kinds"—but one that Plato sees now as incorrect (or at least incomplete). His goal here, as I see it, is to *modify* the classical theory so as to account for a new range of phenomena, not to jettison it. Prior's arguments against Ketchum (1980, nn. 7, 16) do not seem to apply to my construal of what the "forms" and their "friends" are. More about "kinds," and Plato's new "theory of kinds," will be given in chapter 5.

Among the views which might be held by the various god-schools, we can distinguish three sorts: (1) the view that allows no "mixing" or "blending" or "communion" among any of their forms; (2) the view which insists that every one of their forms "blends," "mixes," et cetera with every other form; and (3) the view which holds that some forms "blend," "mix," et cetera, with some other forms, and some forms do not "blend," "mix," et cetera with some other forms.

Plato quickly disposes of the first two kinds of views as applied to the god-schools. If no form has the capacity for combination with any other form, then every god-school is impossible; hence, no god-school can embrace this view of interrelations of their forms. For, as Plato puts it at 252A5–B6:

> This admission seems to make short work of all theories; it upsets at one blow those who have a universe in motion, and those who make it a motionless unity, and all who say their realities exist in forms that are always the same in all respects; for they all attribute existence to things, some saying they

really are in movement, some that they really are at rest. . . . And further, those who make all things come together at one time and separate at another, whether they bring innumerable things into a unity and out of a unity, or divide things into and combine them out of a limited set of elements; no matter whether they suppose this to happen in alternation or to be going on all the time—however it may be, all this would be meaningless if there is no blending at all.

So, no matter what god-school one belongs to, it is a precondition of stating one's theory that one allow "mixture" or "combination" or "blending" or "partaking" or some such relation among one's forms. To put the point in terms of the philosopher's language, it is an insufficient theory which merely has a naming principle (the having of which is a point upon which all the god-schools agree). If reality is actually constructed (assembled, distributed) in the way the theory claims, it must be so statable in the philosopher's language.[13] But in order to *state* one's theory one must (minimally) string one's names together; and, so as not to be merely uttering a list, one must combine these names into a statement. Now, since such a statement is in the philosopher's language of that theory, the theory must mirror reality exactly as the statement exhibits its form. The statement exhibits combination, so the theory must claim that reality exhibits it also. Thus the sort of theory under consideration here refutes itself. Or, as Plato says of the god-schools which subscribe to the "no forms blend" view: "They needn't wait to be refuted by others; their enemy is in their own house (as the saying goes). They carry within their own bellies a voice always contradicting themselves, like that peculiar Eurycles [a ventriloquist]" (252C6–9).

As far as the second kind of view on the blending of the form goes "even I [Theaetetus] can dispose of that! . . . Because Motion itself would be completely at rest and Rest itself would be in movement, if they could supervene upon (ἐπιγιγνοίσθην) one another" (252D4–8). It is not at all obvious how this conclusion follows, nor for what reason it is taken to be absurd.[14] For the time being, however, we can perhaps be happy with this brief account: if the form Motion blends with the form Rest, then some sentence of the philosopher's language, e.g., 'Rest is in motion' or 'Rest moves', will be true. But these sentences are necessarily

13. This is a statement of (one direction of) premise (3) of Parmenides' Problem: Whatever ("really") is the case can be expressed by a true sentence.

14. In chapter 5, at various places in the section, "A Plausible Story," I make some remarks on how the claim might be understood.

false (for whatever reason),[15] and so any such view about the blending or mixing of forms is inadequate to serve any god-school.

We are therefore left with the third alternative: some will and some won't blend.[16] The discussion now turns to the question of the minimal number of forms necessary to account for the two (connected) tasks which have been set: that of giving a general account of sentences with form-names in subject position, and (thereby) giving an account of not-being.

The conclusion of the section on the distinctness of certain γένη gives us five forms[17]: Motion (κίνεσις), Rest (στάσις), Being (ὄν), Sameness (ταὐτό), and Difference (ἕτερον), each of which have been shown (to Theaetetus' and the Stranger's satisfaction) to be nonidentical to the others. The "proofs" (254D3–255E7) of the distinctness of these γένη seem to be less convincing than simply stating the conclusions. We are told (254D7) that Motion and Rest are "unmixed" (ἀμείκτω), but that being is "mixed" with both. Immediately it is concluded that "then there come to be three": each is other than the remaining two. For the next proof we are given the principle that "anything we can say of Motion and Rest in common can't be either of them" because then "Motion will rest and Rest will move." Presumably the idea is that if Φ is true of both Motion and Rest, and Φ turns out to be identical with (say) Motion, then Motion will be true of Rest—which is impossible. (This is reminiscent of the arguments against those who believe there to be just two things, the Hot and the Cold. They have to admit Being as a third entity or else be faced with an absurdity such as "The Hot is the Cold.") Now, Sameness is "said of Motion and Rest in common" (since Motion and Rest are each the same as itself?), so Sameness is distinct from each of Motion and

15. Perhaps because no form can be in motion? Or because no form F can have a property contrary to F? Or because no *thing* which is at rest can also be in motion?

16. Although it may seem natural to do so, it becomes clear in the sequel that this third option is not to be understood as, "For each form, it will blend with some other forms and not blend with yet others" or as "There are forms that blend with other forms, and there are forms that do not blend with other forms." The existence of "vowel forms," that blend with all forms, shows both of these interpretations to be wrong. Rather, we should understand the third option thus: "Some forms do blend with some other forms and do not blend with still other forms." Into this general formulation, Plato will incorporate the vowel forms.

17. Not, of course, that these are all the forms. They were selected because they are "very important" and "we wouldn't want to get confused in the multitude of all forms" (254C). There is also mention of two further forms, τὸ καθ᾽ αὑτό, and τὸ πρὸς ἄλλο ("by way of itself" vs. "with reference to another"). We shall defer until chapter 4 the discussion of whether these are "really" forms in the same way as the others, or whether they mark some sort of mere "characteristic" or "use" of the "real" forms.

Rest. Similarly, Motion and Rest are different (from each other?), and so Difference is distinct from both Motion and Rest. Next, since both Motion and Rest mix with Being, if Sameness were identical with Being, then Motion and Rest would be the same, per impossible. Difference and Being are "shown" to be distinct because one of them, Being, has a property that the other lacks—namely, of being spoken of by way of itself. Being is both spoken of by way of itself and with reference to another, whereas Difference is always spoken with reference to another. Does this show Plato distinguishing "an 'is' of existence" from "an 'is' of predication"? Or perhaps merely an awareness of two different "uses of 'is'"? Or of something else? It seems clear that the present section of the text (255C–D) cannot decide, for the "proof" only requires *some* difference, no one difference in particular. To determine, for example, that Plato distinguished an 'is' of existence from one of predication, one must look farther afield to see whether such a distinction would fit into the overall refutation of Parmenides. It will be my contention that there is no evidence that he made this distinction precisely because it does not aid in a solution to Parmenides' Problem.

Three of these forms (Being, Sameness, Difference) are said to be vowel-forms, that is, they pervade or blend with all the other forms—and, as we would say, are coextensive (namely they apply to everything). The other two are mutually exclusive, at least in the sense that they cannot apply to the same physical objects at the same time, in the same respect, and so on. It should be also noted that Plato did not supply a "proof" of the distinctness of Sameness and Difference, but merely assumes it. Given the methods of "proof" thus far deployed, it is difficult to see how he could give a proof. Sameness and Difference are, after all, "coextensive," and both are only "spoken with reference to another." A Platonic-sounding argument might be: if Sameness and Difference were the same, then since (e.g.) Motion is the same as itself, it would follow that Motion is different from itself, which is absurd. But one should note that this is only absurd if you already think Sameness and Difference to be distinct. That is, the conclusion here, as in the earlier arguments, is more obvious than the premises that are used to prove it.

With these greatest kinds having been distinguished, the discussion turns to the problem of not-being. This area is, I think, the very center of the dialogue and accordingly merits very detailed exposition. Such is the topic of chapter 4, and by implication, of chapter 5. We shall then look in special detail at the various possibilities open to Plato, especially as they relate to being solutions to Parmenides' Problem. But first I wish to open one pathway for understanding Plato's intent which some scholars have thought he was barred from taking.[18] It is not so much that I think that this pathway *has* to be the one actually taken by Plato; it is rather that I think Plato *could* have taken it and do not wish it to be thought that "the text absolutely prohibits Plato's using this method."

Most writers agree that Plato somehow uses the form Difference in his analysis of negation, and that somehow this analysis will invoke sentences like "Form A blends with the Different from Form B" in the philosopher's language. In some of the earliest of the modern commentaries on this topic, Demos (1939) and Ackrill (1955) suggested that the Different introduced an "incompatibility" reading, so that form A "blended with the Different from" form B if and only if it was impossible for something to simultaneously partake of forms A and B. A few others writers (Lorenz and Mittelstrass 1966*a*; Philip 1968; Kostman 1973; Sayre 1983) have also favored an incompatibility reading. But the bulk of opinion follows Frede (1967, p. 79) that the Different can *never* be replaced by 'incompatible'; it is neither compatible with the train of thought nor justified by the text. For instance, Owen (1970, p. 232n) says, "need it be pointed out that this passage [257B] . . . does not introduce a new account of 'not', and of 'different', in terms of incompatibility?" Lee (1972, p. 290): "all interpretations featuring relations of incompatibility suffer the dual defect of lacking adequate basis in the text and of not allowing Plato to account for negative predication statements." Ray (1984, p. 70): "Besides having little or no support in the text, this reduction of negative predication to statements of incompatibility is intrinsically unpromising."

The reason for this antipathy to an "incompatibility" reading is not hard to find. Before 257B, ἕτερον is used clearly in the sense of "nonidentical" (in fact immediately before, 256C12 and 257A1). Thus the crucial passage of 257B, where the "incompatibility" reading must assign its (new) meaning to ἕτερον, would involve a change of sense. Further complications arise with the use in 257B and later of ἐναντίον (usually meaning "contrary"), and with the use of ἀντιθέσις (usually meaning "opposite" or "contrast") immediately following (257D7). So, the problems are that if Plato already has ἐναντίον at his disposal, why should he redefine ἕρερον? If he *has* redefined ἕρερον, why should he start to use ἀντιθέσις? The "incompatibility" theory seems committed to attributing shifts in

---

18. This discussion follows my note Pelletier (1975). Similar remarks have also been made by Kostman (1973), and by Sayre (1983, pp. 229ff, esp. 233f).

meaning to Plato; and everyone agrees that to attribute unexplained shifts in meaning on such an important point is poor interpretive practice.

I wish here to give the necessary explanation of the shifts in meaning in such a way that it is plausible to suppose that Plato might have done it. It should be emphasized again that this does not constitute a proof that he *had* to have made these meaning-shifts—merely that we could suppose he did and not be doing any violence to the text. As background, let me introduce the notion of polar-contraries along a range of predicates, no two of which can modify the same thing at the same time in the same respect. Typical polar-contraries might be white/black along a range of color predicates, large/small on a size range, just/evil on a moral range, and beautiful/ugly on an aesthetic range.[19] Now, let us turn to some of the text.

> . . . Whenever we speak of not-being, we don't, it seems, mean some ἐναντίον of being; merely some ἕτεϱον.—How?— Just as whenever we call something not-large: do you think we mean small by our words any more than we mean middling-sized?—Surely not. (257B)

Owen (1970, p. 323n) says of this passage: "need it be pointed out that this passage does *not* say that 'not-large' means 'either *middling* or *small*', and hence does not introduce a new account of 'not', and of 'different', in terms of incompatibility? It says that 'small' has no more claim to be what 'not large' means than 'middling' has." This is true enough—the passage doesn't *say* that 'not-large' means '*either* middling *or* small'. But a defender of the incompatibility reading can also say something here: Read ἐναντίον as "polar-contrary," not simply as "contrary" (this is a completely normal meaning of ἐναντίον); continue to read ἕτεϱον as "different." By this account, Plato is saying that we don't *necessarily* mean a *polar*-contrary, but that we *do* mean something other than the predicate. But just what kind of "something other"? The discussion of 257C5–E7 tells us that we mean something which is in ἀντιθέσις, and from there on we are to understand ἕτεϱον, when used in describing not-being, as meaning "something antithetical"—i.e., another predicate along the

---

19. Keyt (1973) cites Platonic and Aristotelian usages of these terms for 'polar-contrary', 'contradictories', etc. See *Symposium* 201E3–202B5, *Lysis* 216D5–7, *Republic* 436B8–9, *Gorgias* 495E, *Protagoras* 332C, *Categories* 11b38–12a25. One might also profitably consider the various doctrines of "opposites" and "generation from opposites" the pre-Socratic philosophers such as Pythagoras, Empedocles, and Anaximines. But this would take us too far afield at this point.

same range. (As in 257D7, we are told that not-beautiful picks out a part of the Different which is *antithetical* to the form Beauty).

Such an interpretation is certainly compatible with the next occurrence of ἕτερον at 257D11: "On each occasion, if we call something not beautiful, this is exactly nothing except what is ἕτερον to the nature of the beautiful."

Page 257E2–4 is a difficult passage on any interpretation, but a sense can be given it on the "incompatibility" reading, namely one wherein ἀντιθέσις is being further used to help us understand ἕτερον:

> the not beautiful is marked off as a part of a single specific kind [viz., the Different] among beings [forms], and again is ἀντιτέθεν to some being [viz., the Beautiful].

(The parenthetical explanations have all been suggested by other writers on grounds independent of whether "the Different" is to mean "incompatibility.") And now 257E6–7 says: "Therefore the being of the not beautiful is an instance of an ἀντιθέσις of one being towards another being." Taken with the preceding statement, this would imply that the not-beautiful can be spoken of, since it merely is that part of the Different which is antithetical to the Beautiful. Under the "incompatibility" reading this would mean: any form which is ἕτερον to the Beautiful (i.e., any form on the same range of contraries, but not necessarily the *polar*-contraries, the ἐνάντια), could be the not-beautiful. The defender of the "incompatibility" reading would at this point refer to 257E9–258A10 which appears to make the same claim.

The real test for any interpretation of the Different is 258A11–B3, where ἕτερον, ἐναντίον, and ἀντιθέσις are all used together. If the "incompatibility" reading can make good sense of this passage, it certainly passes the textual test required of it. There are various syntactical difficulties with the passage (see Lee 1972, pp. 282–83 for a summary), but one of the possibilities left open is this:

> So when a part of the nature of The Different [that part referred to by the negated expression] and a part of Being [the form indicated by the unnegated expression] are set in ἀντιθέσις to one another, they exist as much as each other; we do not ⟨necessarily⟩ assert something ἐναντίον to what exists [i.e., to the form] but merely something ἕτερον.

Now, this translation can go with the "incompatibility" reading; indeed, it is simply a restatement of the "incompatibility" thesis, when ἐναντίον is taken to mean "polar-contrary" and ἕτεϱον taken to mean "incompatible."

It therefore seems to me that it is possible to construe the actual pronouncements made by Plato in such a way as to be an endorsement of an "incompatibility" reading of 'the Different'.[20] However, there may also be philosophical objections (rather than textual ones) to the analysis of negation as incompatibility. Ray (1984, pp. 70–71) says, echoing some famous remarks of Russell's:

> The force of the predication of some incompatible "other," after all, seems to depend on some notion of negativity anyway while lacking the forthrightness of an outright negation. . . . The appeal to incompatibility merely makes negative predications complex . . . while introducing the difficult notion of a range. The futility of the "range" expedient is apparent in such negations as "Courage is not yellow," which does not mean that courage is some other color but only that it is not yellow. . . . Some other types of negative statements cannot plausibly be analyzed into statements of incompatibility anyway. "There is not a hippopotamus in the room" corresponds to a fact surely not to be expressed in the last analysis as "Every part of this room is filled up with something that it not a hippopotamus."

Ray's charge, in these lines, is not that Plato didn't have an incompatibility analysis of negation; but rather, if we are unsure of what analysis he has, it would violate a principle of generosity of interpretation to saddle him with incompatibility, since it has various philosophical shortcomings. But as remarked in chapter 1, this principle is subject to various caveats. For one thing, we might become convinced that Plato was concerned with a specific problem, the solution to which is best achieved with an incompatibility analysis. And he therefore might not have concerned himself at all with shortcomings of the analysis in other respects. Second, it may be the case that *all* analyses have shortcomings of one sort or another. In such a case the principles of generosity of interpretation enjoin us to find the "least philosophically objectionable" one—and

---

20. Keyt (1973) mentions the passage 257B also, but does not go into the difficulties in the surrounding passages, nor is his conclusion quite the same as mine. He thinks that ἕτεϱον and ἐναντίον are so vague or imprecise as to support any of the standard readings. F. Lewis (1976) also discusses the passage in some detail. He too finds it multiply ambiguous, but differs from Keyt in thinking that there is some definite position to be attributed to Plato in spite of the multiple ambiguities. See his pp. 106–8.

this could turn out to be an incompatibility analysis. Third, it is possible that the problems mentioned by Ray *do* admit of an incompatibility analysis. Perhaps, in negations of "category errors" (such as "Courage is not yellow"), the relevant range is not the "normal" incompatibility range of the predicate (here the normal range would be colors) wherein the negation amounts to saying "manifests some color other than yellow," but instead some other incompatibility range. The "normal" range is, intuitively, the "next highest determinable above" the predicate *yellow,* namely color; but there are also "higher determinables" that might be used, such as *property of physical objects* (or maybe *property of surfaces of physical objects*). Then we would analyze "Courage is not yellow" as "Courage manifests some property which is incompatible with manifesting a property of physical objects." But this analysis arises only after we decide that the original sentence is a "category error." The incompatibility analysis just offers us "Courage manifests some property which is incompatible with being yellow." *Red* is such an incompatible property, and we therefore should admit Courage's being red as a possible verifying condition for the sentence. Indeed, I would say that it (and the other colors) are viewed by people as the most likely candidates for verifying conditions. But they are not the only verifying conditions. *Yellow* belongs to many incompatibility ranges, and any one of them might supply a property which is "incompatible with being yellow." The analysis or meaning of a negative sentence is merely in terms of "manifests *some* property incompatible with X." It is habit or custom or common usage, not meaning, that makes us look first to "the next higher determinable." If we decide, for whatever reason, that this is the wrong incompatibility range, then we call the sentence a (negation of a) "category error" and look for a different incompatibility range. But this does not impugn the incompatibility analysis in any respect at all.[21] I do not insist that Plato held the incompatibility analysis; but rather only wish to say that the incompatibility analysis cannot not be entirely ruled out. (We might also wonder about whether Plato did, or could, consider these sorts of examples.)

The remarks made earlier, about "incompatibility" being a possible

21. There is a rich history of the analysis of negations of "category errors." The interested reader might look to Spinoza or Hegel, where such "insignificant negations" are said to have a "negative ground," as opposed to "significant negations," which have a "positive ground." Here, positive versus negative grounds map onto "next higher determinable" versus "much higher determinable." Thanks to Larry Horn (personal communication) for pointing me to this literature.

reading of the relevant text, were given only to show the *possibility* of such a reading on textual grounds. I do not insist that Plato did give such an analysis. We should, I think, look precisely at the philosophical merit of the proposed analyses to discern which is best, since each of them can be gleaned from the text. Similarly, it is not clear to me that negative existentials like Russell's hippopotamus example can't be handled by some incompatibility variant. In any case, it ought to be explored. See chapter 5 for further discussion, where I eventually come down on Ray's side about these sentences. But I would still wish to embrace an incompatibility analysis for others. That is, I disagree with Ray's remark (1984, p. 71), "If negativity is not everywhere reducible to difference or incompatibility, we may as well recognize it and use it where it is useful." I do not agree that there must be just one analysis useful in all occasions.

The upshot of this last section on whether we can read Plato to understand Difference as incompatibility, was that we could. Interpretations which make use of such a reading are therefore not to be excluded as possible understandings of Plato's intent. So we should now turn to an examination of the various interpretations of Plato's views on nonbeing. These views will be held up as possibilities for what Plato thought would overthrow the argument of "Father Parmenides" as presented in chapter 2. Once we can decide upon a reasonable understanding of notbeing, we will turn to the Platonic claim that falsity is not-being blended with speech (260C, 261A) and investigate what this might mean.

Some
Interpretations
of the
συμπλοκὴ
εἰδῶν

I repeat here a version of Parmenides' Problem. Recall that I earlier argued that the various versions given in chapter 2 were equivalent, so it does not matter which one we choose to focus on. I pick this one merely for stylistic ease of exposition. The premises are:

1. For any declarative sentence, either it is true or its negation is true, but not both.
2. (a) The meaning of a sentence is the fact to which it refers.
   (b) the meaning of a singular term (or a predicate) is the object(s) to which it refers.
3. Whatever ("really") is, can meaningfully be stated by true sentences.
4. There are no "negative facts."

Recall also that this argument has as one of its conclusions that all true, meaningful sentences mean the same thing, and that I had claimed this argument to be a possible, even likely, contender for what Plato was arguing against, his solution being the συμπλοκὴ εἰδῶν ("interweaving of forms"). It is in any case clear that such an argument effectively does "do away with the possibility of meaningful discourse," and it is some argument such as this that I think Plato wishes to show unsound. Chapter 3 was given over to laying the groundwork for Plato's rebuttal. We saw there that Plato's resolution of this paradoxical position was to invoke a "philosopher's language"—a language which accurately mirrors reality, and in which Parmenides' Problem would not arise. It is rather as if Plato granted that Parmenides' Problem *seems* to arise for natural language, but this appearance is due to the fact that natural language embodies certain "shorthand" abbreviations which do not truly correspond to reality.

One feature the philosopher's language will have is what I called the naming principle: every general term will name something, which something is the meaning of that term. As I remarked at the end of chapter 3, this seems to be an endorsement of premise (2b) of Parmenides' Problem; and, indeed, I think this is the proper way to look at it. The difference between Parmenides and Plato is in what Plato takes the general terms of the philosopher's language to name, not in a denial of the premise. For Plato, it is the forms. With just this much of a sketch of the philosopher's language, we can see that certain things we were automatically forbidden to say (by the Parmenidean argument) are now permitted. For example, 'Unicorns have one horn' is no longer ruled out on the grounds that there are no unicorns, and hence no meaning to 'unicorns' (via premise (2b)), therefore no meaning to any sentence containing 'unicorns.' Perhaps the sentence would still be meaningless for other Parmenidean reasons, but at least not on these grounds.

Plato's altering of the force of premise (2b) to talk about the forms suggests we change premise (2a) in the similar manner: The meaning of ⌜α is Φ⌝ is the fact *about the forms* to which it refers. But just *saying* this will not solve the problems which are involved in the troublesome negative sentences. Consider for example the sentence 'The Wolf is not ferocious'. If this sentence is to have any meaning (according to the new reading of premise (2a)), there must be some fact (about the forms) of the Wolf not being ferocious. In light of premise (4), what meaning can we attach to this? Are we to say that there *are* negative facts in the world of forms? If Plato still holds his earlier "orthodox" views about the relationship between forms and the physical world, then there will also be negative facts in the physical world, since the world of forms is "mirrored" (imperfectly) into the physical world. On the other hand, we might follow up discussions about "Pauline predication"[1] and claim that 'The Wolf is not ferocious' is somehow an expression to the effect 'All instances of the form Wolf are not ferocious'. But we still have the problem—what could this mean but some negative fact? It is clear that a satisfactory answer to this will depend on some reasonable account of Plato's discussion of not-being at 257–258.

I am going to proceed as follows: I claim that Plato denied premise (2a), and furthermore replaced it with a different analysis of the meaning of such sentences. The commentators have (at times unwittingly) attributed to Plato a number of different analyses, and I want to adjudicate among them. My criteria are (a) the analysis attributed to him must in fact not still involve Plato in Parmenides' problem, at least not obviously, and (b) the analysis must also account for Plato's claim that any discourse we can have owes its existence to the interweaving of the forms with one another. If these two conditions are satisfied, then we shall (c) look to the general philosophical acceptability of this analysis, and (d) judge its textual plausibility.

I broadly classify interpretations of Plato into four camps. The first

---

1. See Vlastos (1972; 1973), and Peterson (1973).

group, the "nonstarters," either take Plato to be doing something different from answering Parmenides, and cannot be converted into such an
answer, or else they *say* they're showing how Plato answered Parmenides, but must have a very strange understanding of Parmenides—because it is clear that he would have scoffed at the answer they supply on
Plato's behalf. Besides those nonstarters who deny that Plato is concerned to refute Parmenides (e.g., Rosen 1983), I have four groups in
mind—A: Peck (1952, 1962), Xenakis (1959); B: Hackforth (1945), Robinson (1950); C: Prior (1980), Neal (1975); D: Lee₁ (1972), Ray₁ (1984).[2]
These writers will be discussed below, at least in enough detail for me to
indicate why I think they should be classified as "nonstarters."

The second group, the "correspondence theorists," are those who
make the claim that for each sentence of natural language, Plato has
some specific sentence of the philosopher's language that "corresponds"
to it—and this is to be taken to be what the natural language statement
"really means" and what it "really asserts about reality." These theorists
advocate, in effect, the replacement of premise (2a) by something else;
in particular, they want to show that Plato had a translation (into the
philosopher's language) of the troublesome negative sentences, and that
in this translation Parmenides' Problem will be avoided.[3] I detect thirteen types of correspondence theorists:

I.	Cornford₁	VIII.	Wiggins₁, Owen₂, Ferg
II.	Ross, Allan	IX.	Wiggins₂
III.	Hamlyn	X.	Philip, Ackrill₁, Seligman,
IV.	Schipper, Bluck		Kostman
V.	Moravcsik, Runciman	XI.	Sayre
VI.	Owen₁, Lewis₁	XII.	Frede₁, Taylor, Bostock
VII.	Cornford₂	XIII.	Lorenz and Mittelstrass₁

The third group, the "backdrop theorists," take interweaving to be
something "behind" language in general. That is, they do not view Plato
as giving a determinate sentence of the philosopher's language to replace (say) the ordinary negations, but rather they view Plato to be
claiming that there exists some reality or other which gives a "ground"

2. The subscripts indicate different interpretations of our commentators. Sometimes it
is I who can read them differently, sometimes it is they who shift their interpretation.

3. Some of the correspondence theorists to be discussed do not, in fact, extricate Plato
from Parmenides' Problem. This is presumably because they do not see Parmenides' argument to be the one given by the standard interpretation. I include them nonetheless, on
the grounds that we can now give a definite reason why they are incorrect in their interpretation of Plato.

for the meaningfulness of statements in general. These "grounds" might be viewed as the *presuppositions* of language—what must happen in order for there to be language at all. Here I shall discuss Lorenz and Mittelstrass₂, Ketchum, Lee₂, Lewis₂, and McDowell.

The fourth group I call "mixed theories." These are theories which have both a correspondence component and a backdrop component. Such theories hold Plato to both be giving some reality which is a "ground" or presupposition for language in general, and also to be giving a specific sentence of the philosopher's language which corresponds to any chosen ordinary statement. These theorists might profitably be viewed as saying (with respect so to some particular sentence) *what part* of the "ground" or backdrop is responsible for *that* sentence meaning what it does. Here, Acrill₂ might point to Ackrill₁; Frede₂ (and Ray₂) might point to Frede₁; and Lee₃ might point to Owen₂.

NONSTARTERS

I have three different kinds of nonstarters in mind. The first kind think that Plato is doing something entirely different than I think. Peck (1952; 1962) and Xenakis (1959) do not think that in the *Sophist* Plato is talking about any theory of forms, whether it be his theory or anyone else's; and while I think this wrong, it would take us too far afield to consider this. (Peck thinks that the whole μεγίστα γένη section is "dialectical" and that Plato is only answering the sophists by pointing out relationships among those concepts that they themselves will admit exist and showing where their theories lead. Xenakis denies that the *Sophist* is about the forms (of any god-school) at all rather than about the conceptual framework of language. Of course, the way I am treating the matter the two overlap, but Xenakis denies that we should understand any of this to be about form and then draw conclusions about language or conversely; rather, we should just understand it to be about rules for language *simpliciter.*)

The second group of nonstarters I wish to exclude from the general discussion on textual grounds. Hackforth (1945) and Robinson (1950) both take Plato to be talking about *words* when he says εἴδη, and never about forms, once the section starting at 259 has begun. In fact they take these words to be akin to proper names, and so the "interweaving of words with one another" becomes "Each sentence is a compound of one noun and one verb. It asserts that this thing signified by its noun has the attribute signified by its verb" (Robinson, p. 11). The problem with taking this view is that it affords no link between all the earlier work on the μεγίστα γένη (which they both admit is about forms) and the present section supposedly on words and sentences. At 259E there begins a self-contained discussion, they say, on the Being of speech which is independent of 251–258 on the relations of forms with one another. The συμπλοκή εἰδῶν at 259E is translated as 'interweaving of parts of speech" by them, looking forward to the συμπλοκή mentioned at 262C6 and D4. Lorenz and Mittelstrass (1966a) claim that this forward-looking is not sound since there was an occurrence of συμπλοκή earlier at 240C where it *clearly* signals a combination of something other than parts of speech.[4] I would not wish to decide the issue merely on this, but it does add to the overall difficulty in attributing this sort of strategy to Plato. Further, the translation of εἴδη here as "parts of speech" means that the distinction carefully drawn at 261D1–2 between εἴδη on the one hand and γράμματα ("letters") and ὀνόματα ("words" or "names") on the other is empty word-play. And this is not the best thing to attribute to Plato.[5]

The third group denies that Plato even tries to give an account of negative prediction. Prior (1980) gives a more-or-less standard account of Plato's analysis according to which Plato gives a "translation into the philosopher's language" of positive existential statements, positive identity statements, negative identity statements, and positive predicative statements (pp. 205–6). He follows this up with this remarkable statement (p. 207): "my analysis can explain what the majority view cannot: why Plato confines his analysis of negation to negative identity." Since he doesn't discuss the passages, it is not clear what Prior's views are about the places that most commentators find negative predication: the discussion of not-tall, not-large, not-beautiful and the discussion of falsity.

In a somewhat similar view, Neal (1975, p. 26) holds that "on the question whether Plato was himself aware of the difference between negative identity and negative predication there is also disagreement. While I accept that from 257B we are concerned with what is in fact negative predication, I do not share Bluck's view that Plato has the distinction clear in this own mind." Neal's position is that (what we would call) negative predications are analyzed as saying that the subject is distinct from the form indicated by the predicate, and that this "distinctness" amounts to "a positive content" (p. 29) for these sentences, which "vindicates the apparently meaningless concept of Not-being" (p. 29). Although Neal would not himself endorse this account of negative predication he attrib-

4. Guthrie (1978, p. 161) echoes this objection with approval.
5. Cf. Lorenz and Mittelstrass (1966a, pp. 116–17).

utes to Plato, he does believe that the defect one perceives in it "exists only if we insist on treating negative predication as a separate thing. Plato's own answer could well be to assimilate statements of this type to that of 'Change is not Being', and to argue that 'Helen is different from Beauty' gives a positive and true meaning to the statement in question [= 'Helen is not beautiful']: we must not fault him for not answering twentieth-century problems." While I agree with the sentiment expressed in the last clause, I believe that the problem which requires an answer in the form Neal believes Plato did not provide was in fact a fifth-century (B.C.) problem.

The fourth group of non-starters is to be ruled out on philosophic grounds. I insist that Plato did not invent "negative" forms; that is, the mere addition of a negative prefix to a predicate does not directly generate a name for some form. So, for instance, Plato would not answer Parmenides' objections to 'John is not a cat' simply by saying that its meaning is that John partakes of the form Non-cat. However the analysis of negation comes out in the end, it is nothing so simple as that. If the analysis by the standard interpretation of Parmenides' argument is anything near correct, such a gratuitous addition of forms would merely amount to Plato's replying to Parmenides: "Of course we can make negative predications—you see, there are these forms. . . ." Parmenides would scoff at such a suggestion. It does not get to the root of the Parmenides problem, as Plato himself saw; the whole program of the *Sophist* is aimed in a different direction—that of convincing Father Parmenides on his own grounds.[6] And in any case, it is most unclear that the version

6. After quoting these last few sentences as they appeared in my 1983 article, Ray (1984, pp. 76–77) says

> Pelletier charges Lee with portraying . . . a frivolous Plato, and since I acknowledge Lee's contribution to my own solution, perhaps I too am obliged to answer the charge of making Plato's response frivolous.
>
> Undeniably the Stranger's solution rests on the reality of contrast, *antithesis:* "There exists a part of the Different that is set in contrast to the Beautiful" (257D8) The meaning of this contrast, which I have identified with predicative Not-Being, cannot be captured extensionally, by presenting all the things other than the Beautiful, but consists in opposition (not mere otherness) to it. They must be thought of as all having reference back to the Beautiful and opposing it. To invoke again the difference between identity and participation, Plato can insist that the nature of *antithesis* is a positive thing in virtue of which participants are thought of as being opposed in character to some F.
>
> The Stranger has affirmed, then, the reality of Not-Being, the relation obtaining between any Not-F and its correlative F.

The idea here, apparently, is that although there are negative forms, this is not a frivolous addition to the ontology, but rather they are "constructed intensionally from positive

of Parmenides' Problem given with the "fused" sense of 'is' even allows this as a solution. Furthermore, *Politicus* 262 explicitly states that there are not necessarily forms corresponding to a simple negation. (And see the Aristotelian comments on Plato: *Metaphysics* 990b13–14, 1079a9–10; Alexander's commentary [in *Meta.* 80, 15–81, 7] where he quotes from *Peri Ideon.*)[7]

Now, some of our commentators think that Plato's claims in the *Sophist* about the not-beautiful, the not-wise, and the like—that is, Plato's apparent adoption of negative forms—are a mere *façon de parler*. According to these scholars, Plato would (and does?) paraphrase them away in terms of "blending with the Different from," which is then to be further analyzed. These believers of the "paraphrase away" school are treated below in accordance with how they believe the further analysis is to proceed, and not as if they believed there to be negative forms as primitive entities in Plato's response to Parmenides. (Among others, I here include Frede 1967, pp. 92–94; and Sayre 1969, pp. 210, 195–96. Many others of the correspondence school, perhaps all, take this view.) However, not everyone believes in paraphrasing away negative forms. Lee₁ (see, inter alia, 1972, p. 275) and Ray₁ (see n. 6 above) explicitly embrace, without paraphrase, the notion of a negative form. Unlike the paraphrasers, Lee₁ and Ray₁ take these forms to be essential in the account preferred, even though they are "derived" and "intensional"—the form Otherness, when directed to the form X, yields the "sense" of not-X. Thus these negative forms are not part of the basic ontology of forms, but are "intensionally constructed" out of the basic, positive ones with the aid of the form Otherness. Lee₁ makes a considerable point about claiming that such forms are nonetheless "definite" (p. 292):

> What 'x is not brown' says is that x (which is) partakes of a certain Part of Otherness (a Part which fully and securely *is*. . . .); it says that x partakes of the Part of Otherness whose "name" is "(the) not-brown" and whose determinate nature consists in Otherness-precisely-than-brown.

---

ingredients"—a ("positive") form and the ("positive") relation of *antithesis*. I must say that I still think this frivolous, but will anyway grant Ray his assertion that these are all "constructed positively." In such a case though, one wonders what to make of the proposed solution to Parmenides' Problem. What, in this view, are we to alter in the premises of the Problem which will make it disappear? For some guesses on this, see below "Ray₂."

7. Although as Frede points out (pp. 92–94), the *Politicus* is later than the *Sophist* and therefore may represent yet another shift in Plato's theory of forms.

No doubt most commentators would want to hold something like this as a *part* of their view. But Lee₁ wants it to be *all* of his view (pp. 293, 295):

> it is no part at all of the sense of the negating proposition that it should refer to any (much less all) particular entities or predicates other than the negated predicate. . . . [The negating statement simply] says that the subject's partaking lies outside of the predicate negated . . . just that it lies outside-that-predicate. . . . The determinate sense of 'x is not brown' thus lies precisely, but lies entirely, in its saying that brown is what x is not. What the statement will signify—and all that it signifies, on Plato's analysis—is that the subject does not partake of *that* predicate.

(This position is in some ways similar to schema I below, but in view of the differences between Lee₁ and the holders of schema I, it is perhaps best to separate them.) Given this statement of Lee's, and the Parmenidean argument of above, it is difficult to see how Lee₁ can believe that such an account could possibly "vindicate the sense of negative expressions by showing that the understanding of any negative statement involves the apprehension only of 'existent', positive, determinate contents" (p. 291), for it does not remove the difficulty that Parmenides finds with Not-being.[8] Referring to these remarks of Lee's, McDowell (1982, p. 121 n. 11) says, rightly in my mind, "this would scarcely cut any ice with Parmenides."

CORRESPONDENCE THEORISTS

A correspondence theorist is one who seeks to show how sentences of ordinary language are to be translated into the philosopher's language so as to exhibit reality correctly. To do this, the theorist must offer us some uniform translation procedure. For example, ordinary sentences like 'Theaetetus is sitting' might be said to translate into 'Theaetetus partakes of (the form) Sitting' or into 'Theaetetus partakes of (the form) Sitting, which blends with (the form) Being'. These later sentences, being part of the philosopher's language, mean whatever (fact) they name or describe. (Or alternatively, name the fact that they mean.) Correspondence theorists thus deny the simple naming principle for ordinary lan-

---

8. F. Lewis (1976) has a view very similar to Lee₁'s (See Lewis' n. 40). I later entertain this view, calling it Lewis₂ and Lee₂. Ray does not always hold the view here called Ray₁; below I consider Ray₂.

guage; instead, they translate the ordinary statement into a philosophic one, and apply the naming principle to it. One way to put this is to say that correspondence theorists find Plato assigning meanings to ordinary sentences which are not "on their sleeves," but are rather worn by their philosophical counterparts. I will adopt the convention that such theorists are attributing to Plato the view that the ordinary sentence *means* what is named by its philosophic translation. Thus 'Theaetetus is sitting' means (according to some correspondence theorists) the fact of the referent of 'Theaetetus' (viz., Theaetetus) partaking of the referent of 'sitting' (viz., the form Sitting).

In the schemata to be given below as explicating what various commentators have attributed to Plato, I shall use quasi quotes and use phrases like 'Ref(Φ)' to mean "whatever the referent of Φ is." Furthermore, I intend most of the terms used to be understood in a nontechnical way. So, although I think Plato uses μετέχειν, κοινωνία, σύμμειξις, and others in a fixed pattern,[9] here I follow several different authors' distinct usages at once, and use (i) 'partakes of' as a relation between individuals and forms, (ii) 'belongs to' as a way of saying the converse of 'partakes of', and for the most part (iii) 'blends' as indicating some relation holding among forms.[10] I use 'blends with the Different from' in a specific manner, indicating "is not identical to"; when I want this phrase to mean something else (e.g., "is incompatible with") I use a formulation explicitly invoking the notion of an incompatibility range (see schemata IX, X, and XI).

Cornford (1935) sometimes (pp. 300–301) holds a position like schema I. That is, he claims that Plato can refute Parmenides' difficulties about not-being if he were merely to recognize that he needs to give separate sorts of translations into the philosopher's language for positive and negative sentences.

Schema I: (Cornford$_1$, pp. 300–301)

2a$_1$. The meaning of ⌜α is Φ⌝ consists in the fact of Ref(α) partaking of Ref(Φ).

2a$_2$. The meaning of ⌜α is not Φ⌝ consists in the fact of Ref(α) not partaking of Ref (Φ).

Immediately, however, we see that this does not solve the problem. Consider 'Theaetetus is not flying': Under the proposed analysis, this

9. This will be the topic of chapter 5.

10. Again, just what relation the various occurrences indicate will be the topic of chapter 5.

would have as its meaning the fact of flying not belonging to Theaetetus; but by premise (4) this purported fact does not exist, so the sentence has no meaning. Thus we can reject Cornford's account of negation and his account of the "interweaving of the forms," since they do not adequately show that Plato has solved the problem he set for himself. Furthermore, schema I does not account for the statement at 259E5–6 where "the interweaving of the forms with one another" is claimed to be necessary for the possibility of discourse. On this point Ross claims (1951, p. 115) that it was an "overstatement"—i.e., that it is false. Cornford simply does not translate τὴν ἀλλήλων ("with one another") and claims (p. 314) that the sentence at 259E5–6 means that every sentence mentions at least *one* form-name. Such moves violate our principles of generosity of interpretation, and should therefore be rejected. These readings of 259E5–6 by Ross and Cornford have been attacked by many people, and I shall not repeat their criticisms; but we should note that even if there were no other reason, we would be justified in rejecting this interpretation of interweaving because it does not supply us an account of how to solve Parmenides' Problem. I might also mention that Cornford does not always hold schema I. I shall give another schema he sometimes resorts to, below.

There is another way along the same lines to make sense out of the "interweaving of the forms with one another" in these sentences where the subject is a proper name, and this can be done with resorting to Cornford's nontranslation and inaccurate paraphrase of "with one another." Ross (1951, pp. 115–16) says, "In the sentence 'Theaetetus is not flying' Theaetetus exists and Flying (the form or universal of flying) exists, so in saying the sentence we are not asserting of him something that does not exist, but simply something that does not belong to him." And Allan (1954, p. 285) says "[a true statement] describes things as they are; i.e., its components must (a) stand for real entities and (b) in their relation to one another, depict the relation between those entities—that is why it is significant—but they will represent them as related in a way which does not correspond to the facts."

It thus seems that such commentators are attributing to Plato the following schema.

Schema II: (Ross, Allan)

2a₁. The meaning of ⌜α is Φ⌝ consists in the facts of Ref(α) partaking of Ref(Φ) and that Ref(Φ) exists (and Ref(α) exists?).

2a$_2$. The meaning of ⌜α is not Φ⌝ consists in the facts of Ref(α) not partaking of Ref(Φ) and that Ref(Φ) exists (and Ref(α) exists?).

I said that such a view makes some sense of the interweaving of forms
with one another, since the philosopher's sentence will contain reference to two forms: Being (which might be referred to by the words 'exists' in the schema) and Ref(Φ). Whether such a relation between Being
and Ref(Φ) should be said to be "interweaving" in Plato's sense of the
word is another question, and one which I shall defer until later. It is
sufficient for us to notice that the proposed (2a$_2$) still has not helped us
to solve Parmenides' Problem, for the problem will now arise again in
the philosopher's language. Thus schema II must be rejected, in accordance with the principles of generosity of interpretation, from being Plato's account.

In their anxiety to satisfy the apparent requirement that each sentence
of the philosopher's language somehow mention at least two form-
names, a number of authors have resorted to supposing the existence of
forms that are nowhere mentioned by Plato. One such method of finding enough forms to perform an interweaving in sentences that are (apparently) about particulars is to look "behind" the subject-term—e.g.,
behind 'Theaetetus'. According to the view of Hamlyn (1955), in the philosopher's language there are no names except those for forms. What
appears to be a proper name of a physical particular is actually a mark of
(what Hamlyn calls) a "characteristic": this is a form which applies to
exactly one single entity. So the "interweaving" behind the sentences
'Theaetetus is sitting' is that between the (unique) form indicated by
'Theaetetus' and the form Sitting. The recommendation for meaning is:

Schema III: (Hamlyn)
2a$_1$. The meaning of ⌜α is Φ⌝ consists of the fact that A blends with
Ref(Φ).
2a$_2$. The meaning of ⌜α is not Φ⌝ consists of the fact that A does not
blend with Ref(Φ)
(where: A is the form or "characteristic" of Ref (α)).

Such an account cannot stand up under scrutiny of Plato's use of proper
names in the *Sophist*, it seems to me, and hence is already implausible as
an account of the *Sophist*. For, at 263, the name 'Theaetetus' is explained
as being "about the Theaetetus with whom [the Stranger] is talking
now"; and this is distinguished from those things which hold of him.

The only place I have ever found Plato to be talking of the unique character of a particular is *Theaetetus* 209, but even then there is no hint that Plato is talking about the forms as opposed to some person's concept of the particular. (Some claims about proper names being akin to predicates are made in the *Cratylus*, but I shall not discuss them now; see below, schema XIII.) Furthermore, such a view cannot possibly account for negative predication in the manner needed, for consider 'Theaetetus is not Flying': this sentence asserts (according to Hamlyn) that the form of Theaetetus does not include anything of flying, that is, Theaetetus' form does not blend with the form Flying. But as we can immediately see, this does not solve Parmenides' Problem.

No one that I know of has explicitly taken up Hamlyn's characteristic-form theory (although Turnbull's (1964) interpretation has something like it), but it has suggested various emendations to some. Schipper, for instance, holds that there are no true individuals at all. What 'Theaetetus' refers to is precisely the set of forms that can truly be said to characterize Theaetetus. Thus there are no individuals which partake of some unique form, as Hamlyn would have it, but rather there are sets of forms corresponding to each proper name. In her (1964), Schipper puts the point (p. 44) that particulars exist only by dint of the forms which characterize them. In her (1965, p. 40), she says:

> Though the name 'Theatetus' may be the grammatical subject of statements about him, the experienced Theaetetus is not a substantial subject existing independently of forms, about whom forms are predicated. . . . Theaetetus may be spoken of, not as an existing object beyond the forms, but as described by the interrelated forms. *Logos* is about them, only.

Bluck's (1957) view is similar, but without the notion that individuals exist only by dint of their characterizing forms. He starts with 262C9–D6, which is taken to give a syntactical definition of meaningful sentences. ("Sounds uttered signify nothing until you combine verbs with names. The moment you do that the simplest combination becomes a statement. . . . It gets you somewhere by weaving together verbs with names.") So it is *we* who interweave words together to make a sentence, and (he says) it is therefore *we* who interweave the appropriate forms. The meaning of 259E5–6 now becomes (p. 182) "That in any statement we make we are in fact weaving forms together, either correctly or incorrectly, and that only so is discourse possible." But now what shall "incor-

rectly weaving the forms" come to? And how shall that become a solution to Parmenides' Problem? The forms involved in the sentence
'Theaetetus is sitting' when we utter it are all the forms Theaetetus partakes of plus the form(s) that "this-individual-sitting-here" partakes of.
Thus in weaving together 'Theaetetus' with 'sitting' we are also weaving
together 'this particular man with such-and-such properties' and 'this-
individual-sitting-here' and therefore we are weaving together the forms
Man, . . . (all of Theaetetus' properties), and the form Sitting. And
when we utter 'Theaetetus if Flying', we interweave the words and so
interweave the forms, but there is not an individual-flying-here, and so
we have a false sentence. I doubt if this is going to solve any of the problems raised earlier on in the text about falsity (that is, "Parmenidean arguments" of 237–241), but here I will just note that even though his focus
is on falsity rather than negative sentences, Bluck commits himself to the
view embodied in schema IV (for true sentences). For, since the meaningfulness of sentences in general is taken to be syntactically defined,
and since 'Theaetetus is not flying' satisfies that criterion, the relationships among the forms *behind* this sentence must be just those behind
any meaningful sentence. And that is just whether or not the forms
holding of the subject are blended with that indicated by the predicate.
These views may be represented by schema IV. Version (i) is Schipper's
(see 1964, p. 42); version (ii) is Bluck's.

Schema IV: (i-Schipper, ii-Bluck)

$2a_1$. The meaning of ⌜α is Φ⌝ is that $Ref(\Phi_1)$, $Ref(\Phi_2)$, $Ref(\Phi_3)$ . . . ,
   blend with $Ref(\Phi)$.

$2a_2$. The meaning of ⌜α is not Φ⌝ is that $Ref(\Phi_1)$, $Ref(\Phi_2)$, $Ref(\Phi_3)$ . . . ,
   do not blend with $Ref(\Phi)$.
   i. $Ref(\alpha)$ = the overlap or intersection of $Ref(\Phi_1)$, $Ref(\Phi_2)$,
   $Ref(\Phi_3)$. . . .
   ii. $\Phi_1, \Phi_2, \Phi_3, . . .$ are all the predicates truly applicable to $Ref(\alpha)$.

Schipper's view clearly contradicts Plato's use of proper names at 263,
where Theaetetus is distinguished from the things that are true of him,
and what is being talked about by 'Theaetetus' is exactly the entity before the stranger and nothing else. Against both Schipper's and Bluck's
view we can point out that it does not solve Parmenides' Problem, and
thus cannot be the correct analysis of 'not-being'. And even though it
can give *some* sense to the "interweaving of forms with one another," it
just doesn't give the *right* sense. (As can also be seen by noting that the

analysis of positive sentences makes them be *necessarily true*, if they are true. For, in any true sentence, for example, 'Theaetetus is sitting', Sitting is one of the forms that defines Theaetetus [Schipper] or that Theaetetus partakes of [Bluck], and so the sentence is analyzed as necessarily true. Even though for Bluck it might be that Sitting is only an accidentally true property of Socrates, still the analysis given for the sentence by (2a$_1$) asserts that Sitting is one such property—and it is necessarily true that it is such a property, if it is true at all. Thus the proposed semantical theory gives no account of the difference to be found between 'man is man' and 'man is good', a difference Plato clearly believes his account to cover in contradistinction to the late-learners of 251).

Another place to look for forms that Plato doesn't mention is the copula. Moravcsik (1960; 1962) and Runciman (1965), for example, suppose that there is a form corresponding to the copula and one corresponding to the negative copula; these Moravcsik calls "Relational Being" and "the negative counterpart of Relational Being" (1960, pp. 107–33):

Schema V: (Moravcsik, Runciman)

2a$_1$. The meaning of $\ulcorner\alpha$ is $\Phi\urcorner$ is that Ref(α) blends with Relational Being with respect to Ref(Φ).

2a$_2$. The meaning of $\ulcorner\alpha$ is not $\Phi\urcorner$ is that Ref(α) blends with the negative counterpart of Relational Being with respect to Ref(Φ).

We should first notice that schema V *does* provide a solution to Parmenides' Problem since the meaning of a "negative sentence" is no longer a "negative fact," but rather something positive, namely, Ref(Φ)'s blending with the negative counterpart of Relational Being. But there are difficulties with it. Let's first see some textual difficulties: I said that Moravcsik merely invented these forms. He points to 255D3–8 where it is said of Being that it participates in two εἴδη, αὐτὸ καθ' αὑτο and πρὸς ἄλλο, and he says that these two forms, when combined with Being and Difference, are represented by the copula and its negative counterpart (1960, p. 125). Now, in order for Moravcsik's interpretation to go through, τὸ καθ' αὑτό and τὸ πρὸς ἄλλο must both be understood as binary relations. But this is difficult, when we consider what use these concepts are put to in the test; namely, 'is' is said to have two uses: an αὐτὸ καθ' αὑτό use (an example of which is 'motion is') and a πρὸς ἄλλο use (an example of which is 'motion is the same (as itself)' or 'Man is a learner'). Further, even if Plato did understand forms as sometimes being two-place relations, there is no evidence that he ever took them to be forms "behind" the copula. For if he did, it would be strange that he didn't directly state this, it being a rather important point.[11]

Furthermore there is a serious philosophical objection to this purported solution. If we are to take seriously the rationale behind the attempt to give a justification for meaning of predicative statements in terms of some ontological counterpart, we find that we'll have to have something that works like "glue" in holding the reality together similar to the way the copula works as a syntactic "glue" in holding sentences together. Normally, Plato is considered to have held that the ontological glue was "blending" or "partaking" (and Aristotle so takes it, while demanding a further explanation). Moravcsik takes the "glue" to be "blends with —— with respect to ——." Now consider negative sentences; could there be any such "glue" between Theaetetus and Flying? Obviously not, since the point of the denial of Flying's blending with something with respect to Theaetetus is merely a denial of there being any ontological glue here. So the proposed schema V certainly could not satisfy anyone; and, following our principles of generosity of interpretation, this is good grounds for denying that Plato held it.

Another thing to notice about schema V is that it does not justify itself, in a certain sense. We are told that the interweaving of the forms underlies rational discourse; when asked how, we are told that (a) for statements of identity (or nonidentity), the form Sameness (or Difference) interweaves with Relational Being, (b) for statements of positive (or negative) prediction, Relational Being (or its negative counterpart) interweaves with the form indicated by the predicate. In what sense can this be said to explain how sentences have meaning? There is no plausibility to it other than that it does make the "interweaving of the forms" claim seem true. The explanation given by Moravcsik is simply, "the meaning of any statement involves an attribute and a connector, and this is surely the essential point that Plato makes." But surely it is *not* the essential point. Plato is trying to overcome a logical problem presented by Parmenides; it is not enough to say in response that the problem is indeed

---

11. See the similar criticism in Lorenz and Mittelstrass (1966a, p. 126, n. 81). For dissenting opinions to my claim that τὸ καθ' αὑτό designates a "complete" use of the term in question and not some relation, see Owen (1970), pp. 225–58; Frede (1967), pp. 12–29; and (with different views) Heinaman (1983), p. 14, and Brown (1986), pp. 68–69. On the opposite side see Bostock (1984). Because of the obvious difficulty involved in grasping Plato's meaning here, I would wish to place more weight on the philosophical problems in schema V than the textual ones.

a problem, and what it shows is that we need to add more forms to our ontology so that we can give negative statements meaning. What *would* be enough would be to show that, on the basis of already-accepted forms, and certain plausible relations between them, we can account for the meaningfulness of negative statements exactly as we do for the positive statements that we accept.

Finally, the Moravcsik/Runciman interpretation of Plato's view does not explain truth and falsity of sentences. One of the things we are supposed to be able to do by means of an inspection of a sentence in the philosopher's language is to see why a sentence is true (or why it can be true). One should be able to inspect the sentence and say, "I see what reality this sentence is asserting." But consider the true sentence, 'John is not a cat'. According to the Runciman/Moravcsik interpretation, the only reason we can give for this sentence being true is that the form Cat is blending with the negative counterpart of Relational Being to John. Certainly this is not a very convincing reason—it strikes one as being merely a repetition of the original (if he understands it at all).[12]

I view schemata I–V as exercises in futility. Somehow we all know (but I won't try to tell you how we know it) that the analysis of negation should bring in the form the Different. Perhaps the simplest way to bring it in is Owen$_1$'s (1970, pp. 232, 237–38) and Lewis$_1$'s (1976, pp. 104–5, 108).[13]

Schema VI: (Owen$_1$, Lewis$_1$)

2a$_1$. The meaning of $\lceil \alpha$ is $\Phi \rceil$ is that Ref(α) partakes of Ref(Φ).

2a$_2$. The meaning of $\lceil \alpha$ is not $\Phi \rceil$ is that Ref(Φ_1), Ref(Φ_2), Ref(Φ_3) . . . , blend with the Different with respect to Ref(Φ),

---

12. Moravcsik has changed his mind on many of the details of his original interpretation in his (1960). Already in his (1962) we can see a difference in the understanding of αὐτὸ καθ᾽ αὑτό and πρὸς ἄλλο, where they become the meanings of 'exist' and the copula, thereby removing one of my criticisms based on his earlier understanding of them both as two-place relations. In his (1976, p. 744 n. 4) he further remarks that many of the details of his position—especially on this issue, which was being criticized in the book under review (Seligman 1974)—have changed. Moravcsik has been kind enough to show me a draft of portions of a new book on Plato which he is writing, wherein the roles of "relational being," "converse being," Being, etc., are further discussed, to a slightly different effect and with further attention to the "building block" versus "ontological glue" metaphor. In discussing Plato's account of negation, Moravcsik's position is that there are a number of options, and that none of them can be attributed with any certainty. They are "not explicitly recognized" as distinct options. Moravcsik now thinks Plato did not attempt any "correspondence approach," but rather held a "backdrop approach."

13. This is not really Lewis' view of the matter, but rather one that results from forcing him to be a correspondence theorist. His true view is what I call Lewis$_2$, and is discussed below under "backdrop theorists."

where: Ref(Φ_1), Ref(Φ_2), Ref(Φ_3) . . . , are all the forms Ref(α) partakes of.

Although schema VI solves Parmenides' Problem by assigning a "positive fact" as the meaning of ordinary negative sentences, it seems to me wrong for the following four reasons. First, it does not account for the apparent force of the συμπλοκή at 259E—namely, that each sentence mention at least two forms—because (2a$_1$) only mentions one form. There are various ways that Owen$_1$ and Lewis$_1$ could take around this objection, so perhaps it is not all that important. (They could say that the doctrine of vowel-forms does the requisite blending, or that Plato was trying to stop Parmenides' Problem from even getting going, and for that we need the interweaving of (2a$_2$).) Second, the (2a$_2$) principle here which says that Ref(Φ) is other than *all* the properties which hold of Ref(α) seems to go against Plato's words at 257B10: a negation signifies *something* (τῶν ἄλλων τί) other than the words that follow. (Cf. Bostock 1984, p. 113. This criticism also holds of various other schemata discussed below.) Third, we should note that Plato is explicitly drawing some analogy between the *ontological* "not-being" and *sentential* "not-being" (i.e., falsity). Under Owen$_1$'s view, this analogy becomes this: In order to determine the falsity of 'Theaetetus is flying' we have to find out *all* the predicates that hold of Theaetetus in order to show that Flying is not one of them. It is not sufficient merely to find out that he is sitting, for, according to Owen$_1$'s analysis, one cannot infer from this that he is not flying. Rather, to show he is not flying we must examine *every* predicate and show that it is not identical to flying. As Owen himself remarks, this makes falsifying statements an interminable business (p. 238 n. 2; see also the similar remarks made earlier by Moravcsik 1962, p. 74). Is this objection just a confusion between truth conditions and verification conditions? Possibly, but I think Plato would not see the matter that way. When discussing the "parts of the Different" (257D–E), the Stranger remarks that the not-Beautiful is marked off as some *one* kind (and he generalizes this to other negated predicates). And we are told that although there are innumerable things that an item is not, we are to look at this *one* kind. The moral I take from this is, Plato would admit that there might be (what we would call) "adequate truth conditions" among these innumerable things an item is not,[14] but he believes such conditions are not what are of interest. I take this to indicate his displeasure

14. Assuming we could express such conditions, something Plato probably thinks would be impossible.

with any analysis of negation that separates truth conditions from verification conditions. Owen finds no difficulty here, but this clearly shows that the analogy has broken down, and hence his analysis of the ontological "not-being" is incorrect. Fourth, and most tellingly, while singular affirmative statements are, according to this analysis, synthetic (the notion of "partaking" being somehow synthetic), we find that true singular negative statements are all necessary. For, under Owen$_1$'s analysis of "blends with the Different with respect to," two forms do so exactly in case they are not identical; therefore, whether or not Ref(Φ_1), Ref(Φ_2), Ref(Φ_3), . . . , are identical with Ref(Φ) (in our singular negative statement) is a matter already settled by our semantics (i.e., by statements about how many, and what kinds of, forms there are), and thus is logically necessary. And surely, whether it is true or false that Theaetetus is not standing is not a matter for our semantics to decide upon. Of course, this fourth objection only holds if the extra clause identifying the predicates which are true of Ref(α) is stated "separately," as an adjunct to clause (2a$_2$) and not as part of the clause proper. And although Owen puts his point as if he meant it in the form given by schema VI, it is possible that he really meant it otherwise. For this interpretation—Owen$_2$—see below, schema VIII.

One way around the objections that schema VI makes falsification "an interminable business," makes singular negative sentences analytic (if they are true), and illegitimately imports a universal quantifier where Plato calls for an existential quantifier, is to adopt a view sometimes held by Cornford (1935, pp. 314–15):

Schema VII: (Cornford$_2$, pp. 314–15)
2a$_1$. The meaning of ⌜α is Φ⌝ is that Ref(α) partakes of Ref(Φ).
2a$_2$. The meaning of ⌜α is not Φ⌝ is that Ref(α) partakes of some form F which blends with the Different with respect to Ref(Φ),

where "blends with the form Different with respect to X" is to be understood as not being identical with X.[15]

Cornford's explanation of "not-being" when he is discussing falsity (pp. 314–15) exactly fits this schema. He is still committed, by dint of (2a$_1$) not mentioning two forms, to understanding (per impossile) 'in-

---

15. Keyt's (1973) comment, that Cornford's explanation here is "incomplete" and that Cornford really meant "contrariety" and not "nonidentity," seems to me incorrect. Cornford *explicitly* wants "blending with the different from" to be nonidentity (p. 290), although it is true that his later discussion of "falsity" (on pp. 311–17) does not make much sense for the reasons noted in the next paragraph.

terweaving of forms with one another' as 'at least one form', but at least it does not commit him to other difficulties found in schema I (which he otherwise advocates). But there are some difficulties with this kind of account, which fails to assign the correct properties to negation. For example, this account makes contradictory sentences true. Suppose Socrates is a white man; 'Socrates is a man' is true by (2a$_2$) and since White blends with the Different from Man (i.e., are not identical), it follows that 'Socrates is not a man' is also true. As Wiggins (1970, pp. 293–94) notes, this account also cannot be correct for another reason. Simple difference between Ref(Φ_1) and Ref(Φ_2) cannot suffice to make them exclude one another. Theaetetus' having some quality distinct from flying can hardly in itself rule out the possibility that Theaetetus flies. He would have a distinct quality even if he were flying.[16]

We can avoid at least some of the difficulties raised in connection with the Owen$_1$/Lewis$_1$ and Cornford$_2$ views by reimporting a form behind the copula a la Moravcsik (but not one for the "negative copula"), and always mentioning that the subject is partaking of these forms (as is not done by Owen). This is one of the accounts given by Wiggins (1970, pp. 288–90, 294) and Ferg (1976, pp. 339, 341):

Schema VIII: (Wiggins$_1$, Ferg, Owen$_2$)

2a$_1$. The meaning of $\ulcorner \alpha$ is $\Phi \urcorner$ is that Ref(α) partakes of Being with respect to Ref(Φ).

2a$_2$. The meaning of $\ulcorner \alpha$ is not $\Phi \urcorner$ is that for all forms F, if Ref(α) partakes of Being with respect to F, then F blends with the Different with respect to Ref(Φ).

The wording of this schema is taken from Wiggins and Ferg, rather than Owen, who would not add 'Being' to (2a$_1$). Citing this as being Owen$_2$'s view is due to uncertainty over the understanding of the qualifying clause in schema VI (2a$_2$), one way being as in schema VI, the other way as here. Thus Owen$_2$'s view is the schema VI (2a$_1$) plus the schema VIII (2a$_2$); hence the "minor objection" raised against schema VI (2a$_1$) would still apply to Owen$_2$. The schema VIII (of Wiggins$_1$ and Ferg) is not susceptible to this minor objection, since (unlike schemata VI and VII) it satisfies the criterion that each sentence mention an interweaving of the forms (here, the form Being and at least one other form). Second, again

16. Frede (1967, pp. 78–79) makes a related criticism based on his analysis of two uses of 'is' in the *Sophist*. He claims that there is such a use of 'is not,' but that it is so rare and artificial that one can hardly expect Plato to try to interpret all uses of 'x is not y' according to it. Schema VII (2a$_2$) is Frede's 2(b) on p. 78.

unlike schema VI, the meaning of negative sentences is not such that they are logically true or false.[17] Nor does it make contradictory sentences true as schema VII did. We might furthermore note that this account actually does solve Parmenides' Problem, since the meaning of a negative sentence is now some "positive fact."

What can be said against it? Well, first, like schema VI, it still uses the universal quantifier rather than an existential, and therefore goes against the Platonic dictum that a negation signify something other than what follows. And second, again like schema IV, it still makes falsification of sentences "an interminable business." Wiggins (p. 301) is sensitive to these sorts of objections, and wishes that Plato had replaced it by schema IX:

Schema IX: (Wiggins$_2$)

2a$_1$.   The meaning of ⌜α is Φ⌝ is that Ref(α) partakes of Being with respect to Ref(Φ).

2a$_2$.   The meaning of ⌜α is not Φ⌝ is that there is a form F other than Ref(Φ) such that F belongs to the same incompatibility range as Ref(Φ) and Ref(α) partakes of Being with respect to F,

where "belongs to the same incompatibility range as" is the meaning of the Platonic "blends with the Different with respect to," and is taken to imply that nothing can be characterized by two predicates in the same range at the same time. (The existential quantifier in (2a$_2$) makes the procedure terminate.) However, Wiggins just does not believe that Plato makes this move, even though all his examples (not-large, etc.) are consistent with it.[18] I think it quite clear that schema IX is preferable to schema VIII on philosophic grounds; and as I argued at the end of chapter 3, there is no legitimate textual reason to disallow the incompatibility reading of schema IX. We therefore should apply the principles of gen-

---

17. Note that (2a$_2$) of schemata VI and VIII are not the same, in spite of their superficial similarity. Schema VI says: "Here's a number of forms, Φ$_1$, Φ$_2$, Φ$_3$ . . . ; are they distinct from Φ?" The answer is "Yes (or No)—and necessarily so." The parenthetical remark after (2a$_2$) merely tells us how to grasp the forms Φ$_1$, Φ$_2$, Φ$_3$ . . . , but is not a part of the condition proper. This is not the case with schema VIII. Here, thanks to the bound variable F, we have a non-necessary claim, in spite of the fact that the consequent is necessary for all substitution instances of F.

18. Keyt (1973) of course claims there is no decisive way to decide the issue on textual grounds. He feels that an ambiguity in ἕτερον will allow both sides to have their day in text. Many writers (e.g. Owen, Frede) find absolutely no justification for (2a$_2$) of schema IX. Frede (p. 79) says that ἕτερον can never be replaced by 'incompatible'; that it is neither compatible with the train of thought nor justified by the text. The discussion at the end of chapter 3 (following Pelletier 1975) is intended to blunt this kind of view.

erosity of interpretation and attribute schema IX to Plato, at least provisionally, pending investigation of any other interpretations or considerations).

Yet, there are some problems with schema IX which seem to me to show the desirability of finding some other account. When I discussed Moravcsik, I pointed to two difficulties in understanding there to be forms corresponding to the copula and the "negative copula." The first was that a distinction between "positive Relational Being" and "negative Relational Being" could not be gleaned from the text, that is, that τὸ καθ' αὐτό did not mean "positive Relational Being" since it corresponded to a "complete" use of 'is,' not a two-place relation. The second objection was of a more philosophic nature; Moravcsik's proposal seems to involve a misconstrual of the point of constructing a philosopher's language. It made names of *all* the words in a sentence, and hence turned the sentence into a list. What is needed is some kind of "ontological glue" to hold the "ontological building blocks" together, corresponding to the "syntactic glue" (provided by 'is' and the like in ordinary discourse) which holds the "syntactic building blocks" (the ὀνόματα and the ῥήματα) together.

Here Wiggins is not making Moravcsik's distinction between kinds of "Relational Being" (he in fact agrees that τὸ καθ' αὐτό must be "complete" and not "relative"); but rather he is pointing to τὸ πρὸς ἄλλο (Moravcsik's "negative Relational Being") as needing to be understood as "being with respect to something else," and then glossing this as "the form Being blending with some other form." This seems unobjectionable until he makes the further move of applying this to particular sentences, parsing 'Theaetetus is a man' into 'Theaetetus partakes of the form Man' and then claiming that this is merely a contraction of 'Theaetetus partakes of the form Being blended with the form Man'. He is therefore vulnerable to the second of the objections of Moravcsik. Either Wiggins is claiming (on Plato's behalf) (a) that we have to look "behind" the copula to find a form, or (b) that Theaetetus is partaking of "some special version of the form Being, namely the Man version," or (c) that 'partaking of F' is always equivalent to 'partaking of Being blended with F'.

I cannot see that Plato ever said any of these things, although I do not see this as a decisive argument against schema IX. It is certainly true that Being is a vowel-form and hence "runs through all forms," but it is far from clear that this is equivalent to (c) of the last paragraph. It is also true that when Plato discusses "the Different" (another vowel-form) he claims that "running through them all" gives rise to "parts of the Different" (257C–D), but I still do not see that this implies (b) above. Furthermore, such a view merely pushes various philosophical problems one step further back. Since 'is' is our "syntactic glue," if the ontology-sentence analogy is to hold up, we shall not want to assign 'is' a "building-block" ontological rule but rather a "glue" role. In Wiggins₂'s account we have to invent another glue, namely "partaking" glue—a glue that does not correspond to any syntactic element.[19] For these sorts of reasons, I think we should look for another interpretation.

To avoid the sort of objections of the last few paragraphs, one might consider simply dropping the reference to Being in the formulations of (2a₁) and (2a₂). This would result in the sort of view held by Philip (1968, p. 319), by Kostman (1973), and by Seligman (1974, p. 83). (I also call it Ackrill₁, although the real Ackrill is not a correspondence theorist but rather a mixed theorist. I attribute it to him merely because he might be willing to point to that part of reality indicated by the schema, if he were asked, "what portion of the backdrop makes *this* sentence true?" and also because this position is traditionally identified with him.)

Schema X: (Philip, Kostman, Seligman, Ackrill₁)

2a₁. The meaning of ⌜α is Φ⌝ is that Ref(α) partakes of Ref(Φ).

2a₂. The meaning of ⌜α is not Φ⌝ is that there is a form F other than Ref(Φ) such that F belongs to the same incompatibility range as Ref(Φ) and Ref(α) partakes of F.

This schema does not involve us in the difficulties involved in assigning to 'is' some entity which plays a "building block" role rather than a "glue" role, but on the other hand it fails to make sense of the "interweaving of the forms with one another." On this point Philip gives the following peculiar comment (p. 231): "[This doctrine of blending] puts a stop to eristical discussions. . . . To argue in the eristical way is quite barbarous and would put an end to philosophical discourse, which come to pass 'through the mutual (or two-way) weaving together of

---

19. I am not too sure exactly how this argument should run. If we consider the sentences given by Plato (Θεαίτητος κάθηται and Θεαίτητος πέτεται), there is no word corresponding to 'is' (the sentences could best be translated 'Theaetetus sits', 'Theaetetus flies'), and thus the so-called "syntactic glue" is not there as a unit but merely in the words' interweaving. So we have to invent our "ontological" glue anyway. But if this is the case, it is indeed unclear why anyone would want to put the form Being into every predication. Moravcsik's reason was to get it "behind" the copula, but if there is no copula, there seems no reason to get it at all.

kinds'." He then concludes that ordinary discourse will, in virtue of this interweaving, not be affected by the "Parmenidean denial of not-being, [whereby] identity is denied, difference is ignored, and opposite predicates are attached without regard to the principles [of blending]." This is clearly a misunderstanding of Parmenides. Philip's attempt here to give a sense in which $(2a_1)$ of schema X *does* invoke interweaving seems misguided. On the other hand, if Philip does not mean this, but rather means something along the lines I have been indicating all along, he is indeed unable to account for the interweaving. For *not* every sentence specifically illustrates an interweaving of forms. The Kostman (1973) view of the matter is considerably better thought out; but so far as I see, still has the same unfortunate consequence of not accounting for the interweaving of the forms with one another in every sentence. For a correspondence theorist, the interweaving must be indicated in every sentence, and schema X just doesn't do the job. (Of course, the backdrop portion of the mixed theory of Ackrill is not subject to this criticism. It is a hallmark of such a theory that *not* every individual sentence must indicate a specific interweaving; only the backdrop must. But matters are different for correspondence theories.)

Sayre (1969, p. 210) offers an account which has the advantages of the $(2a_2)$ of schema X, but explicitly embraces an interweaving for its $(2a_1)$. Sayre is one of those who will happily "paraphrase away" talk of negative forms, and so I have done it (see Sayre, 1969, p. 210 n. 89, and the discussion on pp. 195–96, especially n. 68). There is, however, a problem in this "paraphrasing away." Sayre wants to say that $\ulcorner \alpha$ is not $\Phi \urcorner$ becomes $\ulcorner \alpha$ partakes of not-$\Phi \urcorner$, but paraphrasis depends on what it is to partake of not-Φ, not-Φ being in his view a set of forms. Sayre has throughout his writings maintained that this is to partake of (at least) one of the forms in not-Φ. So now the question is, just what forms are in the set not-Φ? In his (1970, p. 82) Sayre said, "any form A has its complement not-A which comprises every form different from itself"—that is, as context makes clear, "different from A," rather than the impossible "every form which is distinct from itself." But as he notes in his (1976, p. 585), this will make $\ulcorner \alpha$ is $\Phi \urcorner$ and $\ulcorner \alpha$ is not $\Phi \urcorner$ both true, as remarked above in regards to schema VIII. So in his (1976) he more explicitly demands that not-A be "an exclusive and exhaustive set" of forms, which he then further elucidates as consisting of an incompatibility range of forms. This is also the account offered in his most recent (1983, pp. 223–38), and is therefore presented here as his official view.

Schema XI: (Sayre, p. 210)

$2a_1$. The meaning of ⌜α is Φ⌝ is that every form Ref(α) partakes of is compatible with Ref(Φ).

$2a_2$. The meaning of ⌜α is not Φ⌝ is that there is a form F other than Ref(Φ) such that F belongs to the same incompatibility range as Ref(Φ) and Ref(α) partakes of F.

I wish to reject this schema, even though it has all the advantages of schema X and lacks its disadvantage (namely, the disadvantage of not being able to account for the συμπλοκή requirement). One reason for casting a wary eye on it is that it makes verification an interminable business: we have to look at every one of the properties of Ref(α) in order to decide whether it is in fact compatible with Ref(Φ). This seems a little too much. One can directly observe that Theaetetus is sitting without having to know or even take cognizance of any other property of Theaetetus, as seems clear enough to 263A5. I think it safe to say that Plato nowhere discusses any such necessity, nor does it seem "to constitute a likely and reasonable interpretation of Plato's own distressing brief discussion," as Sayre claims (p. 211).

But if we reject schema XI, it simply looks as though we will have to face the fact that there is insufficient interweaving happening to account for the συμπλοκή requirement. So perhaps we should look elsewhere.

Frede (1967) advocates a different sort of view, first propounded, I believe, by Taylor (1926), p. 389, and followed by Bostock (1984). Instead of locating the difference "behind" the predicate (or copula), they find it "behind" the subject.[20]

Schema XII: (Frede$_1$, Taylor, Bostock)

$2a_1$. The meaning of ⌜α is Φ⌝ is that Ref(α) partakes of Being in relation to Ref(Φ).

---

20. Taylor (1926) p. 389 says, "'A is not x' does not mean that A is nothing at all, but only that it is something other than anything which is x." Frede's position is somewhat more convoluted. In the cases I am considering, where α is taken to indicate an individual, Frede uses '— is$_2$ —,' which indicates that the predicate does not express what belongs necessarily to the subject (p. 33). This I have expressed by 'partakes of Being in relation to,' which seems to be what follows from his discussion on, e.g., pp. 33–44, especially 37–38 and 43, and p. 82. (2a$_2$) is stated on p. 79 as his (1'), but see also his discussion on p. 78. The 'partakes of Being in relation to' in (2a$_2$) may be slightly incorrect, for Frede intends not only '— is$_2$ —' but also his '— is$_1$ —,' where the predicate indicates *precisely* what is indicated by the subject. For the case of individuals as subjects, however, this seems to make no difference. It is in any case probably more accurate to treat Frede as a mixed theorist. See below, Frede$_2$.

2a$_2$. The meaning of $\ulcorner \alpha$ is not $\Phi \urcorner$ is that for all x, if x partakes of Being in relation to Ref(Φ), then x is different from Ref(α).

Frede recommends this (2a$_2$) over the (2a$_2$) of schemata VI–IX because his specifically illustrates Not-Being as a difference from Ref(α), not simply that something is different from something that applies to Ref(α) (as schemata XI–XI would have it). Frede claims that this is decisive (p. 79); but in the spirit of Keyt (1973), we can say that at best this is an indicator. Such a move on Frede's part requires understanding 257B10–C3 in a tendentious way. It reads: "what we get by placing 'not' before a term indicates something other (τῶν ἄλλων τί) than the following words; or rather, from the things indicated by the words pronounced after the negation." First it should be remarked that we are told that negation indicates *something* other, not that it indicates *everything* other, as schema XII claims. Of course, being told that it means "something other" does not by itself preclude its meaning "everything other"; but since Plato prefixes this with "we shall admit no more than this", it would seem that such a suggestion is blocked. Frede's tendentious reading comes from his interpretation of the last qualifying clause of 257B10–C3. This clause, which Frede crucially relies on, perhaps admits of two interpretations, that corresponding to Frede's interpretation—where the "things indi-cated" are the (physical) entities falling under the negated concept, and the Owen-Wiggins-Lewis-Philip-Kostman-Cornford interpreta-tion—where the "things indicated" are the forms corresponding to the predicate. Now, both interpretations can make sense of Not-Being as a particular kind of difference; Frede as "difference from the subject" or alternatively "difference from what falls under the predicate which was negated," and the opposing theorists as "difference from the predi-cate which was negated." I fail to see how the first alternative is so clearly Plato's meaning that the second alternative can be decisively ruled out.[21]

Bostock (1984, p. 115) also supports schema XII as being "the only one which makes good sense of Plato's account of 'not'." He, however, charges that the whole analysis rests on a confusion by Plato between an abstract term's being in a "naming (of a form) role" or a "generalizing (over instances of a form) role." As he puts it,

---

21. At the end of chapter 3, I tried to justify yet another possible reading of this passage in terms of "incompatibility." I think that the strict textual evidence does not rule any of these out. For similar feelings see Keyt (1973).

Whether the "is" is one of identity or of predication, we can explain 'is not Φ' as meaning 'is other than what the word "Φ" stands for'. But . . . where the 'is' is in fact an 'is' of identity, we assign the word 'Φ' its naming role, as standing for the form; and . . . where the 'is' is in fact an 'is' of predication, we assign the word 'Φ' its generalizing role, as standing for whatever is an instance of that form.

We will return, in chapter 5, to this distinction between naming and generalizing roles. For now we just note that this is one way to arrive at schema XII: start with $\ulcorner\alpha$ is not $\Phi\urcorner$, transform it to $\ulcorner\alpha$ is other than $\Phi\urcorner$, and then read Φ here in "its generalizing role" to yield $\ulcorner\alpha$ is other than everything which manifests $\Phi\urcorner$, from which the $(2a_2)$ of schema XII comes quickly.

As I have remarked on various occasions, a point in the favor of $(2a_2)$ in all of schemata VI–XI is that they give a clear-cut understanding to "interweaving of the forms with one another" in negative predications. For, they claim, *all* forms blend with the Different relation to one another, and through that they make discourse possible. The weakness of VI and X is that their $(2a_1)$ does not illustrate an interweaving. A weakness of schemata VII–IX seems to me also to lie in $(2a_1)$ where, although there is interweaving of a sort, it amounts only to the form Being blended with the form corresponding to the predicate. Now, schema XII has the same $(2a_1)$ as schemata VII–IX, and is therefore suspect for this reason; but furthermore, $(2a_2)$ reduces even the interweaving for negative sentences to this same "weak" type of blending. The only interweaving in $(2a_2)$ is exactly that of $(2a_1)$: the form Being with the form corresponding to the predicate when unnegated. The difference between its $(2a_1)$ and its $(2a^2)$ is merely which subjects partake of this blending. It is hard to see why such a "weak" type of interweaving should be so important as to "make all discourse possible." Frede too, notices a difference between these two notions of interweaving. On p. 43 he gives them as

1.   The interweaving between predicate-concepts[22] and the form of Being.
2.   The interweaving between the concepts which are mentioned in the sentence.

22. I shall here treat this term (*Prädikatsbegriff*) as if it meant the form corresponding to the predicate, since his explanation immediately after seems to demand it ("Die erste Art vonVerbindung von Formen wird von allen Sätzen vorausgesetzt. Dem Prädikat muß in sinnvollen Sätzen immer eine Form zugeordnet sein, die ist"). But he does not always seem

The first kind of interweaving, says Frede, is presupposed by all sentences. The predicate must always have an associated form which exists. The second type of interweaving, he continues, is not presupposed by all sentences—e.g., not by 'Theaetetus flies'; thus Plato must have been thinking of only the first type when he insisted that all discourse is due to such interweaving. This explanation sounds suspiciously like the discredited view of Ross. Recall Ross: "In the sentence 'Theaetetus is not flying' . . . the Form or universal of flying exists, so in saying the sentence we are not asserting of him something that does not exist, but simply something that does not belong to him." Now, Ross's position has been refuted already by many people, one of whom is Frede (p. 80), who says that any interpretation which identifies the meaning of 'is not' with that of 'is different from' will be unable to find an adequate analysis of negative predication, but only of negative identity claims. The interweaving presupposed by the (2a$_2$) of schemata I and II on the one hand, and schema XII on the other, are identical, and thus his own schema XII is as susceptible to this criticism as schemata I and II are.

The distinction Frede makes between, on the one hand, the interweaving of the predicate form and the form of Being, and on the other hand an interweaving between forms named in the sentence, and his claim that not every sentence illustrates the latter, seems to me to make his final and official position one of a backdrop, or mixed theorist. Enough people (e.g., Keyt and Lewis) have, however, interpreted him as a correspondence theorist to make it worthwhile to explore the possibility of attributing schema XII to Plato and comparing its virtues and defects with those of schemata VI–XI.

It seems to me that there is a series of related, philosophic difficulties with schema XII; and that this should make us chary of attributing it to Plato. First, let us notice that in order to verify that Theaetetus is not

---

to have this in mind. Immediately before (p. 42) he seems to distinguish 'Begriff' from 'form': "Und insofern sind alle diese Theorien sinnlos, wenn es keinen Begriff oder keine Form gibt, mit Bezug auf die Ausdrüke wie 'σύμμειξις,' 'Mischung' usw.sinnvoll sind." This seems to presuppose a "building block" role for 'blending'—something we have already discarded. Frede goes on to say (p. 42): "die Verbindung von Ruhe und Bewegung einerseits und dem Seienden andererseits im ersten Argument [251E7–252A11] genauso zu verstehen ist wie die Verbindung zwischen Mischung und dem Seienden im zweiten Argument [252B1–252B6], nämlich als eine Verbindung zwischen dem Prädikatsbegriff und der Form des Seienden, die—wie die voraufgegangene Diskussion 242–250 gezeigt hatte—verschieden sind, wenn nicht gerade das Prädikat '. . . ist seiend' lautet. Erst auf Grund dieser Verbindung sind Sätze sinnvoll, in denen das entsprechende Prädikat gebraucht wird."

flying, one must find every flying object and determine that Theaetetus is not any of them. Although this kind of "interminableness of verification" is different from that discussed earlier (where one had to look at all of Theaetetus' *properties* to determine that flying wasn't one of them), it still seems to me that any kind of "interminability of verification" is suspect. But interminableness of verification is not the only difficulty with schema XII. Consider just the consequent of its ($2a_2$), which Frede paraphrases (p. 78) as: 'x is not y' means '(x is different from z) and (z is y)' where 'z' stands for the class of things that fall under y or else the form y itself. So in order to determine whether this consequent is true, one must first make some sense of (say) 'Theaetetus differs from the members of the class of flying things' before 'Theaetetus is not flying' can be understood in the way Frede gives as his ($2a_2$). Now, I think it fair to say that Plato nowhere in the μεγίστα γένη section discusses difference between individuals, or between an individual and all members of a class. As I mentioned above, Frede's evidence for this is 257C1–3 where 'the not large' could be taken to denote the class of things which are not large. But as I also mentioned above, this is not the only interpretation possible. And while it is not so forced here to read in Frede's manner, doing so here lends itself to reading other areas in the same way—areas in which it is implausible (e.g., 256E7 see Frede p. 80; 257B3–4 see Frede pp. 83–84). Related to this (as Wiggins points out, 1970, pp. 299–300), such a view will inevitably lead to contradiction because it presupposes the well-definedness of the complement of every class. We can bring this criticism down to a more Platonic level by wondering how it is that Plato thinks (as he would have to if he accepted the present view) he can identify an individual well enough to be able to distinguish it from others, when he has no identifying characteristics or properties to help him. For example, in 'Theaetetus is not flying', if we have absolutely no characterizing properties with which to pick out Theaetetus, how is it that we can ever know that the consequent of ($2a_2$) is satisfied?—as we are able, since we can (according to Plato) understand the original negative predication. It seems to me that such considerations show the implausibility of attributing to Plato any interpretation in which 'is different' holds between physical objects.[23]

Lorenz and Mittelstrass (1966*a*) are really backdrop theorists. Like all

---

23. I believe that Frede actually attributes to Plato the idea that the complement of every well-defined set exists. On p. 86 he says that 'not-y' belongs to the things that have a proper essence (*eigenes Wesen*). This may also account for his belief that the *Sophist* makes use of "negative" forms.

such theorists, they believe that language is given legitimacy in virtue of some pre-existent blending which occurs among the forms. They are, however, quite certain that for any specific sentence they can indicate some blending. In this sense they can (for the time being) be classed as correspondence theorists.[24] In order to make each sentence indicate specifically an interweaving, they claim that we must understand what we call proper names as examples of a Kind: that to an individual must be specified a characteristic Kind under which the individual falls. They say that the word 'Theaetetus' refers to the *man* Theaetetus, and it has sense only insofar as one knows *a priori* that Theaetetus is a man. They give the following schema.

Schema XIII: (Lorenz and Mittelstrass$_1$)

$2a_1$. The meaning of ⌜α is Φ⌝ is that Ref(Aα) blends with Ref(Φ).

$2a_2$. The meaning of ⌜α is not Φ⌝ is that Ref(Aα) blends with some Form F in the same incompatibility range as Ref(Φ),

where by 'Aα' we are to understand something analogous to "the *man* Theaetetus" (if 'Theaetetus' were substituted for α).

In their ($2a_1$), "blends with" means "is compatible with"; and (as with other authors who believe this) I have replaced their "blends with the Different from" by "is incompatible with." It is the "A part" of 'Aα' that does the blending with Ref(Φ), so it is somehow "Man blends with Sitting" that gives the "ground" for the meaning of 'Theaetetus is sitting'— but not the *sufficient* grounds. For that, say Lorenz and Mittelstrass, we need to add the "necessarily true" 'Theaetetus is a man'.

There seem to me to be several difficulties with schema XIII. First, even if it *is* necessarily true that Theaetetus is a man, the blending of the form Sitting with the form Man will not be sufficient ground for the *truth* of 'Theaetetus is sitting'. For he could be standing while he is still a man, while the eleatic Stranger (who is also necessarily a man) is sitting. Thus the supposedly sufficient "grounds" are satisfied, while the sentence is false. Lorenz and Mittelstrass$_1$ want to separate the issue of truth and falsity of a sentence from the issue of the meaningfulness of a sentence. They admit that the blending of Man with Sitting gives only the *necessary* grounds for 'Theaetetus is sitting', but claim that this is all that is re-

24. That is, here we shall only concentrate on the blending they think gives legitimacy to language, and treat it as if it gave the precise sentence of the philosopher's language that would be required if they were correspondence theorists. Thus construed, they are Lorenz and Mittelstrass$_1$, to be distinguished from the actual position they hold, Lorenz and Mittelstrass$_2$.

quired—it gives *meaningfulness conditions* but not *truth conditions*. But for a correspondence theorist (as we are imagining Lorenz and Mittelstrass to be here), matters are not so simple. Consider a sentence like 'Theaetetus is flying': here, by their lights, for the sentence to be meaningful, the form Man would have to blend with the form Flying. But, since no man flies, the blending does not occur, and so they are forced to say the sentence is meaningless. Clearly, however, the sentence is *false*, not meaningless. The relationship between truth and falsity on the one hand and the meaning of positive and negative predications on the other, is clearly this: a meaningful sentence is false just in case its negation is true. Thus if we are to account for the truth or falsity of sentences we shall first have to assign a definite meaning to them. It cannot be sufficient in affirmative sentences to use 'compatible' as Lorenz and Mittelstrass$_1$ do in (2a$_1$), for this will give rise to precisely the same problem that allowing 'blends with the different' to mean 'non-identical' in (2a$_2$) of schema VII (Cornford$_2$) did.[25]

A second difficulty, of course, is their assertion that one is unable to understand a proper name unless one can fit it under a characteristic Kind. Two questions arise: Does Plato ever hold such a doctrine? And can any sense be made out of it? To the first, the authors refer to the *Cratylus* where such a proper name as 'Hermogenes' supposedly occurs clearly as a predicate. I do not propose to discuss that issue here,[26] but I think we can see that even if Plato did hold that silly position then, he no longer holds it in the *Sophist*. He gives the example of the proper name 'Theaetetus' as being of the one who is here before me now, and not necessarily as being characterized as a man. Further, Plato is fairly clear on the distinction between ὄνομα and ῥῆμα such that an ὄνομα names an entity of which we will then attribute some ῥῆμα. But if Lorenz and Mittelstrass$_1$ are right, Plato is horribly confused, since there are no ὄνομα but rather everything is (at least in part) a ῥῆμα. And this clearly

25. Thus (2a$_2$) does not give the required *correspondence* for (say) 'Theaetetus sits'; rather it gives something like "Man is compatible with Sitting" (or in their terminology, Man I-partakes of Sitting). In some sense this gives the "grounds" for the truth of the sentence, or gives a presupposition of the sentence, but does not give necessary and sufficient truth conditions nor does it give the meaning of the sentence. Since Lorenz and Mittelstrass are really backdrop theorists, such objections needn't tell against them, but they do tell against our straw-people Lorenz and Mittelstrass$_1$ who take schema XIII as a correspondence theory.

26. In fact I do not think that the *Cratylus* gives us such a doctrine, but will not discuss that here. For their justification, see Lorenz and Mittelstrass (1966*b*). Other interesting, but non standard, views can be found in Pfeiffer (1972), Weingartner (1970), and Richardson (1976).

contradicts Plato's present use of the terms at 263A5. Theaetetus says of the sentence 'Theaetetus sits', that "it is about me and of me." There is no hint whatsoever that it is about the form Man, nor about an instantiated characteristic of Man-in-Theaetetus. (Compare the criticism above of schema IV.) It thus seems clear that Plato didn't hold this view in the *Sophist*.

Furthermore, the whole view seems incoherent. Why was 'Man' picked out for Theaetetus? Perhaps Lorenz and Mittelstrass have some view about "essential properties"—something that I think no one has ever attributed to Plato of the *Sophist*,[27] something that is acknowledged to be new with Aristotle. In a confusing footnote (p. 138) they say that the form Wise or perhaps the form Philosopher might instead be used as the "characteristic" for Socrates. If so, it would be tautologous to say that Socrates is wise, or that he is a philosopher; and surely that will not do. Why did we not use the form Sitting in talking about the sitting Theaetetus? Obviously Lorenz and Mittelstrass₁ do not have anything like Aristotle's doctrine of essential properties, or anything like *anyone* has ever held (an essential property of X must at least be a property of X that X always has, and their examples of 'philosopher' and 'wise' do not fit this). We should not saddle Plato with an indefensible theory which in any case does not appear in the text under consideration. For similar remarks, see Guthrie (1978, p. 161) and Sayre (1969, p. 209, n. 87).

SOME CONCLUSIONS ABOUT CORRESPONDENCE THEORIES

What then should be our conclusions concerning correspondence theorists? That is, if we were to grant that Plato's thought here is to be explicated as his use of the philosopher's language in the way called for by a correspondence theory, which of schemata I–XIII should he be viewed as holding? I think that if we continue to view the *Sophist* as a refutation of Parmenides' Problem in the form presented by the standard interpretation, we can apply the principles of generosity of interpretation given in chapter 1 to come up with an answer. Reasons have been adduced along the way, but perhaps we should here adjudicate among them.

First, it seems clear, we should rule out schemata I–IV on the grounds that they do not solve Parmenides' Problem. (This alongside any textual problems one may find with them.) The other schemata all give *some* solution to Parmenides' Problem, so we must look to other features of

---

27. Arguably Plato's "characters" of the *Phaedo* might be essential properties, but that is a different doctrine than what we require here, and in any case there seems to be no carryover from the *Phaedo* to the *Sophist* on this matter.

these schemata to determine whether Plato is to be credited with them. Schema V is to be ruled out, I think, for various reasons. For one thing there is some textual difficulty in attributing to Plato a "negative counterpart of τὸ πρὸς ἄλλο." But also, on philosophic grounds, there are the problems involved with finding a "connector form" (this "negative counterpart") for sentences concerned with *denying* that there is any connection (e.g., negative existentials), and problems concerned with introducing forms that the "opposition" wouldn't recognize. Schema VI makes all true negative sentences necessarily true, and makes the determination of the falsity of false affirmative sentences "an interminable business." For these reasons it should be rejected if no better account is available. (We might also note in passing that according to schema VI, not every sentence explicitly mentions an interweaving of two forms. For a correspondence theorist, this failure amounts to an inability to account for the συμπλοκὴ εἰδῶν. I shall return to this issue shortly.) Schema VII is inadequate because it assigns the wrong properties to 'not'. (And it too cannot account for the συμπλοκὴ εἰδῶν.) Schema VIII is inadequate because it too makes falsification "an interminable business." It furthermore assigns to 'is' an ontological correlate, the form Being, thereby leaving us with no syntactical correlate to the "ontological glue" of partaking. I found this quite a serious problem above, so serious that in discussing schema IX (which I found to have only this one drawback), I recommended against it in favor of schema X, even though schema X is unable to account for the συμπλοκὴ εἰδῶν. The role of "building blocks" versus "glue" both in syntax and in ontology is crucial to a proper understanding of the point of the philosopher's language. I find that commentators who assume that the form Being will turn the trick for συμπλοκὴ εἰδῶν just haven't thought enough about the whole point of a "correspondence theory of language/ontology," or else they would realize that this move effectively undercuts the whole project. (More on this point in the "mixed theories" section below.) I found schema XI inferior to schema X even though it *could* account for the συμπλοκή requirement and even though schemata X and XI had the same account of negative predication. Its fault was making the meaning of a positive sentence be intolerably difficult. Schema XII guarantees inconsistency because it assumes the well-definedness of the complement of every class, and thereby commits Plato to thinking he can identify "all members of the class of non-flying objects" in the complete absence of any other identifying features. We should therefore reject schema XII. Finally, schema XIII would attribute to Plato some (incoherent) doctrine of essential properties; it furthermore confuses falsity with meaninglessness, and (if taken strictly as a correspondence theory) confuses truth with presupposition-satisfaction.

In sum then, the best of the correspondence theories is, in my opinion, schema X, despite its inability to explain the συμπλοκὴ εἰδῶν. But before we wholeheartedly embrace this interpretation, we must consider backdrop theorists and the whole question of whether Plato is to be considered a correspondence theorist or a backdrop theorist.

BACKDROP THEORISTS

I have characterized (Platonic) backdrop theorists as those who believe that the world of forms exhibits some particular interweavings which give legitimacy to language, but that these interweavings are not to be correlated in any one-to-one way with individual sentences as demanded by the correspondence theorists. This has become a rather common view of the *Sophist*, although different commentators have taken this route for different reasons. One reason to take it would be if one wanted to be a correspondence theorist but felt that $(2a_1)$ did not mention enough forms to perform a συμπλοκή. For instance, an advocate of schema VII or schema X might recognize this shortcoming and might invoke the backdrop to show that, say, the predicate form was blended with Being and hence the συμπλοκή requirement was satisfied.[28] Another sort of justification for a backdrop theory is the view that the backdrop gives us *preconditions* for the use of language. Behind *no* sentence should we look for a particular συμπλοκὴ εἰδῶν. Rather, we should view the relationships among the forms as a general presupposition for the possibility of any language. There must be, such a theorist might say, concepts available for us such that we can use them in comparing two things, and other concepts available so that we can distinguish things, in order for us to carry on discourse. Ackrill$_2$ (1955) officially views the role of the forms and their interconnections as providing us with just that; the general words in language that refer to the forms "pick up" these interconnections, and guarantee meaningful discourse. So the "interweaving of forms" is, in a way, antecedent to language; and thus we need not force ourselves to look at each sentence to find some interwoven forms lurking about. In a similar vein, Lorenz and Mittelstrass$_2$ (1966a) view the interweaving behind (say) singular affirmative sen-

---

28. It is possible to read many of our correspondence theorists in this manner, e.g., the holders of schemata VII–IX; but none of them are explicit enough on the point to decide how to take them, and so I have simply read them as correspondence theorists.

tences where the subject is a man as being given legitimacy by the form Man I-participating[29] in the predicate form. This is a presupposition of the sentence in this sense: if the sentence is true then this participation must happen. But it is unclear what Lorenz and Mittelstrass$_2$ attribute to Plato in case the requisite participation does not hold—whether the sentence is simply false, necessarily false, meaningless, or "the issue of truth and falsity does not arise." Finally, here, there are the views of Lee$_2$ and Lewis$_2$ who hold (Lewis 1976, p. 105):

> Plato is little concerned either with the truth-conditions of a negative sentence, or with supplying the details that will give a materially adequate account of such sentences. Instead, he is concerned almost exclusively with stating what is needed if we are to understand a negative predicate, and if it is to have a determinate meaning.

And the similar view of McDowell (1982, p. 120) who says:

> This unconcern with analysis [i.e., giving a correspondence account] need not seem a defect, if we see the ES's project as what it is: not to give an account of the sense of phrases like 'not beautiful', but rather to scotch a mistake about what entitles us to our confidence that they are not idle chatter, that they do indeed have the precise sense we take them to have. (No need, in executing this project, to produce any substantive theory about what that sense is.)

The idea here is that Plato will construct enough to the backdrop ("say what is needed if . . . [a negative predicate] is to have a determinate sense" or "say what entitles us to our confidence that they are not idle chatter"), that the details of "a materially adequate account" of negative sentences could be straightforwardly formulated.

The first two kinds of backdrop theories mentioned in the last paragraph—those where a συμπλοκὴ εἰδῶν is achieved in virtue of Being interweaving with the predicate form but where the determinate meaning of sentence can be given a la some schema's (2a$_1$) and (2a$_2$), or those where the συμπλοκὴ εἰδῶν is more pervasive than this but still the determinate meaning of a sentence is still to be accounted for by a (2a$_1$) and

---

29. Reminder: (form) X I-participates in (form) Y if and only if X is compatible with Y. (That is, if and only if some X is Y.)

(2a₂) type of correspondence—are more profitably viewed as *mixed theories*, and will be treated in the next section.

Let us deal here with the other two kinds of theories, which are more properly called "backdrop theories." We should spend some time trying to decide whether any of these theories can form an answer to Parmenides' Problem.[30] The question we must ask is how these theories propose to deal with the troublesome negative sentences. It is rather difficult to deal with backdrop theorists here, since they could all have a very complex backdrop in mind—one complex enough to embrace any or all of the interweavings mentioned by our correspondence theorists. Thus Ackrill, for example, might not only believe that there is the sort of interweaving mentioned explicitly in schema X, but also that there is interweaving of Being with every form, and also the interweaving mentioned explicitly in schema VI.[31] When the theory has so many possible kinds of interweavings that could be worked into it, it is difficult to know exactly where to criticize it. For this reason we shall attribute to the theories under consideration only the minimal interweavings that are mentioned by their authors, and act as though the theory denied any further interweavings. Possibly this is unfair to some of the theories, but at least it will have the effect of forcing such theorists to be more explicit in their account of the συμπλοκὴ εἰδῶν.

The backdrop theory of Lorenz and Mittelstrass₂ does not, it seems to me, show either how the philosopher's language can be said to exhibit reality nor how Parmenides' Problem is to be solved. According to Premise (3) of Parmenides' Problem, if some state of affairs exists in the world, some true sentence can express it. And by Premise (2), this true sentence

---

30. It might be objected here that I have begged the question against Lee₂, Lewis₂, and McDowell, since (as Lewis and McDowell say in the quotes given) they hold that Plato is not concerned with trying to formulate truth conditions for negative sentences (i.e., is not trying to give any replacement for Parmenides' premise (2)). The charge against me is accurate, but is one that any of the commentators under consideration might bring up in his defense. For, I suppose all the commentators would think that the failure of their Schemata to solve my Parmenides' Problem merely showed that Plato wasn't concerned with Parmenides' Problem as I gave it. To them I reissue my challenge: give a possible interpretation of Parmenides such that your schema shows how the problem is to be solved, and not just dark mutterings about Parmenides having denied the intelligibility of not-being. *Why* did he deny it? and what was so superficially convincing about the denial that Plato felt he had to devote a dialogue to it? How *precisely* is that argument seen (by Plato) as overthrown by the proposed schema? Just *what* does the backdrop do to solve it?.

31. Since the schema VI interweaving is a logical consequence of the schema X interweaving.

must designate a fact which is its meaning. In a god-school (of the sort discussed in chapter 3), this will amount to describing the relations among particulars and forms, and among the forms. The fault with the Lorenz-Mittelstrass₂ backdrop is that it does not give sufficient structure to do this. Consider again 'Theaetetus is sitting'. The relevant part of the backdrop has Theaetetus partaking of Man, and Man I-participating with Sitting. But far from giving the *meaning* of the original sentence, this backdrop does not even get sufficient truth-conditions (since the sentence could be false and the backdrop occur anyway). What needs to be added to their account is that it is the Theaetetus "part" of the form Man which blends with Sitting.[32]

The view of Lee₂ and Lewis₂ can be similarly criticized. Lewis does not really hold the view expressed in schema VI; indeed, he thinks that any such "particularization" drastically overinterprets the text, and that Plato should not be seen as trying to formulate any such account which might be "materially adequate." So according to Lewis₂, it is an inappropriate criticism of any interpretation of Plato here to point out that its account of negation will not work; rather, he says, Plato is only trying to give "a definite sense" to negative sentences and not trying to give their truth conditions. However, according to the standard interpretation of Parmenides' Problem—the version given in chapter 2—the two cannot be separated. According to that formulation, it is required that any successful counterproposal be able to specify precisely the "fact described by the negative sentence." And this simply amounts to giving the truth conditions for a negative sentence.

One can criticize McDowell in a similar manner. The claim he makes concerning the backdrop is this (p. 120):

> We may put the ES's point about 'not beautiful' thus: 'not beautiful' is to be understood . . . in terms of that part of the nature of otherness that is set over against it . . . 'Understood in terms of' . . . is best not taken as promising an analysis. 'Not beautiful' means exactly what it does, viz., *not beautiful;*

---

32. Lorenz and Mittelstrass note that they haven't given sufficient conditions (e.g., see pp. 142–43), but they do not see a problem here. They apparently have a different conception of what the philosopher's language is supposed to be like than what I am advocating here. (See their discussion on pp. 133–34 which, nonetheless, does not seem to me to adequately confront the issue. Indeed, it seems only to be an argument in favor of having *some* backdrop or other, and not an argument about whether correspondence theories are a necessary adjunct.) Again, I place the burden upon them explicitly to interpret Parmenides in such a way that their remarks about a backdrop (and in particular, their specific kind of backdrop) become relevant.

the role of the notion of otherness is in an explanation, at a
sub-semantical level, of why we do not need to fear that such
a semantical remark is condemned to vacuity.

So far as I understand this remark, it is precisely denying that Plato will
answer Parmenides' Problem. But if that is what it means, then surely
the principles of generosity of interpretation demand that we refrain
from attributing it to Plato. Such a criticism holds against any pure backdrop theory. One holds a pure backdrop theory only if one denies that
Plato is going to provide an answer to Parmenides Problem; so unless
and until some other, equally plausible, account of Parmenides is given,
we should not attribute a pure backdrop theory to Plato.

I indicated at the end of chapter 3, when discussing the god-schools,
that here may very well be a sense in which Plato is discussing "kinds"
throughout this section of the *Sophist*, when he says γένη or εἴδη or ἰδέα.
The sense I mentioned was that these might be concepts, or whatever,
that gave meaning to general terms. All that was required I said, is that
Plato's classical theory be included as one of the possible god-schools.
Ketchum (1978) and Teloh (1981, pp. 189–99) each give an account of this
view of Plato's goals. They would seem an excellent place to find the
requisite backdrop, or the backdrop portion of a mixed theory; unfortunately, neither Ketchum nor Teloh seem much inclined to do so. Rather,
they expend their energies on trying to prove that Plato was never talking about classical forms, only "kinds," instead of explicitly stating what
the backdrop is (or what the correspondence portion of the theory is, if
mixed theorists they be). Ketchum (p. 58) seems to think that the examples given using "blending," et cetera, in the arguments describing
which γένη blend, "were intended in part to explain what is meant by
'blending.'" But without further explanation of the "backdrop" there
can be no reason to accept this as a backdrop. And in any case, viewed
as a pure backdrop theory, without a correspondence component, it certainly cannot form an adequate answer to Parmenides' Problem.

It thus appears that the ploy taken by Lorenz and Mittelstrass$_2$, by
Lewis$_2$, by Lee$_2$, and by McDowell, of understanding the backdrop as
giving necessary conditions for the meaningfulness of sentences (i.e.,
for the possibility of their being either true or false) cannot serve as a
solution to Parmenides' Problem. Such a backdrop simply does not
touch upon the heart of the difficulty as stated in the Problem. What is
further required is precisely what these writers deny: a statement of the
precise configuration of "reality" that gives meaning to the troublesome

sentences. Without this, Parmenides' Problem continues undiminished in force in precisely its original form.[33] This perhaps gives some further sense to Bostock's complaint against backdrop theories (1984, p. 114), that they "seem to me totally unconvincing." It might have been better to say that they would have seemed totally unconvincing to Parmenides, and Plato knew it.

MIXED THEORIES

The upshot of the preceding discussion would seem to indicate that backdrop theories are doomed as accounts of an adequate response to Parmenides' Problem, since, if it does give "a precise characterization of reality" for every sentence, it is no longer a backdrop theory, but instead is a correspondence theory. But this is not *quite* right. One can have a correspondence theory "tacked on" to a backdrop theory. The backdrop is to give the "grounds" or "presuppositions" of language in general (and incidentally account for the συμπλοκὴ εἰδῶν requirement), while the correspondence part is to give a determinate portion of the backdrop as the meaning of each ordinary sentence.

Let us start by recalling the remarks of Frede (p. 43). He says that there are two types of interweaving. (1) the interweaving between predicate-forms and the form of Being; and (2) the interweaving between the forms which are mentioned in the sentence. Frede$_2$ points to the first type of interweaving as meeting the requirement that discourse demands an interweaving of forms with one another. Any commentator who holds a correspondence theory can adopt this view and thereby become a mixed theorist. For example, the holders of schemata VI and X, who do not explicitly make Being part of their correspondence theory, might adopt this to account for Plato's insistence on a συμπλοκὴ εἰδῶν.

But will it do the job? What's at issue at this stage with these kinds of mixed theories is not how well they solve Parmenides' Problem, for that is a job for their (2a$_2$) to tackle. Instead, they have to show how the interweaving of Being with every form would lead Plato to say "the possibility of any discourse we can have *owes its existence*" to this kind of interweaving. As I said in discussing schemata IX and XII, such a weak claim as "Being blends with every form" simply does not give sufficient reason for Plato to make this bold assertion. After all, *that* kind of interweaving was introduced without objection as being "obvious" to everyone, so if

---

33. Of course, a different understanding of Parmenides might make this sort of backdrop theory relevant. These writers therefore owe us an account of Parmenides which does this.

this were all there is to Plato's insistence on interweaving, he could have deleted the intervening parts of his discussion. I will not dwell further on this "weak" backdrop theory; at the very least it needs to have further kinds of blending included in its backdrop in order to account for the "necessity" of having such a συμπλοκὴ εἰδῶν. And I would say that such "further blendings" cannot merely be that each form blends with the Same and blends with the Different, at least not if these are understood simply as meaning that each form is the same as itself and different from any other form. Once again this is simply not enough to account for Plato's very strong claim about the effect of interweaving. Frede$_2$'s decision (p. 434) also to include these blendings in his account still seems to me, therefore, not to capture the full force of 259E5–6.

One might try to "beef up" the background portion of Frede$_2$'s theory by annexing to it Lee$_1$'s theory where the interweaving amounts to "the intensional construction of parts of the Different." Such an account, it seems to me, is a considerably better attempt to account for the entire strength of the συμπλοκὴ εἰδῶν requirement, at least if it could be made more precise as to what it amounts (more than saying it is "irreducible and *sui generis,*" as Ray 1984, p. 72, puts it). Of course, to be a mixed theorist, one must choose some correspondence theory to demonstrate how the backdrop generates an account for any particular sentence, to give thereby an answer to Parmenides' Problem. One could, I suppose, pick any of our thirteen correspondence accounts. Lee$_3$ picks schema VI, as we have seen; Ray$_2$ (1984, p. 71) picks Frede's schema XII. Now, I have already argued against schemata VI and XII as not being as philosophically good as certain other schemata, particularly X and XI. It therefore follows that, unless there be some reason that these last schemata cannot be married to Lee's account of "intensional negation," such a marriage should be given preference over one to schema VI or schema XII. But rather than endorse any such mixed theory, I would like to point to the obscurity of the Lee backdrop. It is hard to see how such an account is supposed to be considered so obvious to the opponents that they will adopt it as a truism. Until such an issue can be resolved, we should look at other backdrops to annex our correspondence theories to.

Teloh (1981, pp. 189–99) adopts the sort of backdrop envisaged by Ketchum (1978), presumably where the backdrop amounts to "truths about kinds." But he adds to it a certain correspondence component (p. 198): "Later in the *Sophist* the stranger also forges an analysis of negative predications . . . , and this further enriches the senses in which x can be F and not-F. Joan does not partake in Beauty, and hence is predicatively, not-beautiful, although there are many things that Joan is predicatively." As I understand this, Teloh recommends that the correspondence component to be added to Ketchum's backdrop is schema I. Besides endorsing a completely opaque backdrop, Teloh appears to be endorsing that correspondence schema which is least likely to form an answer to Parmenides' Problem.

One way to add the further blendings required from Frede$_2$'s account, but not to get involved in the obscurity of an "intensional" account of negation is the manner of Ackrill$_2$. Ackrill$_2$ (1955; 1957) claims that the backdrop contains all of the various relations that hold among the forms. For example, it includes the blending of Being with every form, it includes the establishment of incompatibility ranges of forms by their blending with the Different with respect to one another, and it perhaps also includes the relation among forms that has variously been called "Pauline predication" (by Peterson [1973] and Vlastos [1972; 1973]), or "A-participation" (by Lorenz and Mittelstrass [1966a]), or "B-participation" (by Lewis [1974]). The structure of this backdrop will be more fully investigated in chapter 5, especially in connection with how it is to be expressed in the philosopher's language, but for now we simply note that, according to this mixed theory, the Platonic insistence upon a συμπλοκὴ εἰδῶν is understandable. Certainly if there were none of these kinds of interweaving, then, indeed, language would be impossible. It is quite clear, therefore, that this mixed theory is preferable to the other mixed theory mentioned above. And since it accords the συμπλοκὴ εἰδῶν this prominent role in accounting for discourse, it clearly is preferable to those correspondence theories which do not have a sufficient amount of interweaving (i.e., do not have at least two forms blending for every sentence)—such as schemata VI and X.

I have said before that I believe schema X is the best of the correspondence theories. The present considerations make the Ackrill$_2$ mixed theory preferable to any of the correspondence theories, so long as it retains all the advantages of schema X. It does, of course, retain all these advantages because the correspondence portion of this mixed theory is precisely schema X. The backdrop is to give all the relations among the forms (chapter 5 will go into this in more detail, showing what sentences of the philosopher's language describe the backdrop), but for sentences about physical objects (e.g., Theaetetus) schema X yields a translation into the philosopher's language that shows which "partakings" are to be superadded to the backdrop in order to describe reality adequately. For this reason, the Ackrill$_2$ mixed theory is clearly preferable to any of the pure backdrop theories, since they do not address themselves to the issue of sufficient truth conditions (or, as we might say in light of Parmenides' Problem, to the issue of sufficient meaningfulness conditions).

A few more things in favor of this view should be mentioned before I attempt to deal with the traditional criticisms. (a) It solves Parmenides' Problem, at least with regard to negative predications. (Further problems about nondenoting subject terms will be discussed later in this chapter). A part of the "concept network" provided by the forms includes the relation of incompatibility of certain predicates. Thus, 'Theaetetus is not flying' can be treated as though it meant that Theaetetus did something incompatible with flying. (When applied to some particular sentence, the account looks very much like schema X, but it is incorrect to say that this account is merely an account of interweaving "behind" each individual sentence. It is rather an account of what happens "behind" language in general.) (b) The account of the truth of such sentences is at least as straightforward (in contrast to say, Moravcsik's or Lorenz and Mittelstrass$_1$'s—in schema V or schema XIII): Theaetetus is sitting (say) and that precludes his flying. (c) It does not make "synthetic" sentences "necessary," as some of the other semantical accounts did. (d) It does not force recourse to properties known *a priori*, or to "unique characteristics." (e) It does not force us to look to "all the properties a thing has," nor does it assume the well-definedness of the complement of every well-defined class—thereby neither making falsification "an interminable business," verification "an interminable business," nor guaranteeing a contradictory system. (f) It does not gratuitously add new forms to the ontology, either in the way Moravcsik (schema V) or the believers in "negative" forms (Lee$_1$, and Ray$_1$) want to add some unusual forms. Remember that the existence of forms of any kind has not really been granted yet by the sophists—they are waiting to see if a coherent theory can be built up out of them. If we had to make up unusual forms, especially ones Plato's opponents would naturally be inclined not to believe in ("negative" forms), the sophist will have won. Ackrill$_2$'s account causes Plato merely to have to point to relations which we are prepared to admit prior to philosophic wondering.

Let me now mention some of the traditional criticisms of this view, and try to ease anxieties on at least a few points. The usual criticism is that Ackrill's account presupposes an "incompatibility" reading, and that this is impossible. I have already dealt with this objection in chapter

3, trying to show that it is possible to read the account of negation given in the *Sophist* in an "incompatibility" manner (although it is not necessary to do so). It is true that Ackrill did not try to justify it, but he could—perhaps along the lines I suggested. The same criticism, although perhaps from a slightly different perspective, is made by Lorenz and Mittelstrass (1966*a*). They object that, while there is incompatibility presupposed in 251–259, "interweaving" cannot be taken to include "incompatibility" since the blendings, partakings, communions, and so forth, mentioned in 251–259 are all "positive" and never meant as "separation" (pp. 121–22). Moravcsik makes a related objection (1960, p. 122): He claims that the "blending and communion of forms" in 253–258 is nonsymmetric, whereas "incompatibility" is symmetrical. Thus, interweaving cannot mean any of the relations to be found earlier.

The answer to this was already to be found in Ackrill (1957). The phrase 'weaving together of forms' is obviously supposed to be a very "broad" concept (i.e., to contain many different subconcepts), and the concepts so contained are all the relations that have been mentioned as holding between the forms (e.g., 'partakes of', 'blends with', 'blends with the Different from'). Even though the first relation might not be symmetrical, the second sometimes is, and the last clearly is. This last, which is explained in 257–258C, is part of the key to the concept of 'weaving together of the forms'. While the first two show which (and how) forms blend together, the last shows which (and how) forms do not blend together. With this full sense of 'weave together' we can see how it is that this relation can be symmetrical and yet the particular subrelations into which it can be broken up (like 'partakes of') not all be symmetrical. And furthermore, we now know where the "separation" sense of "interweaving" is to be found: "blending with the Different from." (Ackrill's example of this is 'is a relative of' which is symmetric, whereas particular kinds of consanguinity relations, e.g., 'is a father of' are not.)

Lorenz and Mittelstrass (1966*a*, p. 122) also object that Ackrill's account cannot explain the later discussion of falsity. Above, I objected that neither Lorenz and Mittelstrass's schema XIII nor their backdrop theory can make sense of the meaningfulness of affirmative singular sentences, or else they cannot make sense of the falsity of them. We note here that Ackrill can make sense of both. First, the account of not-being as applied to negative predication (given above); and secondly, the falsity of a sentence consists in its negation being true. Or, as the formula at 260C puts the matter, falsity consists in not-being combining with *logos*.

Conclusions About Premise (2a)

It seems clear that a mixed theory is preferable to either a pure correspondence theory or a pure backdrop theory. Pure backdrop theories are unable to deal adequately with Parmenides' Problem because they do not give a determinate sentence of the philosopher's language (which displays the "reality" asserted by the ordinary sentence of which it is a translation) that will show how the Parmenidean argument can be avoided. And if they do give this, they are no longer backdrop theories, but rather mixed theories. Pure correspondence theories either have Plato giving philosophically implausible accounts of how to avoid Parmenides' Problem (and are thus to be ruled out by the principles of generosity of interpretation), or if they give adequate accounts of this matter, find themselves unable to explain Plato's insistence on the συμπλοκὴ ἐιδῶν. Only the mixed theories can do both; and of the mixed theories considered, Ackrill's is superior.

So we have found a way around Keyt's (1973) textual problems. Just because a number of divergent readings can be given to the text, all of which are self-consistent, it does not follow that there is no way to choose among them. We find the problem Plato thought he solved, and the principles of generosity of interpretation tell us that, of the textually possible solutions, pick the best. In my opinion, of the published works, this is still Ackrill$_2$'s.

Negative Existentials: Premise (2b)

There are however some problems remaining. For instance, I have occasionally mentioned that the structure of the backdrop needs to be more fully specified. These sorts of inadequacies seem best summed up under the heading, "What is the meaning of sentences with form-names in subject position?" This forms the topic of the next chapter. Another problem that is as yet unresolved is what to replace Premise (2b) of Parmenides' Problem with. Given either a pure correspondence theory, or the correspondence portion of a mixed theory, there still remain difficulties with Premise (2b). Without any story about this, only statements of the form ⌐α is (a) Φ⌐ and ⌐α is not (a) Φ⌐ have been accounted for, and we would be forced to conclude that the general theory is incomplete.

How is one to rephrase ⌐α exists⌐? Presumably by ⌐α partakes of the form Being⌐. But if this is so, what sense are we to make of ⌐α's do not exist⌐? We cannot say that there are any α's to partake of the form Nonbeing (even if there were such a form), so it seems that it cannot be anything like ⌜Ref(α) partakes of the Nonbeing⌝. I think it is fair to say that nowhere in the work under consideration does Plato ever consider noninstantiated forms—or even give so much as a hint that he believes there are noninstantiated concepts. However, from this we should not conclude, as McDowell (1982, p. 129, n.27) does, that there is no good reason to try to find some Platonic-like position which could have been adopted by Plato. If we are in the business of attributing a semantic theory to Plato, it is only fair to speculate how he might answer certain objections that can be raised to the theory (if only he were around today to do it).

Owen (1970, p. 246) speculates: "We can describe centaurs. They have hooves, not fishtails; they are made of flesh and blood, not tin; and they are fictitious, not found in Whipsnade Zoo." Taking at least the last clause seriously, we can be an analogue of an "incompatibility" reading of $(2a_2)$.[34]

Schema XIV: (Owen)

$2b_1$: The meaning of ⌜α exists⌝ is that Ref(α) partakes of the form Being.

$2b_2$: The meaning of ⌜α does not exist⌝ is that Ref(α) partakes of some form which is incompatible with the form Being.

One such form might be Owen's "occurs in works of Fiction only"; another might be "occurs in Cynthia's imagination only." Of course, there are other things of which we say that they do not exist, for example, "Socrates does not exist (anymore)." Also, entities in other possible worlds which do not occur in works of fiction, or in anyone's imagination. Perhaps we could have a form like "Existence in possible worlds i, j, k, . . . ," where *a* (the actual world) is not one of the listed possible worlds. Perhaps the above "time claim" about Socrates can be handled along the same line (by "reducing" tense logic to modal logic).

Heinaman (1983, pp. 12–13) recommends such a scheme with, however, a claim I would not endorse, that Plato actually advocated this view. (Heinaman claims that for Plato negative existentials only arise for tense claims, never for fictional objects. See his pp. 12–13 and n. 31.) Heinaman attributes the following to Plato.

Schema XV: (Heinaman)

$2b_1$: The meaning of ⌜α exists⌝ is that α partakes in Being with respect to the present.

34. I continue the numbering from before, but the present schemata should not be taken as alternatives to those given earlier; rather, they are supplements—they could be annexed (more or less naturally) by any of the others.

2b$_2$: The meaning of ⌜α does not exist⌝ is that α partakes in some F
which blends with the Different with respect to the present.

It seems clear that Heinaman wants "blends with the Different with respect to the present" to mean "is incompatible with partaking of Being
with respect to the present," and the types of forms which are supposed
to fall into this incompatibility range are "Being with respect to the past"
and "Being with respect to the future." (If they are not incompatible with
"Being with respect to the present," then schema XV does not count as
an appropriate analysis.) But on the surface, it seems that the three alleged forms are *not* incompatible; after all, some things which now exist
used to exist in the past and will exist in the future, such as Heinaman
himself. Perhaps there is some patch that can be placed on schema XV; I
will let advocates of schema XV worry about that.

But schemata XIV and XV, with their reliance on incompatibility between forms, are not the only contenders here. Swindler (1980) advocates a view that amalgamates the (2b) replacement with the "difference
from all instances" of Frede's schema XII. To understand this schema,
we first note that Swindler advocates the view that anything self-
identical has being; that is, all *possible* entities have being. In a more Platonic turn of phrase, "Being is expressed as 'participates in Sameness
with respect to itself'." (We note, as Swindler does, that although this
makes such items as Vulcan and Pegasus have being, it withholds being
from "impossible entities" such as the largest prime. Therefore, Parmenides' Problem will reassert itself with respect to these, since we will not
be able to say meaningfully, "The largest prime number does not exist.")
When one wishes to move from the realm of the (merely) possible into
that of the actual, Swindler wishes always to add some qualification,
such as "exists for astronomy," "exists for biology," et cetera. Using now
the "difference from all entities," we get such translations into the Philosopher's Language as: 'Vulcan does not exist' → 'Vulcan does not exist
for astronomy' → 'Vulcan participates in some form (e.g., Planet) all of
whose instances blend with the Different form (i.e., are not identical to)
Vulcan' (p. 742). Presumably, similar translations hold for general terms:
'Unicorns do not exist' → 'Unicorns do not exist for biology' → 'Everything which participates in Unicorn blends with the Different from (is
not identical to) everything which participates in Biological'. Also, presumably, sentences like 'Some animals (e.g., unicorns) do not exist (for
biology)' would be translated 'There is a form (e.g., Unicorn) all of those
instances blend with the Different from (are not identical to) everything
which participates in Biological'.

I will not attempt to give an explicit schema for Swindler's account of negative existentials; the reader is urged to try to find an account which gives the correct sense to a positive existential and yet follows Swindler in having a "exists for X" phrase. For instance, what can possibly block the addition of 'exists for Arlene'? But surely Arlene might think that there *is* a largest prime number, so how can we make it so that there is some possibility that Arlene is incorrect? Can an account be given which does not have the consequence that ⌜α exists⌝ and ⌜α does not exist⌝ both come out true (contrary to premise (1))? Does this matter? In any case, I think Swindler's account can be more perspicuously cast in term of the "different types of participation" to be discussed in the next chapter. This would show that, although I will continue to advocate an "incompatibility" portion for the correspondence portion of my mixed theory, the backdrop portion could be used by many different theorists—such as those who advocate Schema XII.

Another way to account for negative existentials is to introduce two "superforms," that is, forms which have only other forms partaking of them. Call them 'the E' and 'the E*'. Now, a form F partakes of the E if and only if there are F's in the physical world; and a form G partakes of the E* if and only if there are not any G's in the physical world.[35]

Schema XVI: (Furth)

2b$_1$: The meaning of ⌜α's exist⌝ is that Ref(α) partakes of the form E.

2b$_2$: The meaning of ⌜α's do not exist⌝ is that Ref(α) partakes of the form E*.

Of course, this is not quite enough; actually we will need an infinite hierarchy of forms corresponding to the numbers so that we can say such things as "There are three billion people." With such addition, Plato's theory takes on quite a resemblance to Frege's. Schemata XIV and XV seem best suited for cases where the subject is a singular term—such as 'Pegasus'; schema XVI seems best suited to cases where the subject is a general term—such as 'Unicorns'. And perhaps we can marge schema XV with schema XVI to give an account of "Dodos do not exist (anymore)." I shall not do this here, for my interests are elsewhere. In fairness to Platonic theory, however, perhaps we should let him have all these last schemata (even if none of this is actually to be found in the historical Plato).

My interests lie more in discovering what Plato thought was the ap-

---

35. This way of treating premise (2b) was suggested to me by Monte Furth. A similar suggestion is made by Wiggins (1970, 286 n).

propriate backdrop for his mixed theory, and it is to that topic I wish to turn. I close this chapter with a summary of the various schemata that have been discussed with respect to correspondence theorists. Chapter 5 will make reference to various of these schemata.

A SUMMARY OF CORRESPONDENCE SCHEMATA

Schemata I: (Cornford$_1$)

$2a_1$. The meaning of ⌜α is ⌝ consists in the fact of Ref(α) partaking of Ref(Φ).

$2a_2$. The meaning of ⌜α is not Φ⌝ consists in the fact of Ref(α) not partaking of Ref(Φ).

Schema II: (Ross, Allan)

$2a_1$. The meaning of ⌜α is Φ⌝ consists in the facts of Ref(α) partaking of Ref(Φ) and that Ref(Φ) exists (and Ref(α) exists?).

$2a_2$. The meaning of ⌜α is not Φ⌝ consists in the facts of Ref(α) not partaking of Ref(Φ) and that Ref(Φ) exists (and Ref(α) exists?).

Schema III: (Hamlyn)

$2a_1$. The meaning of ⌜α is Φ⌝ consists of the fact that A blends with Ref(Φ).

$2a_2$. The meaning of ⌜α is not Φ⌝ consists of the fact that A does not blend with Ref(Φ)
(where: A is the form or "characteristic" of Ref(α)).

Schema IV: (i-Schipper, ii-Bluck)

$2a_1$. The meaning of ⌜α is Φ⌝ is that Ref($Φ_1$), Ref($Φ_2$), Ref($Φ_3$), . . . , blend with Ref(Φ).

$2a_2$. The meaning of ⌜α is not Φ⌝ is that Ref($Φ_1$), Ref($Φ_2$), Ref($Φ_3$), . . . , do not blend with Ref(Φ)
i: Ref(α) = the overlap or intersection of Ref($Φ_1$), Ref($Φ_2$), Ref($Φ_3$)
. . . ,
ii: $Φ_1$, $Φ_2$, $Φ_3$, . . . , are all the predicates truly applicable to Ref(α).

Schema V: (Moravcsik, Runciman)

$2a_1$. The meaning of ⌜α is Φ⌝ is that Ref(α) blends with Relational Being with respect to Ref(Φ).

$2a_2$. The meaning of ⌜α is not Φ⌝ is that Ref(α) blends with the negative counterpart of Relational Being with respect to Ref(Φ).

Schema VI: (Owen$_1$, Lewis$_1$)

$2a_1$. The meaning of ⌜α is Φ⌝ is that Ref(α) partakes of Ref(Φ).

$2a_2$. The meaning of ⌜α is not Φ⌝ is that Ref($Φ_1$), Ref($Φ_2$), Ref($Φ_3$), . . . , blend with the Different with respect to Ref(Φ), where: Ref(Φ_1), Ref(Φ_2), Ref(Φ_3), . . . , are all the forms Ref(α) partakes of.

Schema VII: (Cornford$_2$)

2a$_1$. The meaning of ⌜α is Φ⌝ is that Ref(α) partakes of Ref(Φ).

2a$_2$. The meaning of ⌜α is not Φ⌝ is that Ref(α) partakes of some form F which blends with the Different with respect to Ref(Φ).

Schema VIII: (Wiggins$_1$, Ferg, Owen$_2$)

2a$_1$. The meaning of ⌜α is Φ⌝ is that Ref(α) partakes of Being with respect to Ref(Φ).

2a$_2$. The meaning of ⌜α is not Φ⌝ is that for all forms F, if Ref(α) partakes of Being with respect to F, then F blends with the Different with respect to Ref(Φ).

Schema IX: (Wiggins$_2$)

2a$_1$. The meaning of ⌜α is Φ⌝ is that Ref(α) partakes of Being with respect to Ref(Φ).

2a$_2$. The meaning of ⌜α is not Φ⌝ is that there is a form F other than Ref(Φ) such that F belongs to the same incompatibility range as Ref(Φ) and Ref(α) partakes to Being with respect to F.

Schema X: (Philip, Kostman, Seligman, Ackrill$_1$)

2a$_1$. The meaning of ⌜α is Φ⌝ is that Ref(α) partakes of Ref(Φ).

2a$_2$. The meaning of ⌜α is not Φ⌝ is that there is a form F other than Ref(Φ) such that F belongs to the same incompatibility range as Ref(Φ) and Ref(α) partakes of F.

Schema XI: (Sayre)

2a$_1$. The meaning of ⌜α is Φ⌝ is that every form Ref(α) partakes of is compatible with Ref(Φ).

2a$_2$. The meaning of ⌜α is not Φ⌝ is that there is a form F other than Ref(Φ) such that F belongs to the same incompatibility range as Ref(Φ) and Ref(α) partakes of F.

Schema XII: (Frede$_1$, Taylor, Bostock)

2a$_1$. The meaning of ⌜α is Φ⌝ is that Ref(α) partakes of Being in relation to Ref(Φ).

2a$_2$. The meaning of ⌜α is not Φ⌝ is that for all x, if x partakes of Being in relation to Ref(Φ), then x is different from Ref(α).

Schema XIII: (Lorenz and Mittelstrass$_1$)

2a$_1$. The meaning of ⌜α is Φ⌝ is that Ref(Aα) blends with Ref(Φ).

2a$_2$. The meaning of ⌜α is not Φ⌝ is that Ref(Aα) blends with some form F in the same incompatibility range as Ref(Φ).

Schema XIV: (Owen)

2b₁: The meaning of ⌜α exists⌝ is that Ref(α) partakes of the form Being.

2b₂: The meaning of ⌜α does not exist⌝ is that Ref(α) partakes of some form which is incompatible with the form Being.

Schema XV: (Heinaman)

2b₁: The meaning of ⌜α exists⌝ is that α partakes in Being with respect to the present.

2b₂: The meaning of ⌜α does not exist⌝ is that α partakes in some F which blends with the Different with respect to the present.

Schema XVI: (Furth)

2b₁: The meaning of ⌜α's exist⌝ is that Ref(α) partakes of the form E.

2b₂: The meaning of ⌜α's do not exist⌝ is that Ref(α) partakes of the form E*.

The
Philosopher's
Language

In chapter 4 I considered some re-placements that Plato might have found congenial for premises (2a) and (2b) of Parmenides' Problem. It might also be recalled that, so far as the correspondence portion of Plato's theory goes, I urged schema X ("incompatibility") for predications, although I also mentioned that this might only marginally be better than schema XI which in turn is only slightly preferable to schema XII. And I recommended all of schemata XIV, XV, and XVI for existentials. But this is not at all the whole of the story. As I also claimed in chapter 4, it seems clear to me that we shall have to have a "mixed theory" in order to account for much of what Plato seems to desire and need, in particular, the requirement of a συμπλοκὴν τῶν εἰδῶν. Therefore I wish to further the account of the "background" portion of such mixed theories; and in so doing I will, I hope, show that schemata such as XIV, XV, and XVI are not required in the form presented—rather they will emerge as possible additions to a more general theory of predication in Plato.

DIFFERENT TYPES OF 'IS'

There are various reasons why I find it implausible to say that Plato did actually make conscious distinctions among an 'is' of predication, an 'is' of existence, and an 'is' of identity. For one thing, he nowhere says he was making such distinctions. For another, it is not presupposed by anything he does say. While it is true that he used ἔστιν in different ways, for example, a "complete versus incomplete" use and a "regular versus converse" use, such uses would show up in any philosophical/conceptual discussion (and probably in ordinary discussion also). He just seems to be unaware that there is anything more to the matter than different uses of the same word with the same sense. Furthermore, if Plato had seen a distinction between an 'is' of existence and an 'is' of predication, he surely would have made a point of considering remedies for premise (2b). The fact that he did not do this, but rather concentrated on (2a) indicates he thought that by replacing (2a) he *ipso facto* replaced (2b); and he therefore could not have "distinguished the copula from the existential 'is'." Finally, as F. Lewis (1975) has remarked, a minimal condition for disambiguating a word is to hold it up for consideration. Instead, when Plato considers sentences like 'Motion is the same' and 'Motion is not the same', it is the entire sentence which is paraphrased so as to remove the appearance of paradox. Thus, the best that could be said is that identity sentences are distinguished from predicative sentences. But there is no hint there that any ambiguity is found in 'is', as opposed to a sentential ambiguity.

But, one might well ask, if Plato didn't find different senses of 'is' but did disambiguate sentences, what roles in these disambiguated sentences did he assign the ordinary 'is'? The answer to this will return us to the backdrops mentioned in chapter 4, and to the question of just what is the structure of the philosopher's language. But before this, we should look at some phenomena of English semantics.

Generic Statements in English

Generic statements are statements which, in some sense, are about "kinds." Just what makes a statement be about a kind is a complex interaction between the type of noun phrase used and the type of verb phrase that is predicated of it.[1] Since our study is Greek as Plato used it, we needn't embark on a detailed study of this phenomenon in English; but still, there are some general features of generics that can be equally well illustrated in English as in Greek, and I believe that pointing out some of these will aid in our understanding of Plato's talk about the forms.

One way to guarantee that one is talking about a "kind" is to use the phrase *the kind, X* (or any of a number of synonyms for "kind," such as *element, substance, species, sort*). For example, one might say "the element, gold, is rare," or "the species, Dodo, is extinct." But this is a relatively unusual way to put the thought. Far more common would be to say, "Gold is rare," or "The Dodo is extinct," or "Dodos are extinct." This clearly shows that mass terms (like *gold*), species names (like *the Dodo*), and bare plurals (plural common noun phrases without a determiner, such as *Dodos*) all can be used to designate kinds. (Or at least, can be used in a sentence which is about that kind, and about it because of the presence of that term.)[2] In these sentences, the verb phrase is of the type

---

1. The most thorough study of the phenomena of genericity in English is that of Carlson (1980), but see also Dahl (1985), Schubert and Pelletier (1987), and Krifka (1987).

2. These are certainly not the only sorts of noun phrases that can be used to make claims about kinds. Below I discuss indefinite singulars, such as *a cat* in *A cat is an animal*. Furthermore, in the right circumstances both demonstrative noun phrases and quantified noun phrases can be used to make generic claims, as for example *This car* (pointing) *is made in nine different countries*, or *Every car in this lot is made in nine different countries*. Clearly, the demonstrative or quantified noun phrase is being use here to talk about *kinds* of cars. Further types of examples can be found in Lawler (1973) and Nunberg (1977).

which does not "trickle down" to the instances of the kind. *Being extinct* or *being rare* (in the relevant sense) is not the sort of property which can be enjoyed by individual manifestations of the kind. But not all properties attributed to kinds are like this. For example, according to modern analyses of the semantics of bare plurals, the sentence *Electrons are negatively charged* is a predication of "is negatively charged" to the kind, electron. But because of its type of predication, this property is allowed to "trickle down" and apply indirectly to individual electrons.

Not every possible noun-phrase/verb-phrase is to be analyzed as predication of the verb phrase to a kind. Most quantified noun phrases (except of the sort described in the previous footnote) do not allow this: *Every electron is negatively charged* directly predicates "being charged negatively" to all individual electrons, and *Some snowflakes are hexagonal* directly attributes "hexagonality" to certain individual snowflakes. However, indefinite noun phrases sometimes show one face and sometimes the other. *A whale is a mammal* predicates "being a mammal" to the kind, whale (but is one of those predications which allow it to "trickle down" to individual whales), whereas *A whale is in the tank* predicates "being in the tank" to a certain whale. Not even using bare plurals or mass terms guarantees that it will be a kind predication. *Snow is falling, Gold is in my teeth, Dogs are barking outside*, and the like, all are about some individual manifestation(s) of the bare plural or mass term.

What distinguishes, in these cases, the attribution of a property to a kind from the attribution of that property to instances of that kind, is, under modern analyses, taken to be the type of verb phrase it is. Verb phrases which are "episodic"—that is, describe an episode such as the progressives *is falling, are barking*—and verb phrases that describe being in a location—such as *being in a tank* or *being in my teeth*—usually limit the sentence to individual instances. On the other hand, "nonepisodic" verb phrases generally are taken as making a predication to the kind indicated by the subject (*being hexagonal, being a mammal, being negatively charged*), when the subject term is a mass term, bare plural, or indefinite noun phrase (but not when it is a quantified noun phrase).

It has also been noted widely that a generic statement of the type that allows the verb phrase to "trickle down" to instances, does not require this "downward trickling" necessarily to affect all the instances of the kind. Thus: *The Lion has four legs, Dogs are loyal, A guppy gives live birth* are all true statements about kinds despite the existence of amputee lions, disloyal dogs, and male guppies. Just how many "exceptions" can be tolerated while the generic statement remains true is a very complicated matter having to do with the kind under discussion, its predicate, and "knowledge about the world." The converse phenomenon can also happen: all instances may be true, but the generic false nonetheless. For example, it may be the case that all children who have been born in Rainbow Lake are right handed, and yet *Children born in Rainbow Lake are right handed* is false. Similarly, it is known that almost all crocodiles die before the age of two weeks, but *Crocodiles die before they reach the age of two weeks* is false.

Why are statements like *Crocodiles die before they reach the age of two weeks* false despite the predicate's holding of the vast majority of them, and why are statements like *Dogs are loyal* true despite the existence of some that aren't? This is a deep question in the semantics of generics, and not one to be answered with any definiteness here. Fortunately, we don't have to give any hard-and-fast answers in order to understand Plato's views. One answer is to appeal to the notion of a "normal" instance of the kind. But the notion of normalcy being invoked here is itself quite difficult. (How is it that almost all crocodiles are abnormal?) Another answer is to appeal to a stereotype. Again, though, this is a notoriously difficult concept. A third answer might have to do with law-likeness. Rather than trying to answer these issues, perhaps we should just try to classify the different types of generic statements, and see what emerges.

Let us look again at the types of generic statements mentioned above. One type (the first type discussed above) directly attributes a property to a kind with no "trickle down" effect. I call these "direct kind predications" or DK-predications. Intuitively speaking, a DK-predication "talks about a kind *qua* kind," or (in other terminology) uses the subject term "as a name of a kind." In English, these subject terms might be any of a definite article plus common noun, a mass term, or a bare plural (and also, the sorts of examples mentioned in the preceding footnote). It cannot, for whatever reason, be an indefinite noun phrase: *A dodo is extinct* is ungrammatical.

Another type of generic statement allows the property to "trickle down" to manifestations of the subject term. This should not be viewed as an abbreviation of, or alternative way of saying, the sentence with an explicit quantifier. Rather, the sentence is well and truly about the *kind*, but some property of the verb phrase (or, the verb phrase in conjunction with that kind) decrees that it will also apply to the instances. Now, in some examples of this type of predication the property is inherited by all instances, and (usually, it seems) so inherited as a matter of scientific or nomic necessity. Thus we have *Whales are mammals* or *Electrons are nega-*

tively charged. In fact, even in this type of nomically necessary predication, one can relax the restriction that the property be inherited by all instances, if one employs a context-dependent notion of "most" and retains the requirement of nomic necessity. Under such an analysis, *The lion has four feet* would be grouped with *Electrons are negatively charged* on the grounds that, as a matter of nomic (biological?) necessity, most lions have four feet, where "most" is context-relative. If it were to turn out that most of the relevant group of lions did not have four feet, then we would be prepared to claim that the initial generic statement was false, not true. Details of such an approach can be found in Schubert and Pelletier (1987). The details are not important for the study of the *Sophist;* what *is* important for this study is to recognize a group of generic statements, different from the DK-predications, wherein the property "trickles down" to all (or to a context-dependent most) individual instances as a matter of (scientific or nomic) necessity. In the linguistics literature, especially since Lawler (1973), such generic statements have been called "universal-like" or (in recognition of their allowing exceptions) "quasi-universal." The point is that, despite the fact that a property is predicated of a kind, the property is inherited by all (most) instances, and that this inheritance is nomically necessary. I propose to call them "universally necessary, indirect, object predications," or UNIO-predications. In English the subject term can be a definite article plus common noun, an indefinite article plus common noun, a mass term, or a bare plural. As remarked, there is a complex interaction between the type of verb phrase used and the kind referred to which determines whether a given sentence is a UNIO-predication.

A third type of generic statement superficially has the form of UNIO-predications, but the property does not "trickle down" as a matter of nomic necessity in the same way. Instead of being inherited by all instances, the statement merely says that some (or a context-dependent notion of "many") of the instances manifest the property. Thus there are generic statements like *Hurricanes arise in that part of the Pacific,* which in no way predicate a property necessarily true of all (most) hurricanes. If we were to import a notion of lawlikeness into this, we would want to say that the sentence asserts, "it is nomically compatible with being a hurricane to have arisen in that part of the Pacific." In other words, this sort of generic has the force of saying that the subject and predicate are jointly instantiated, and that this is no mere accident—scientific laws predict or allow that this should happen. In the linguistic literature, such generic statements are usually called "existential-like" or "quasi-existential." The point, once again, is that despite the property being predicated of a kind, this property is inherited by some instances, and that this inheritance is nomically necessary. I propose to call such generic statements "existentially necessary, indirect, object predications," or ENIO-predications.

As remarked at various places in the foregoing discussion, English grammar uses a diverse group of devices to keep straight which type of generic statement is being made. It is not to be expected that every language will use the same devices. A shortcoming of the English method is that it can sometimes be difficult to determine which type is intended. Consider *Ice cream comes in many different flavors*, which has as its normal interpretation the DK-predication statement that the kind, ice cream, has many distinct subkinds. Yet there is an interpretation, a UNIO-predication, which says that each sample of ice cream contains (mixed together, perhaps) many different flavors. (This is a false statement, but still an interpretation of the original generic sentence.) Still a third interpretation of the sentence is as an ENIO-predication: among the objects one can get that contain many different flavors is ice cream. That is, some samples of ice cream contain many different flavors. Similar remarks might be said of a sentence like *Atomic bombs are produced in five different countries*, which may be taken as a DK-predication (which would assert that there are five subtypes of atomic bombs), as a UNIO-predication (which would assert that each atomic bomb has some of its components come from one country, some from another, . . . ,), or as an ENIO-predication (which would assert that at least one atomic bomb has some components from one country, some from another, . . . ,).

As I remarked, different languages are likely to distinguish these different types of sentences in distinct manners. For example, a language might use different adverbs, or different verbal affixes, or different case markings, or different determiners, or different particles to draw these distinctions more clearly than English does. (For discussion of how this works in different languages, see Krifka 1987.) It should be expected that in a "philosopher's language" such constructions will somehow be differentially marked. We shall now turn to the topic of whether in Plato's philosopher's language we can discern these distinctions. My claim will be that he does make the relevant distinctions, and that some of them are syntactically marked.

I take it that it is some such story as this that Ketchum (1978) and Teloh (1981) are urging when they claim that Plato is discussing "kinds" in the *Sophist*. Unfortunately, their account of what sort of "kind predication" they believe Plato to be discussing is left woefully underspecified: they give no account of how any sort of "kind predication" can overcome Parmenides' Problem, and their main justification for attributing it seems to be that Plato's classical theory of forms is believed by them to have been discarded. Most of the argumentation is then devoted to such issues as the dating of the *Timeaus*. My belief is that the classical theory of forms *is* a theory of kind-predication—just an incomplete theory. It can be completed in various ways, and the *Sophist* sets out to give us certain conditions on this completion. A theory of kinds and kind-predication is what is referred to as a "god-school of thought," and anyone who holds such a view is a "Friend of the Forms." Most, but perhaps not all, of the claims made in the classical theory can be retained in the theory of kinds to be developed here in the *Sophist*.

DIFFERENT TYPES OF PREDICATION/PARTICIPATION IN PLATO

Plato uses various locutions in the philosopher's language to replace our ordinary copula: κοινωνία, μείγνυσθαι, συμμείγνυσθι, μετέχειν, συναρμόττειν, μεταλαμβάνειν, προσγίγνεσθαι, ἐπιγίγνεσθαι, προσάπτειν, συμφωνεῖν, δέχεσθαι, προσαρμόττειν, κεράννυναι, προστίθεναι, συντίθεναι, προσφέρειν, among others. Most commentators do not attach any significance to the choice of word used. Thus Cornford (1935, p. 256): "Plato . . . wisely refuses to allow any one metaphor to harden into a technical term." This sentiment is echoed by Sayre (1969, p. 182 n. 45) and Guthrie (1978, p. 150), who suggest that any subtle differences one might detect among the terms is of little consequence.[3] It has furthermore been noted by various commentators that Plato sometimes uses these with the genitive

---

3. Van Fraassen (1969) also has a theory about differential use of terminology in Plato. It is that Plato has three relations: 'partakes of', 'blends with', and 'combines with'. 'Partakes of' is "a relation between individuals and forms," 'blends with' is a relation between forms which holds "if and only if some individual actually participates in both," and 'combines with' is a relation between forms which holds "if and only if it is possible" for the forms to blend. This is an ingenious account of Plato, and the first (so far as I am aware) to try to give a logic-based explanation of the *Sophist*. But it does have shortcomings. According to van Fraassen, μετέχειν is not uniformly to be translated as 'partakes', since sometimes it is said to be a relation between forms; and of the very important distinction between blending and combining, it is said that "Plato does not seem to have honored this distinction with a consistent terminological distinction." Clever though the resulting theory may be, it does not accord very closely with Plato's actual use of the terms in the dialogue (as van Fraassen is aware). It is more of a "Plato *ought* to have said . . ." than an account of what he did say. Of course, I do not for that reason think the reconstruction ought to be ignored (for the reasons given in chapter 1), but I do think it gives us reason to look for another equally clever account more in accord with what the text gives us. It is this account that I intend to give in what follows.

and sometimes with the dative construction. Some of these commentators do not take this to indicate anything important. Thus Ross remarks (1951, p.111 n. 6), "Though Plato uses the two different constructions, he does not seem to attach any importance to the difference between them"—a remark cited approvingly by Guthrie (1978, p. 150 n. 1) and Sayre (1969, p. 196 n. 69) who adds. "I see no reason in such grammatical considerations to conclude that Plato was attempting to distinguish particular forms of predication." By contrast, other commentators have made much of the distinction. Ackrill (1957, p. 220) says

> κοινωνεῖν followed by the genitive (e.g., θατέρου) is used where the fact being asserted is that some εἶδος is (copula) such-and-such (e.g., different from . . .); that is, it is used to express the fact that one concept *falls under* another. The dative construction, on the other hand, occurs in highly general remarks about the connectedness of εἴδη, where no definite fact as to any particular εἴδη is being stated. Surely this confirms—what ordinary Greek usage would suggest—that Plato consciously uses κοινωνεῖν in two different ways. Sometimes it stands for the general symmetrical notion of 'connectedness', sometimes it stands for a determinate non-symmetrical notion, 'sharing in'.

Lorenz and Mittelstrass (1966a, p. 131 n. 60) say, in translation

> Plato distinguished two different meanings of κοινωνία . . . , which are exhibited by different grammatical constructions. . . . The construction with the genitive . . . represents a 'participation' phrase, or as we want to say, represents an A-relation (e.g., when the Forms Man and Mortal are in an A-relation, all men are mortal); while the construction with the dative . . . represents a 'compatibility' relation, or as we want to say, are in an I-relation (e.g., when the Forms Man and Laughter are in an I-relation, some man laughs).

Ackrill and Lorenz and Mittelstrass apparently agree to some extent on the import of the dative construction, at least when it follows κοινωνία.[4] (I shall shortly illustrate the fact that this assessment holds for the other metaphorical words also). However, they disagree on the force

4. I say "apparently" here because Ackrill's "general symmetric notion of 'connectedness' " might be something other than the attribution of properties to individuals (as the Lorenz and Mittelstrass I-relation has it). But Ackrill is unfortunately vague as to what exact relation he has in mind, so it is difficult to tell whether he holds the same view as Lorenz and Mittelstrass do. This is discussed in more detail below.

of the genitive construction, Ackrill holding that it represents an "ordinary" copulative predication while Lorenz and Mittelstrass holds that it represents what they call A-relation and what has since become known as "Pauline predication."[5] Vlastos (1973) also sees a distinction at work here in the *Sophist* (and other places besides). He separates what we might call ordinary predication (Ackrill's notion of "falling under") from what he calls "Pauline predication" (the Lorenz and Mittelstrass notion of "A-relation"); but in his published works, he does not single out the dative use of the blending metaphors.[6]

In order to standardize reference to these different kinds of predication or participation, I am going to conflate the distinction between predication and participation, always using a participation phrase, and trusting the context to determine whether a linguistic relation or an ontological relation is meant. I shall use the following terminology:[7]

Φ DK-participates in Ψ	iff	Ref(Φ) is an instance of Ref (Ψ).
Φ UNIO-participates in Ψ	iff	As a matter of nomic necessity, everything which is an instance of Ref(Φ) is also an instance of Ref(Ψ).
Φ ENIO-participates in Ψ	iff	As a matter of nomic necessity, something which is an instance of Ref(Φ) is also an instance of Ref(Ψ).

The participation sentences (on the left of the 'iff') are supposed to be translations into the philosopher's language of different kinds of natural

5. The term is from Peterson (see her 1973) and popularized by Vlastos (see n. 88 of his 1972). A-predication of the Lorenz and Mittelstrass sort is the same as Peterson's original usage; but in Vlastos's hands, in addition to this A-predication, it includes such features as necessity, making it more like the UNIO-predication described above. (It also includes the feature of "categoricity," making it unlike UNIO-predication.)

6. Frank Lewis (personal communication) tells me that Vlastos has made the distinction in lectures, although he (Lewis) does not remember Vlastos's final position on the dative. (That Vlastos recognizes the construction is not in doubt. See his [1973], nn. 49, 62, and 65. In n. 65, it is apparently claimed that the dative is to be replaced by "is$_{op}$," that is, our DK-participation). More about the Vlastos distinction occurs below.

7. F. Lewis (1974) has also drawn a trichotomy here. He used the terminology A-, B-, and C-predication where I use DK-, UNIO-, and ENIO-participation (except that his distinction is without the addition of the "nomic necessity" clause, making the three types of predication be wholly extensional). Unfortunately, he has decided against publication of this paper. The account given here follows closely Lewis's discussion in that paper, although there are differences of detail at many places. But credit (a) for the trichotomy, and (b) for the recognition that the interpretive differences among those commentators who

language sentences—those kinds of sentences whose truth conditions might be given by the right side of 'iff'.[8] It is to be emphasized that these sentences of the philosopher's language are statements about *forms* blending—they are not to be viewed as a clumsy way of putting the ordinary language sentence, and they are not directly about individuals,

---

find some genitive/dative distinction at work here is due to its being a trichotomy rather than a dichotomy, is owed to him. The main advance of the present work is a consideration of *all* the occurrences in the text rather than just the fourteen cited by Ross, and a consideration of how the trichotomy interacts with negation. (Lewis chose to exclude from consideration "negative contexts" since his interests in that paper were elsewhere.)

8. The UNIO-participation bears a very strong resemblance to Vlastos's (1973) "Pauline predication," rather than to Peterson's (1973) notion of the same name. His is "intensional," hers "extensional" like Lewis's (1974) B-participation. So here, if Man UNIO-participates in Mortal, then it is a matter of nomic necessity that men be mortal. And I have also added this to ENIO-participation, since I also see these as "intensional," so that if Man ENIO-participates in Laughter, then (the kinds/concepts) Man and Laughter nomically allow some man to laugh. Should these types of predication have this nomic element? There are in fact two questions here: (1) Should a correct account of these types of predication as they are manifested in some natural language (e.g., English) have nomic necessity? (b) In Plato's philosopher's language should they have nomic necessity? My view of question (a) is that, yes, an adequate description of (e.g.) English would attribute this law-likeness to UNIO- and ENIO-predications. Consider the examples given in the previous Section: *Babies born in Rainbow Lake are right-handed* is not a true UNIO-predication despite its being true that all such babies are right-handed; *Dogs are in the yard* is not a true ENIO-predication even if there are dogs in the yard. The reason is that these are accidental generalizations rather than nomic truths. But when it comes to discerning Plato's actual intents, matters are not so clear, for he seems simply not to distinguish between accidental generalizations and law-like statements. One possible explanation for this may be that the only types of predication he finds of interest here are relations among the forms—and perhaps he views all such relations to be nomically necessary. Possibly, also, Plato views (what we would call) accidental generalizations to be, in reality, nomically necessary: he might say that they all "follow from" truths about the forms. I think that very little of what I propose below hinges on a difference between accidental generalizations and law-like statements. Generosity of interpretation suggests that we therefore allow the law-likeness requirement to stand in the philosopher's language.

When Vlastos discusses (what we call) DK-participation, he also adds the requirement of "categoricity," so that when one form DK-participates in another, some important properties about formhood are described. I do *not* wish to add this requirement: it seems to me that DK-participation is the same regardless of whether a form or a physical object is the subject of the participation. On this point one should consult Owen (1968) on the distinction between "A and B predicates" and the further subdivision into "B_1 and B_2 predicates," although Owen does not wish to accord recognition of this to Plato by means of any explicit grammatical construction. Owen's distinctions, though similar, are not identical with the ones I am drawing here.

I should also emphasize again that I always use "DK-, UNIO-, ENIO-*participation*" regardless of whether I am talking about the linguistic construction or the ontological correlate of blending among the forms. As we shall see, sometimes this relationship is symmetric. I do not wish my use of 'participates in' to be taken to imply otherwise.

but rather are about individuals only indirectly. They are viewed on a par with Plato's earlier pronouncements about forms, and are ontologically revealing in the sense that these kinds of blendings provide the underlying ontological explanation for the states of affairs indicated by their truth conditions. Furthermore, given DK-participation, UNIO- and ENIO-participation can be paraphrased in terms of it:

Φ UNIO-participates in Ψ iff   of nomic necessity, everything which DK-participates in Ref(Φ) also DK-participates in Ref(Ψ).

Φ ENIO-participates in Ψ iff   of nomic necessity, something that DK-participates in Ref(Φ) also DK-participates in Ref(Ψ).

Thus I include in the notion of DK-participation both the relation between a physical object and a form (when the object exemplifies the form)—more or less as the classical theory held,[9] and also the relation which holds between forms when one exemplifies the property named by the other. (And is not to be "transferred to the instances.") This latter type of DK-participation is new to the theory being developed, and is the first step toward answering questions about what it means to predicate one form of another.

Given that the ordinary language sentence does not explicitly have such phrases as "DK-participates," and given that sometimes such ordinary language predications are ambiguous between a DK- and a UNIO-participation (for example), when I wish to emphasize in the ordinary language that it is the DK-participation sense in which I am interested, I will sometimes use phrases like "Φ (qua form)." This is to be understood as making Φ take "its naming role," or as I would prefer to say, it forces a DK-interpretation on the sentence. Thus a natural language sentence like *Reading is interesting* can be seen as meaning either that all (most) actual cases of reading something are interesting experiences, or that the concept of reading is an interesting concept. When I wish to emphasize that it is the second meaning we are analyzing, I will say *Reading (qua form) is interesting*.

Is it possible to find these different kinds of participation in this section of the *Sophist*? I think it is. Of course, Plato never draws our atten-

9. This is at odds with F. Lewis (1974) and Vlastos (1973), who restrict it to a relationship between forms.

tion to any such distinctions, but perhaps one reason for this is Ackrill's "[it is] what ordinary Greek usage would suggest," and therefore Plato's audience would understand it merely by reading it. Now, for reasons of the sort described in chapter 1, I would not wish to put much weight on such a claim. Rather I think the way to find out if he was in fact employing these distinctions is to look at what examples he gives, whether he thought these example sentences were true or false, and then decide what kind of participation he must have had in mind in order to account for these true/false judgments of his, and for his beliefs that certain consequences follow from the participation examples.

This task is difficult for the various reasons. For one thing, it is often difficult to decide whether Plato considers the example sentence to be true or false. Even when a statement is known to be (say) false, it could be so for a variety of reasons—some favoring the reading of one kind of participation and others favoring another kind of participation. A similar sort of problem occurs when we know that Plato considers an example to be false, but also considers it to follow from positions that are hypothetically accepted for purposes of argument. Still another challenge to the importance of the differential uses of the cases comes from Greek grammar; it is just more common to use the genitive with a certain set of words and the dative with another set of words. If Plato's usage corresponds to this common practice, then it might be argued that there is really nothing here that needs explaining.

I therefore propose to do the following: I shall construct a "plausible account" of the uses of the various blending metaphors by starting with the clearest cases and assigning them meanings in accordance with the DK-, UNIO-, ENIO-participation model above. I then attempt to assign meanings to less clear cases, of the sort mentioned in the last paragraph. At the end I shall have tried to make the theory yield an explanation of all the uses. As we shall see, this theory is consistent and has various interesting consequences for Plato's claim that he can answer Parmenides' challenge. However, in accordance with the "indeterminacy of interpretation" thesis advocated in chapter 1, I would not claim that this is the only way to interpret this portion of the *Sophist*. Rather, I view the plausibility of this interpretation and the way it nicely fits into the other apparatus being used as adding further evidence to an *overall* interpretation. Although the justification for any one portion of this larger interpretation may seem slight or even circular, the accumulation of these smaller portions reinforce one another and make the circle of explanation larger and larger. When a circle is large enough, it takes on a life of its own, and can withstand attacks aimed at only one point. Here I hope to have given a large enough circle of explanation and interpretation that an attack on the interpretation of Parmenides of chapter 2, or on the account of Plato's naming principle, or on the explanation of the Friends of the Forms, or on the correspondence understanding of the συμπλοκή, or on the account of blending and the philosopher's language, cannot succeed. The entire circle would need to be overthrown at once by a reinterpretation of all these issues.

PARTICIPATION PASSAGES: 249D9–264B8

At 249D9 the Stranger abruptly breaks off the train of thought which forced Friends of the Forms to admit 'the children's prayer' (that being is both what moves and what is at rest), and he proceeds to the so-called constructive part of the dialogue, wherein he is going to provide an account of both being and not-being on behalf of the Friends of the Forms. This section closes when, at 264B9, he returns to the earlier task of defining the sophist by division. Between these lines occurs a densely argued account of how the forms/kinds blend, mix, harmonize, and partake of one another. It is in this central portion of the *Sophist* that I think we can find Plato making use of the "different kinds of participation." I therefore start by providing a list of all these passages, at first broadly divided into four types.

(a) There are those cases where the items which are blending are not forms (or kinds). Sometimes these other, incidental things are examples such as letters, sounds, or words. I will not attempt to assign them a type of participation, but the reader can verify that the present interpretation extends nicely to them: some letters ENIO-blend with others, some sounds ENIO-blend with others, some ὀνόματα ENIO-blend with ῥήματα. Still other passages on this list are cases where, seemingly, a blending term is being used in a way not indicating "blending proper." For example, 251D8 uses συναγάγωμεν to mean "we gather a bunch of forms together and consider them all" (this sentence also has ἐπικοινωνεῖν in it being used as a normal blending metaphor).

(b) There are cases where clearly forms are doing the blending, but the sentence does not specify an "object of blending," and therefore one cannot apply any grammatical criterion to tell what kind of participation is used. In English such a phenomenon occurs in sentences like, "X and Y blend" where there is no "object of blending." This is contrasted with "X and Y blend with one another" where the 'one another' is the "object of blending." It should be noted that occasionally in the type (a) passages of blending of incidental nonforms, this phenomenon occurs also.

(c) There are uses of "all pervasiveness" or "running through all the forms," which neither the grammatical criterion nor the sense attached to the different types of participation covers, strictly speaking. Perhaps a phrase like "kind X pervades all forms" means something like "kind X has all the types of participation with all forms," but this is a speculation I cannot back up. There is also a kind of "opposite" to this, meaning that a form separates off or divides up another form into pieces. (When either of these sorts of blending occur with nonforms, they appear in group (a), as with 253A4.) Along these lines, Plato sometimes makes reference to "all the different types of blending there are," for instance, 253B9: "Since we have agreed that the kinds have the same relations to one another with regards to partaking [μείξεως]." Here it seems that Plato is talking about all the types of partaking or blending, rather than any one in particular. In group (c) below, I distinguish these two kinds as "all pervasive" versus "reference to all types of blending."

(d) Finally, I give a list of passages in which the blending terms are used in the "usual" way, and with an "object of blending."

I give all these lists in English, but with the "blending" term untranslated. (Sometimes this makes for a mismatch between the Greek form and what is required for English, but I trust this will be tolerated.) Where appropriate (group (d)), I state what case the term denoting the "object of blending" occurs in, and what sort of participation I take it to be. Justification for the latter will be in the form of a "plausible story" which makes the overall account ring true. This "story" follows the lists. Within any of these groups, the passages are given in the order in which they occur in the text, with their page and line numbers, but, as indicated above, when I move on to give my "plausible story" (especially of the entries of group (d)), I will discuss them in a somewhat different order. Here then are the occurrences of the blending terms in 249D9–264B8.

Group (a): Blending of non-forms, and 'blending' used metaphorically

page	translation
251D8	Are we to συναγάγωμεν them all ⟨the forms⟩ up. . . .
253A1–2	For also of these ⟨letters⟩, some ἀναρμοστεῖ with the others in any way, but others συναρμόττει
253A4	The vowels, in contrast to the others, δεσμός through them all as a bond . . .

Group (a): Blending of non-forms, and 'blending' used metaphorically
(*continued*)

page	translation
253A6	so that, without one of them ⟨vowels⟩, the others cannot ἁρμόττειν with others.
253A8	Does everyone know with ⟨letters⟩ are able to κοινωνεῖν with which . . .
253B2	One who has the art of knowing which things ⟨sounds⟩ are συγκεραννυμένους is musical.
261A2	. . . and having proved that falsehood is, ἔνοχος the sophist in it . . .
261D5	. . . whether all ⟨words⟩ συναρμόττει with each other.
261E1	. . . some ⟨words⟩, spoken in order and indicating something, συναρμόττει, . . .
261E2	. . . while others signifying nothing in that succession, ἀναρμοστεῖ.
262C4	. . . until someone κεράσῃ verbs with nouns.
262C5	But then they ⟨verbs and nouns⟩ ἥρμοσεν . . .
262C6	. . . and their ⟨verbs and nouns⟩ first συμπλοκή immediately becomes discourse.
262D4	. . . does not merely name, but finishes something, by συμπλέκων verbs with nouns.
262E1	So also in the area of vocal signs, some don't ἁρμόττει . . .
262E2	. . . but others of them, ἁρμόττοντα, cause discourse.
262E12	I'll give you a statement by συνθείς of a thing and an action, by means of a noun and a verb.
263D3	. . . it really seems as if such a σύνθεσις, made of both nouns and verbs, really and truly has become false discourse.
264B1	What we call "seems to be" is a σύμμειξις of perception and belief.
264E2	. . . getting ahold of the κοινωνίας of the sophist . . .
264E3	. . . until we have stripped him of all κοινά about him.

Group (b): Blending of forms, but no "object of blending"

page	translation
250B8	Rest and Motion are περιεχομένην ⟨by being⟩
251D6	. . . but treat them ⟨Motion and Rest⟩ as things which are ἄμεικτα?
252B6	. . . if there is no σύμμειξις.
252E2	And one of these is necessary: either every ⟨kind⟩, or no

Group (b): Blending of forms, but no "object of blending" (*continued*)

page   *translation*

	⟨kind⟩, or some ⟨kind⟩ does while others do not, want συμμείγνυσθαι.
253C2	. . . so that they ⟨the forms⟩ are capable συμμείγνυσθαι.
253E1	. . . and this is knowing how to distinguish, by kind, in what way they can and in what way ⟨they⟩ cannot κοινωνεῖν.
259A6	. . . and on the one hand Difference, μετασχόν [see group (d) below] Being, is, because of this μέθεξιν.
260C2	But if it ⟨not-Being⟩ does μειγνυμένου, false belief and speech will come to be.
260D8	. . . and that Speech and Belief are amongst those that don't μετεχόντων.
260E3	. . . for falsehood is not at all if this κοινωνίας has not been put together.

Group (c): "All pervasive" [= type 1] and "Reference to all kinds of blending" [= type 2].

page/type   *translation*

253B9 [2]	Since we have agreed that the kinds have the same relation to one another with regards to μείξεως.
253B12 [2]	. . . and which sorts ⟨of kinds⟩ do not δέχεται one another.
253C1 [1]	If there are some ⟨kinds⟩ that συνέχοντ' all
253D5–D9 [1]	He who can do this ⟨division by kinds⟩ sees clearly a single idea [ἰδέαν] entirely διατεταμένην through many, each one lying separately, and of many ⟨ideas⟩ different from each other περιεχομένας from without by one ⟨idea⟩, and again one ⟨idea⟩ συνημμένην in one through [Fowler: by the union of] many wholes, and many ⟨ideas⟩ διωρισμένας completely apart.
257C7 [1]	The nature of the Different seems to me to be κατακεκερματίσθαι, in the same way as knowledge.
258E1 [1]	. . . having shown that the nature of the Different is, and also is κατακεκερματισμένην over all the things which are relative to one another
259A5 [1 and 2?]	. . . both Being and Difference διεληλυθότε all things and each other
260B8 [2]	Not being has shown itself to us as some one kind, which is, amongst the others, and διεσπαρμένον in all that is.

Group (d): Participation phrases with "an object of blending"

page	object case	participa- tion type	translation
250B9	genitive	UNIO	Noticing their ⟨Motion and Rest⟩ κοινωνίαν in Being, you speak of them as being
251D5	dative	ENIO	Shall we neither προσάπτωμεν Being to Motion and Rest . . .
251D6	dative	ENIO	. . . nor ⟨προσάπτωμεν⟩ anything to anything . . .
251D7	genitive	UNIO	. . . and without the power to μετα- λαμβάνειν with each other?
251D9	dative	ENIO	Or shall we collect them all up as being able to ἐπικοινωνεῖν with one another?
251E8	dative	ENIO	Let's suppose they first say that nothing has any power for κοινωνίας with anything in any re- gard.
251E9	genitive	UNIO	Then Motion and Rest don't μεθέ- ξετον with Being.
252A2	genitive	UNIO	Will either of them ⟨Motion and Rest⟩ be, if not προσκοινοῦν in Being?
252B9	genitive	UNIO	. . . those ⟨theorists⟩ who never al- low us to speak of one thing by an- other's name, even though it is by κοινωνία in the quality produced by that other.
252D3	dative	ENIO	Shall we allow all things ⟨kinds⟩ the power of ἐπικοινωνίας with one another?
252D7	dual	ENIO	Motion itself would altogether be at rest and Rest in turn itself would be in motion, if they ἐπιγιγνοίσθην on one another.
253B11	dative	ENIO	Isn't it necessary for one who in- tends to rightly understand which kinds συμφωνεῖ with each other . . .
254B8	dative	ENIO	We have agreed that some of the

Group (d): Participation phrases with "an object of blending"
(*continued*)

page	object case	participa-tion type	translation
			kinds are willing to κοινωνεῖν with one another, and others not
254C1	dative	ENIO	. . . nothing stops some ⟨kinds⟩ from κεκοινωνηκέναι with any and all.
254C5	genitive	UNIO	. . . consider the capacity some ⟨kinds⟩ have for κοινωνίας with one another.
254D7	dual	ENIO	And moreover we say that two of them ⟨Motion and Rest⟩ ἀμείκτω with themselves in respect to each other
254D10	dual	ENIO	But being μεικτόν with both ⟨Motion and Rest⟩
254E4	dative	ENIO	Are they ⟨Sameness and Difference⟩ two kinds, different from the other three, yet always necessarily συμμειγνομένω with them each?
255B1	genitive	UNIO	They ⟨Motion and Rest, each⟩ will become the contrary of its own nature, because it μετασχόν in its contrary
255B3	genitive	UNIO	Yet both ⟨Motion and Rest⟩ μετέχετον in Sameness and Difference
255D4	dual	ENIO	If Difference were to μετεῖχε in both forms, as being does . . .
255E5	genitive	DK	Each one ⟨kind⟩ is different from the rest, not because of its own nature, but because of μετέχειν in the form of Difference.
256A1	genitive	DK	If ⟨Motion⟩ is, because of μετέχειν in Being.
256A7	genitive	DK	Yet it ⟨Motion⟩ was the same, because everything μετέχειν in Sameness.
256B1	genitive	DK	When ⟨we say Motion is⟩ the same, it's because of its μέθεξιν in Sameness with respect to itself . . .

Group (d): Participation phrases with "an object of blending"
(*continued*)

page	object case	participa-tion type	translation
256B2	genitive	DK	. . . but when on the other hand ⟨we say Motion is⟩ not the same, it's because of its κοινωνίαν in Difference.
256B6	genitive	UNIO	Then if Motion itself were somehow μετελάμβανεν in Rest, it wouldn't be absurd to call it at rest.
256B9	dative	ENIO	Correct, if we agree that some of the kinds are willing to μείγνυσθαι with one another, and others aren't.
256D9	genitive	DK	Then plainly, Motion really is ⟨a?⟩ non-being and ⟨a?⟩ being, ⟨the latter?⟩ because it μετέχει in Being. [Fowler: It is clear then, that Motion really is not, and also that it is, since it μετέχει of Being.]
256E3	genitive	DK	Since they ⟨the forms⟩ μετέχει in Being, they therefore are and are beings.
257A9	dative	ENIO	. . . it is the nature of the kinds to have κοινωνίαν with each other.
259A4	dative	ENIO	The kinds συμμείγνυται with one another.
259A6	genitive	DK	and on the one hand, Difference, μετασχόν in Being, is, because of this μέθεξιν [see group (b) above] . . .
259A7	genitive	DK	. . . on the other hand, ⟨Difference is⟩ not that in which it μετέσχεν, but ⟨rather⟩ is different.
259B1	genitive	DK	Being, having μετειληφός in Difference, becomes different from the other kinds.
259E6	genitive	ENIO	Discourse becomes possible through the συμπλοκήν of kinds with one another.
260A3	dative	ENIO	. . . forcing them ⟨the "separa-

Group (d): Participation phrases with "an object of blending"
(*continued*)

page	object case	participa- tion type	translation
			tists"> to admit different <kinds> μείγνυσθαι with others.
260B1	dative	ENIO	. . . if we had agreed that there was no μεῖξιν of anything with anything . . .
260B11	dative	ENIO	Next we must consider whether it <not-being> μείγνυται with Belief and Speech.
260C1	dative	ENIO	If it <not-Being> doesn't μειγνυμένου with them, necessarily everything must be true.
260D3	genitive	UNIO	<The sophist says> it is impossible for not-being μετέχειν in Being in any way at all.
260D5	genitive	UNIO	But now this <not-Being> has shown itself μετέχον in Being.
260D7	genitive	UNIO	Perhaps he <the sophist> would say that some of the kinds μετέχειν in not-being, but others don't.
260E2	genitive	UNIO	<The sophist might contend> that Belief and Speech do not κοινωνεῖ with not-being, . . .
260E5	dative	ENIO	So we must first investigate Speech, Belief and Appearances in order that we may discern also their κοινωνίαν with not-Being.
261C8	genitive	ENIO	Let's take up Speech and Belief first, . . . so as to more clearly infer whether not-Being ἅπτεται to them . . .
262D9	dative	ENIO	Thus, just as with the things <kinds>, where some ἥρμοττεν with each other and others don't, . . .

A "PLAUSIBLE STORY"

The basic idea behind the assignment of DK-, UNIO-, and ENIO-participation to the blending sentences of group (d) is the grammatical criterion:

A genitive construction used singularly is a DK-participation.
A genitive construction used generally is an UNIO-partici-
pation.
A dative construction (which is always used generally) is a
ENIO-participation.

The fact that DK- and UNIO-participations both use the genitive
means that there will be times when it is difficult to decide which is intended; but on the whole, the decision comes directly from the context.
The reader might note the preponderance of UNIO- versus DK-
participations in 249D9–264B8. This seems to indicate that Vlastos's
(1973) remarks to the effect that Plato had a bias toward seeing interform
relations as Pauline predications (= UNIO-participation) is correct. But
it is not just a "bias" in the *Sophist,* as I hope to show. The way for Plato
to make the relevant points here is to state most of his claims in terms of
UNIO-participation.

Five of the passages do not strictly obey the grammatical criterion:
252D7, 254D7, 254D10, 255D4, and 259E6. The first four of these are in
the dual, and in the dual, the genitive and dative cases are identical, so
that one cannot tell which is employed. In what follows I will try to justify the particular assignments I made to them on other grounds,
namely how they fit into what I take to be the overall thrust of Plato's
argumentation. The other place where I have departed from a strict
understanding of the grammatical criterion is at 259E6. Here the object,
"one another" (τὴν ἀλλήλων), is in the genitive, but for reasons to be
given below, I would prefer to read this as "really" a dative. The reason
that this is not an out-and-out violation of the grammatical criterion is
that the "one another" is immediately adjacent to the genitive "of the
forms" (τῶν εἰδῶν), and it is a well-known tendency of Greek to allow
this kind of adjacency to affect the case of the following phrase. Thus,
even had Plato wanted to put "one another" in the dative case, considerations of style and euphony would have made it become genitive.
Forty-one of the other forty-two entries in group (d) straightforwardly
obey the grammatical criterion; and as I have just said, the five just discussed do not disobey it. The remaining one is 261C8 about which I
defer discussion until the end of this section.

I will now attempt a "plausible story" according to which each of the
passages in group (d) makes good sense when read in the manner proposed by their assignment to a specific participation type. Of course, the
"indeterminacy of interpretation thesis" put forth in chapter 1 precludes
my claiming that this is the only way to read the passages. Indeed, at

various points there are other accounts that will occur to the reader as "better" or "simpler" or "more in keeping with overall Platonic doctrine." Still, mine *is* a plausible reading, taken overall; and at various specific points it seems to me that it has strikingly strong credentials, on the grounds that alternative interpretations are unable to account for the passages at all without attributing obvious contradictions or hopeless confusions to Plato. In fact, I believe this is the only reading which is unified in the sense of having some one justification for readings of all the passages, rather than being a series of individually possible, even plausible, "short term" readings which fail nonetheless to cohere into a larger story with one fundamental point.

Let's start the "story" with the thesis, considered four times by Plato, that Motion rests (252D6, 254D7, 255B1, 256B6). As Vlastos (1973) and Moravcsik (1962) note, the thesis that Motion rests, when considered as a DK-participation, follows from the 248A4–249D8 claim that all forms rest.[10] Thus the present four claims—which are clearly taken to be false (or their negations true)—must be either cases of UNIO- or ENIO- participation. The present interpretation assigns to 252D6 the claims that if Motion ENIO-participated in Rest, then some resting object would be in motion. I will later come back to explain why Plato would use the intensifiers "motion *itself* would *altogether* be at rest." The answer will provide further support for assigning this dual an ENIO-participation. The context of 252D6 is the refutation of the "monists" who believe that all forms blend with each other. To refute such a position, it is necessary to find a pair of forms and a type of participation which makes this false. And Theaetetus here has done just that. I remark again that if there were only DK-blending, then one of the two conjuncts here ("Motion blends with Rest" and "Rest blends with Motion") would be true, not false; and although the argument would still be valid on account of the other conjunct, it still seems most unlikely that Plato would have said both in such a case. It seems also unreasonable to say Plato used the "stronger" UNIO-participation here when all that's needed is the simple ENIO-participation. The interpretation assigns to 255B1 and 256B6 the claim that if Motion UNIO-participated in Rest, then all moving things would be at rest. It will be recalled from chapter 3 that 255B1 occurs embedded

---

10. Whatever the final upshot of the discussion with the Friends of the Forms (248A8–249D8), it is clear that they at least hold that the forms DK-participate in Rest. This statement is first given in their initial characterization at 248A10–11 and again at 249B10-C1. Whether the entire argument is going to force them also to admit that more things than forms are "real beings," it is never withdrawn that the forms DK-participate in Rest.

in a proof that Motion and Rest are each distinct from Being, on the grounds that "whatever we say of both Motion and Rest in common has to be different from each" (and we say "is <a?> being" of both). The principle is supposed to be correct because otherwise (if, say, Rest were identical to Being) we could "substitute" and get that Motion participates in Rest. But notice that the general principle appealed to does not hold of DK-predications. Thus, both Motion and Rest DK-participate in Rest, yet Rest is not distinct from each of Motion and Rest. Or, to take a different example, Difference and Being both DK-participate in Being, yet Being is not distinct from both. Any attempt to read the "say in common" here as a statement of DK-participation will be unable to account for Plato's belief that the principle is true.

The reason for assigning 256B6 a UNIO-participation rather than an ENIO-participation (besides its agreement with the grammatical criterion) will emerge below in the discussion of 256B9. At 254B7 Plato asserts (using the negative ἀμείκτω) that "we say that Motion and Rest are unmixed with themselves in any regard." The "we say" harkens back to 250A10, where Motion and Rest are claimed to be "most contrary." Now, this sentence, 250A10, does not contain a blending term, nor is its context completely clear as to the regard in which Motion and Rest are most contrary, but it is used, apparently, to show that Being must be a third thing distinct from Motion and Rest, very much like the argument of 255B1. But as I argued with regards to 255B1, the blending mentioned there cannot be understood as DK-participation, but must rather be UNIO-participation. Now, if 255B1 is UNIO-participation, and the argument there is an elaboration of the one surrounding 250A10, and if 254D7 is intended to recall 250A10, then the participation at 254D7 must be of an appropriate sort to make these connections hold together. What is this sort? Well, it depends on whether we're talking about the entire negative word ἀμείκτω or the positive stem μείκτω. Intuitively, in keeping with the train of argumentation from 255B1 through 250A10 to 254D7, this should say that nothing which moves is at rest and that nothing at rest moves. That is, the entire negative term should indicate some kind of "negative" UNIO-participation. But if we are interested just in the positive term, which type of participation is appropriate? The answer is ENIO-participation: it is not true that Rest ENIO-participates in Motion and it is not true that Motion ENIO-participates in Rest. (In the last section of this chapter I explain in more detail how negation interacts with the various types of participation. Here we operate just on the intuitive level, and on that level this sentence must assign ENIO-participation to the positive blending term in order to keep it meaning what context says it must.) The conclusion of these four passages asserting the nonblending of Motion and Rest, then, is that Motion cannot either UNIO- or ENIO-participate in Rest—although it does DK-participate in Rest. The present account can consistently, and in accordance with the grammatical criterion, assign sense to these passages. Furthermore, it makes sense of the arguments in which 252D6 and 255B1 occur, shows how the train of thought from 250A10 to 254D7 to 255B1 runs, and also reconciles Plato's insistence on the falsity of "Motion blends with Rest" with the truth of "Motion DK-participates in Rest." No theory that recognizes DK-participation as the only type of participation can do any of these. Nor can any theory (such as that of Lorenz and Mittelstrass) that does not recognize DK-participation account for the sense in which it is true that Motion is at rest—the sense embraced by the Friends of the Forms.

At 250A8-C8 it is argued that, while Motion and Rest are "most contrary to each other," they nonetheless are. As I argued above, this should be understood in a UNIO-manner, saying that although the inhabitants of the world of motion (physical objects) are "most opposed" to the inhabitants of the world of rest (the forms), nonetheless the inhabitants of both worlds are beings. That is, both Motion and Rest UNIO-participate in Being, as 250B9 says. Were this to be understood as DK-participation, then the point would be lost, for it would only say that the forms Motion and Rest exist. Not only is this statement not yet proved (it is argued for later, in 254D3-E1), but if the DK-participation were meant, it would be quite unclear what the point of the discussion of "the children's prayer" could be. For certainly the children's prayer says that what has being are both what moves and what rests—and it certainly seems as if the Stranger is setting out to make the children's prayer his own.

Although many, indeed most, of the genitive constructions are to be read as UNIO-participation, there are times when it should be read as DK-participation, as for example when the talk is about the distinctness of the five great kinds. In these passages it seems clear that we are talking about the kinds' DK-properties, rather than UNIO-properties which transfer to the instances. For example, Being and Sameness are properties enjoyed by individual objects, according to Platonic doctrine here, yet they are manifested by exactly the same objects, namely all of them. Therefore, a UNIO-predication of a property (such as "being different from Sameness") to Being would be exactly the same as a UNIO-predication of that property to Sameness; but, Plato clearly thinks that "Being is different from Sameness" is true while "Sameness is different from Sameness" is false. So predications asserting the distinctness of the kinds must, at least in the cases of Being, Sameness, and Difference (where they are all coextensive in their instances), be taken as DK-participation. And once the principle in used for these three forms, it seems natural to extend it to predications of distinctness involving Motion and Rest. One might also claim, following Vlastos (1973), that the properties described here are the sort any form must have if it is to count as a kind. Therefore the statements about the distinctness of the forms, and many of the statements about properties the forms have in the proofs of their distinctness (but not all, see below about 256B6, 256B9 and 257A9), should be taken as DK-participations in the section between 255E5 and 257A12 and in the recapitulation of it in 258D6–259B6. In this group I include as DK-participations 255A5 ("Each kind is different from the rest . . . because it DK-participates in the form Different"), 256A1 ("Motion is, because it DK-participates in Being"), 256A7 ("Motion is the same, because everything DK-participates in Sameness"), 256B2 ("When we say Motion is not the same, it's because it DK-participates in Difference"), 256D9 ("Motion is a being because it DK-participates in Being"), 256E3 ("Since the forms DK-participate in Being, they therefore are and are beings"), 259A6 ("Difference is, because of its DK-participation in Being"), 259A7 ("Difference is not that in which it DK-participates, but instead is different"), and 259B1 ("Since Being DK-participates in Difference, it is different from the other kinds").

ENIO-participation is not (*pace* Ackrill 1957, pp. 219, 220) merely the "rather indeterminate symmetrical relation 'being connected with'" which occurs "in highly general remarks about the connectedness of εἴδη, where no definite fact as to any particular pair of εἴδη is being stated." Rather, it is the particular relation—having a common instance or, more accurately, being compatible as a matter of nomic necessity. If one form UNIO-participates in another, then it ENIO-participates in it also (though not vice versa). Because of this stronger/weaker relationship between UNIO- and ENIO-participation, one would expect "general remarks about the connectedness of εἴδη" to be phrased in terms of ENIO-participation, in spite of the fact that ENIO-participation is also used for the determinate relation of nomically necessary, extensional overlap. In addition, if Plato wished to deny that either of these relations held between a pair of forms, he would do it by denying that there is

ENIO-participation between them. This denial amounts to saying that it is impossible that there should be joint instantiation, which explains, I would say, why Plato is so emphatic in the claims he makes when he is denying that Motion and Rest blend with one another. At 252D6, for example, he emphasizes the nonblending by using various intensifiers in his statement: ὅτι κίνησις τε αὐτὴ παντάπασιν ἵσταιτ᾽ ἂν καὶ στάσις αὖ πάλιν αὐτὴ κινοῖτο ("Motion *itself* would *altogether* be at rest and Rest in turn itself would be in motion"); in 255A11–B1 he emphasizes by another method: περὶ γὰρ ἀμφότερα θάτερον ὁποτερονοῦν γιγνόμενον αὐτοῖν ἀναγκάσει μεταβάλλειν αὖ θάτερον ἐπὶ τοὐναντίον τῆς αὐτοῦ φύσεως ("they each will become the *contrary* of its own nature"); and in 256B6 the point is made by pointing out that it is *absurd* to say that Motion was at rest. Now, there is a problem with many of these "negative" passages in that it is not clear what is intended by denying UNIO- or ENIO-participation (or asserting the negation of one of these types of sentence). Vlastos (1973, pp. 274–275) takes "B and C are contraries" to mean that B UNIO-participates in not-C (which entails, given only "non-empty forms," that 'B UNIO-participates in C' is false); and he takes "B does not UNIO-participate in C" to mean that, of nomic necessity, it is not the case that B does UNIO-participate in C. This last is ambiguous perhaps, on the one hand allowing for B to ENIO-participate in C and on the other hand not allowing it. Vlastos's discussion here apparently takes it in the latter way, more or less equating "being contraries" and "does not UNIO-participate." It is not exactly clear how Vlastos intends negation to interact with UNIO-participation (for example, what is the form "not-C?"; and why should negating a "necessary statement" such as UNIO-participation result in another necessary statement?), especially in the formalism he employs which lacks explicit quantifiers. Thus, "Motion UNIO-participates in Rest" is represented as (M is$_{pp}$ R), which is to mean N(M→R), i.e., "necessarily, everything in motion is at rest." But is negation is to mean N − (M→R), he says; and by analogy one would think this is "necessarily not everything in motion is at rest," that is, "necessarily, something in motion is not at rest." But far from being impossible, or absurd, contrary to their natures, it is true and trivial. I conclude that Vlastos has some other, subtle, way of handling the interaction of negation and UNIO-participation. My own account of this interaction will emerge below in the section called "The Philosopher's Language." It involves claiming that in the philosopher's language, negation of UNIO- and ENIO-predications is internal negation. So, to negate 'B UNIO-participates in C' (i.e., to negate 'necessarily, everything which DK-participates in B also DK-participates in C') we generate sentences meaning 'necessarily, everything that DK-participates in B does not DK-participate in C' or 'necessarily, no B is C'. The details below show how the negations that thereby get introduced are to be analyzed away, but for the present purposes it is necessary only to know that the negations are internal.

So, 251D5–7 rhetorically asks a (negative) question of the form, "Shall we neither allow the forms to do X nor indeed to do Y, but rather insist that they can't do Z?" where Y is a "generalization" of X. In particular it asks "Shall we neither attach Being to Motion and Rest, nor attach anything to anything, but rather are we to say they're unmixed and incapable of blending with each other?" Now, notice that the Z part of the sentence schema ought to be different from the point being made in the "neither X nor Y" part, or else it is a mere repetition. In the actual sentence we then would prefer that being incapable of blending with one another mean something different from not allowing them attachment with one another. The present interpretation assigns ENIO-participations to προσάπτωμεν ("attachment") in the "neither X nor Y" part of the question, and UNIO-participation to μεταλαμβάνειν ("blend") of the Z part. The distinction between UNIO- and ENIO-participation thus nicely explains an issue that has troubled commentators: how is it that the two parts of the question are distinct?

Following this question, at 251D9 the Stranger asks another question: "Or shall we say that they all can blend with one another?" This should be read as the "opposite" supposition from the Y part of the "neither X nor Y" question of 251D5–6. But then this requires 251D9 to be ENIO-participation: every form has ENIO-participation with every other form, that is, every form is compatible with every form. (As the Stranger points out, the two suppositions are not contradictory, since they can both be false if some forms ENIO-participate in some forms while other forms do not ENIO-participate in yet other forms).

Now, 251E8 ("Let's suppose they first say that nothing has any power to blend with anything in any regard") is the taking up of the first alternative, and so it must receive the same participation type as 251D5–6; and 252D3 ("Shall we allow all kinds the power to blend with one another?") is the taking up of the "opposite" supposition and so it must receive the same participation type as 251D9. Therefore the present interpretation assigns them all ENIO-participation. Of course, if no forms ENIO-participate, as 251E8 is supposing, then they cannot UNIO-participate. In particular, it would follow that Motion and Rest don't UNIO-participate in Being (251E9). But this in turn would mean that nothing at rest and nothing in motion have being (as 252A2 says)—

which is taken to be absurd and contrary to the children's prayer; thus 251E9 and 252A2 should be read as UNIO-participation. Note that if they were read as DK-participations, their "obvious falsity" would not follow from the suppositions—after all, Motion does not ENIO-participate in Rest, but it does DK-participate in it (i.e., the form, Motion, is at Rest).

252B9 again recalls the "separatists" of earlier (e.g., 251E8) who refuse to allow any ENIO-participation. A reasonable charge to hurl at them is they won't let one kind of thing (e.g., Man) be called another (e.g., Good) even if all men are good. That is, even if the UNIO-participation statement says that it is nomically necessary that all men be good. This is precisely the characterization given them at 252B9, according to the present interpretation.

253B11–12 ("He who intends to understand correctly which kinds blend with each other and which kinds do not attach") recalls again the opposition set up earlier among the three types of god-schools. As I argued earlier, to understand this as a real trichotomy, one should take the "separatists" as denying any ENIO-participation and the "universal blenders" as insisting on every form's ENIO-participating with every other form. Here we are presented with what the third party must do: on the one hand he must discover which forms ENIO-participate (253B11), and on the other hand he must know "which do not attach to each other." This latter part I have placed in group (c) on the grounds that it looks as if he is being enjoined to know all the different types of nonparticipation among the forms.

At 254B8 the Stranger remarks that they have already agreed that some forms blend with one another. If this is to make sense, it must be the type of blending already agreed to, and that is ENIO-participation. Thus 254B8 is assigned ENIO-participation. But of course, the Stranger continues, just because it's ENIO-participation that we have been talking about, this does not prevent a form from ENIO-participating with all kinds of other forms, and maybe even with all of them. If this is the thrust of the Stranger's remarks, then 254C1 should also be read as ENIO-participation, and the present interpretation so does.

According to the present interpretation, when in the next lines the Stranger turns to a consideration of certain great kinds, he no longer is interested in the "indeterminate" question of whether there is any blending at all (i.e., whether any forms are compatible), for that question has already been answered. Instead he should be seen as asking a somewhat different, "stronger" question: What kinds of UNIO-blending hold amongst these great kinds? So, we are to understand 254C5 as asking us to consider the capacity some of the kinds have for UNIO-blending with one another. This "considering" is to be built upon certain facts already present. For example, says the Stranger at 254D7, we say that Motion and Rest are unmixed with one another but that (254D10) Being mixes with both Motion and Rest. As remarked, the present interpretation takes these to be reiterations of already-admitted ENIO-statements. Further confirmation for this comes from considering the alternative possibilities of what kind of participation these might be. With regards to the latter, 254D10, we note that this participation *must* be ENIO-participation: first, Being does *not* DK-participate in Motion, and second, if Being were to UNIO-participate in Motion and also to UNIO-participate in Rest when everything would both be in motion and at rest—which is surely absurd by Plato's lights. For, as Plato remarks at 255B1, this would entail that every moving thing would be at rest, and conversely, because of such "blending with a contrary." As for 254D7, the term used is ἀμείκτω, a negative, 'unmixed'. It should be noted that a *pair* of statements is being made here, one about Motion's relationship to Rest and another about Rest's relationship to Motion (but that whatever relationship is under discussion, it must be the same kind of blending for both parts). Let's look at one of the pair, Motion's relationship to Rest. We should concentrate on the positive term here, and ask what is being denied by the negative. As remarked above, it can't be a DK-participation which is being denied since it's true, not false, that Motion DK-participates in Rest. As for UNIO- and ENIO-participation, according to my previously mentioned, intuitive explanation of negations of these types of predication, we are asking which of the following is Plato saying: that (a) necessarily, no moving thing is at rest? or is he saying (b) necessarily, some moving thing is not at rest? Since 254D7 is a dual, we cannot use the grammatical criterion. According to Plato, both (a) and (b) are true, and so to decide between them some other consideration must be brought to bear. As I see it, the only plausible consideration to use is the fact that this statement is one whose truth has already been admitted—but what has already been admitted, according to the present interpretation, is that they do not ENIO-participate in each other. Therefore, the positive term at 254D7 should be assigned ENIO-participation.

In 254E4 ("Are Sameness and Difference two kinds, different from the other three ⟨Being, Motion, and Rest⟩, yet always necessarily blending with them each?"), it is taken as presupposed that Sameness and Difference always blend with Motion, Rest, and Being. The only understanding under which this can be true is with ENIO-participation. For, first notice that if it were meant that Sameness and Difference DK-participated in each of Motion, Rest, and Being, then the forms Sameness and Difference would both move and rest—surely an unacceptable consequence by Platonic standards. And in any case, such an eventuality is not even contemplated here enough for Plato to argue against it. Notice second that if it were meant that Sameness and Difference UNIO-participated in each of Motion, Rest, and Being, then everything that DK-participated in Sameness (namely, everything—since Sameness is all-embracing) would DK-participate in both Motion and Rest. Once again, surely this is unacceptable to Plato and not even contemplated here. But, understood as ENIO-participation, the claim is obviously true: if Sameness and Difference ENIO-participate in each of Motion, Rest, and Being, then some of the Sameness-instances (i.e., some things) are at rest, some in motion, and some have being. (Of course, this last clause could be strengthened: they *all* have being; but Plato does not produce this UNIO-participation sentence). ENIO-participation is symmetric, and 254E4 can therefore also be read as saying that Motion, Rest, and Being ENIO-participate in both Sameness and Difference. This is interesting because *all* of the sentences generated here could be strengthened to UNIO-participations; and Plato *does* strengthen all of them (except the ones involving Being) at 255B3 ("Motion and Rest UNIO-participate in Sameness and Difference"), according to the present interpretation.

The current interpretation also has happy consequences for understanding two notoriously difficult pieces of our text. The first has to do with the two εἴδη: τὸ πρὸς ἄλλο and τὸ καθ' αὐτό of 255C–D. At 255D4 Being is claimed to partake of both these εἴδη—a remark difficult to understand if taken as DK-participation. (Since presumably the form of Being qua form does not have these two characteristics in the manner required by a DK-participation, that is, the form itself is not simultaneously "by way of others" and "by way of itself.") Rather, the claim that Being partakes of both forms should be read as a conjunction of ENIO-participations: Being ENIO-participates in τὸ πρὸς ἄλλο and Being ENIO-participates in τὸ καθ' αὐτό, in other words, some things that DK-participate in Being (i.e., some beings) are, merely by this participation, πρὸς ἄλλο, others are καθ' αὐτό. However, as 255D4 says, Difference does not ENIO-participate in τὸ καθ' αὐτό; that is, there are no things which

DK-participate in Difference that are, for that reason alone, καθ' αὑτό. I am not completely convinced by this account, though. A lot of weight must be put on the phrases 'merely by this participation' and 'for that reason alone' in the preceding two sentences. For, as remarked above, Being and Difference are coextensive in their instances—everything DK-participates in each. Therefore a statement like "some things that DK-participate in Being are πρὸς ἄλλο and others are καθ' αὑτό" would be true if and only if "some things that DK-participate in Difference are πρὸς ἄλλο and others are καθ' αὑτό" were true—because those very same things would be πρὸς ἄλλο or καθ' αὑτό in either case. So we must build in something further, which I've tried to do with the 'because of this participation' clause. I'm not sure it works, but recognizing UNIO- and ENIO-participation opens new avenues of exploration for this difficult passage; it most certainly cannot be DK-participation.[11] As to the choice between UNIO- and ENIO-participation, it seems clear that it must be the latter, since the former would say that everything that DK-participates in Being is πρὸς ἄλλο and is also καθ' αὑτό. But this is clearly incorrect.

The second happy consequence for interpretation has to do with 256B6 and 256B9 ("If Motion were somehow mixed in Rest, it wouldn't be absurd to call it at rest." "Correct, if we agree that some of the kinds are willing to blend with one another, and others aren't."). Various translators (e.g., Cornford[12]) have thought that there must be a lacuna in the text between the Stranger's remark and Theaetetus' response, for, as they see it the train of the argument seemed not to follow at all. In Cornford's version the translation of the lacuna goes as follows:

> STRANGER: . . . . there would be nothing outrageous in speaking of it as stationary. ⟨But it does not in fact participate in Rest at all.
> THEAETETUS: No, it does not.
> STRANGER: Whereas it does participate both in Sameness and in Difference, so that it is correct to speak of it as both the same and not the Same.⟩

11. See Cornford's remark (p. 280, n. 2); and in this regard see Ackrill (1957, pp. 219ff., esp. n. 9); Moravcsik (1962); Frede (1967, p. 22 and *passim*); Owen (1970, pp. 252, 255 ff., "additional note"); Malcolm (1967); and especially Owen (1968), where "x is being πρὸς ἄλλο F" is argued *not* to be a transfer of the property F to the instances of Being, but rather a feature of the form, Being. Needless to say, I thoroughly disagree with this analysis, and think that the explanation of the present text shows me right.

12. See his remarks, pp. 286–87 n. 3; see also the discussion in Owen (1970) about the necessity (or lack of it) for the interpolation.

THEAETETUS: Perfectly correct, provided we are to agree that some of the Kinds will blend with one another, some will not.

It seems to me that we ought to try to obviate the need for such a tortured addition to the Stranger's speech, an alleged response by Theaetetus, and another speech by the Stranger. And under the present interpretation, no such lacuna is called for. At 256B6 the Stranger says that if Motion were somehow to UNIO-participate in Rest, it wouldn't be absurd to call it at rest. That is, if as a matter of nomic necessity all instances of Motion are instances of Rest, then it wouldn't be absurd to say that moving things would be at rest. And Theaetetus responds at 256B9 that this is correct, but only if we recognize that there are any ENIO-participations at all; that is, only if it is nomically possible for some forms (e.g., Motion and Rest) to be jointly instantiated. Surely it is not only true that this possibility must be admitted first, but it is relevant to the conversation and a rather subtle point.

Lines 260A3 ("It was a good thing that we forced the "separatists" to admit that different kinds blend with others") and 260B1 ("if we had agreed that there was no blending of anything with anything") recall for the last time the "separatists" discussed earlier, restating their position and asserting that it has been refuted. Therefore, these must be understood as being the sort of blending that the "separatists" had denied—and that was ENIO-participation. So the present interpretation these also to be ENIO-participation.

According to the present interpretation, Plato emphasizes the overall point he is trying to make three times: 257A9 ("It is the nature of the kinds to have blending with each other"), 259A4 ("The kinds mix with one another"), and 259E6 ("Discourse is possible because of the blending of kinds with one another"). And this point is appealed to again at 262D9 ("just as with the kinds, where some blend with each other and others don't"). Seen in this light, these four ought to be assigned the same participation-type. So what then is the overall point? It seems to me that it is to refute the late-learning "separatists" and to show that there must be *some* kind of blending amongst the forms. And recall that the "separatists" had denied even ENIO-participation. So these four passages ought to be also assigned ENIO-participation.

We are now in a position to look a little more closely at our late-learning "separatists." Just why is it ENIO-participation that they deny rather than one of the other participation-types, and why is Plato so concerned to reinstate ENIO-participation? The answer comes from consideration of what happens if ENIO-participation is denied. Recall that our "separatists" do not allow us to say that <a?> man is good, but only that <a? the ?> good is good or that <a?> man is <a?> man (251C1–3). Their position, as I have earlier argued, is that for any pair of distinct kinds, there is no ENIO-participation, so in particular there is no ENIO-participation between Man and Good. There being no ENIO-participation here, there also can be no UNIO-participation. Can there still be DK-participation? Nothing in their position has yet ruled it out; so perhaps Theaetetus can DK-participate in Man and also DK-participate in Good. But no: this would mean that Man and Good are jointly instantiated, and this is the ENIO-participation between distinct forms which has been ruled out. So one can see that the ruling out of ENIO-participation would prohibit all interrelations among distinct forms, and thereby (given Plato's picture of the philosopher's language) wreak havoc with our discourse. It could not be UNIO-participation that they wish to rule out, since that would not by itself carry over the ruling-out of the other kinds of participation, and therefore wouldn't do the damage Plato thinks their position does. Of course, had it been DK-participation that they were concerned to rule out, this too would infect both UNIO- and ENIO-participation, since they can be defined by means of DK-participation. So why am I so sure that this isn't the "separatist" position, to deny DK-participation? It will be noticed in Plato's characterization of the "separatists" that they *do* allow us to say "man is man" and "good is good." They therefore are not ruling out *all* participations. So what are the late learners allowing? It seems clear that they are committed to allowing UNIO- and ENIO-participation of a kind with itself, but would they also allow DK-participation of a kind with itself? It seems to me that the answer must be no; the late learner's position doesn't allow this sort of "self-predication" whereby a form (qua form) can partake of itself. For, if that were their position, then Plato could bring forth his "third man (or third largeness) argument" against them. And since he doesn't do this, it seems that Plato did not understand them to be affirming self-DK-participation. So, once again we are led to the conclusion that the position of the late-learning "separatists" is the denial of any ENIO-participation among the forms. And once again we see that Plato's strategy here must be to affirm the existence of ENIO-participation.

At 260A1, having disposed of the "separatists," the Stranger comes back to the issue of showing that falsehood is possible. In these next pages, the Stranger talks of mixing among not-Being, Speech, Belief, and Appearance. Now, to the modern ear it perhaps sounds strange to view these, especially the last three, as kinds or forms. Instead, we wish (if we are charitable about how we understand not-Being) to think of not-Being's "blending" with *individual* statements, *individual* beliefs, and *individual* appearances. But this is not the way Plato wishes to talk here. Rather, we are presented with the kinds: Speech, Belief, and Appearance. And it is variously said that each of them blends or partakes of not-Being, and furthermore that not-Being blends or partakes of them. It is this last clause, especially, which shows that Belief, Speech, and Appearance must be forms, for although individuals can partake of (DK-participate in) forms, nothing can partake of an individual in any of the sorts of participation. On the other hand, however, Plato obviously wants his talk of not-Being mixing with Speech, Belief, and Appearance to have consequences for the truth or falsity of individual statements, beliefs and appearances, it seems clear that he must have in mind some sort of participation other than the ("classical") DK-participation. For, were the form Speech, say, to DK-participate in not-Being, this would have no consequences for individual statements—DK-participation just does not "trickle down" to instances.

In accord with his earlier analysis (see the discussion in chapter 3 about Parmenidean arguments in Plato and the summary of *Sophist* 237–241), Plato here views falsity as a problem of how not-Being can be mixed with (the forms) Speech, Belief, and Appearance. The analysis to be given is one where the forms Speech, Belief, and Appearance can be said to partake of not-Being, and this is to yield that some statements, some beliefs, and some appearances are false. But note that the only sort of participation which yields this result is ENIO-participation. As remarked above, if one of these forms DK-participated in not-Being, this would have no consequences for individual instances of the form, such as individual statements, but rather would be making a predication of not-Being directly to the form (whatever this might mean, upon analysis). If it were UNIO-participation, then *all* individual statements, beliefs, and appearances would be false, so this cannot be correct either. Furthermore, Plato often states the point by saying that not-Being partakes of these other forms. If the kind of participation were anything but the symmetric ENIO-participation, this would be unintelligible—not-Being just is not an instance of these other forms (DK-participation), nor is every instance of not-Being an instance of these other forms (UNIO-participation).

For these reasons, when the Stranger is explaining why one should now look at the relationship between not-Being and these three other forms, we must read it as ENIO-participation. So 260B11 ("Next we must consider whether not-Being blends with Belief and Speech") and 260C1 ("If not-Being doesn't mix with them, then necessarily everything must be true") are both read this way. At 260D3 ("The sophist says it is impossible for not-Being to mix with Being in any way at all") the sophist's position (here: Parmenides' position) is recalled. It is that no nonbeings have being. That is, the participation mentioned is UNIO-participation. But, continues the Stranger at 260C5, we have proved the negation of this: "But not-Being has shown itself to be mixed with Being." For 260C5 to be the negation of 260D3 means that we must read this too as UNIO-participation; we have proved that all nonbeings have being. (To my ears this sounds like, anything that we are willing to call a nonbeing actually also has being—that is, from perhaps another standpoint we would say that it exists).

Since we have proved the negation of the sophist's original position, the Stranger continues, perhaps he will change the position somewhat. Rather than saying that not-Being's UNIO-participation in Being is impossible, maybe he will say that some of the kinds do not UNIO-participate in not-Being. That is, perhaps he will say that there are kinds such that none of their instances partake of not-Being. (260D7: "Perhaps the sophist would say that some of the kinds partake of not-Being, but others don't"). This reformed position amounts to saying that some beings (all the ones that are instances of the selected kinds) do not have nonbeing. Which are the selected forms, none of whose instances have nonbeing? 260E2 tells us that our reformed sophist might claim in particular "that Belief and Speech do not UNIO-participate in not-Being." Now, is this position attributed to our new sophist sufficient for him to carry out the Parmenidean argument? Yes. For then there are no false statements, so no true negative ones; hence Parmenides' Problem goes through as before, with the possible exception that since there is not-Being among the forms ("negation in the world") but none in the statements, premise (3), which says that anything in the world can be described by some true statement, has now been shown false. But while this means that the original Parmenidean argument can't be presented as stated earlier, I would not think that Plato can accept this "solution" to the problem. For it *is* a tenet of the god's position that the philosopher's language is "adequate to the world" in being able to describe reality accurately and precisely. Therefore, Plato has to show that the "negations in the world" can be truly stated by means of "negations in speech"—implying that he has to show that false statement is possible. And this means that Plato has to show that Speech and not-Being ENIO-participate. He cannot be content with the modified sophist's position, even if it can no longer generate Parmenides' Problem in its original form.

Thus, Plato's task is to refute the claim at 260E2 that Belief and Speech do not UNIO-participate in not-Being. To show this wrong, says the Stranger (correctly) at 260E5, we would want to prove that Belief and Speech ENIO-participate in not-Being. That is, to show incorrect the claim that no instance of Belief or Speech is an instance of not-Being, we need to prove that there is an instance of Belief or Speech which is an instance of not-Being. As the Stranger puts it (260E5), "So we must first investigate Speech, Belief, and Appearances in order that we may discern their blending with not-Being." The result of this investigation, undertaken through an examination of "elementary syntax" as an analogy (see the examples listed in group (a) above), is said to be that (262D9) just as with the kinds, where some ENIO-participate with one another and others don't, so too some words "blend" with one another and others don't. As I remarked earlier, the kind-blending here must be ENIO-blending if (as is surely the case) it is intended to recall accurately the previous conclusion about what kinds of blending there must be. This lends further weight to the present claim that Plato is concerned here at 260E5 to demonstrate ENIO-participation of Belief, Speech, and Appearance with not-Being, rather than any other kind of participation.

The last passage to be discussed, 261C8 ("Let's take up Speech and Belief first, . . . so as to infer more clearly whether not-Being attaches to them, or whether both of them are always true and never false"), is rather a puzzler. Of course, it is clear what it *should* be saying (or is clear at least if one accepts Heindorf's emendation to read ἀπολογισώμεθα where the manuscripts have ἀπολογησώμεθα, as is widely accepted and as I have done in the translation). It should be a repetition of what we're about to investigate—the 260E5 task of finding out whether Speech, Belief, and Appearance ENIO-participate in not-Being. But here, if we follow the grammatical criterion, the claim would amount to "not-Being UNIO-participates in both Speech and Belief," that is, everything which is a nonbeing is a statement and is a belief. And surely *this* is not what the Stranger is claiming. To get around this problem, one might be tempted to go back to the original ἀπολογησώμεθα of the manuscripts. This would yield a translation like, "Let us take up Speech and Belief first, . . . so that we may defend ourselves more clearly, concerning whether not-Being attaches to them." Here, it might be argued, the Stranger is not putting forth his doctrine to defend, but rather defending himself from the sophist's doctrine that not-Being UNIO-participates in Speech and Belief. But this reading too seems impossible, for this never was the sophist's position, not even our reformed sophist. In fact no one in the *Sophist* has held this position.

It seems to me that the plausibility with which the grammatical distinction has categorized the preceding passages should make us want to find some explanation for this passage's not fitting in. Here is my speculation. First, I think ἅπτω ("attach to") is not, strictly speaking, being used here as a blending metaphor in the same manner that the other terms were being used. Normally a blending sentence has one of the following forms: X blends with Y, X and Y blend with one another, the mixture/blending of X with Y, or the like. But here we are presented with "X is attached to Y." If this were to be rephrased in the same style as the others, presumably it should be "Y blends with X"—where the order is important. After all, as the whole point of these last sections was to show, not all blendings are symmetrical. And therefore, if we choose a canonical representation for any blending sentence (a canonical representation such as "X blends with Y"), then when we are faced with any particular sentence that we wish to recast in this canonical form, we had better be sure what will be the "logical subject" and what will be the "logical object" of the blending. And the grammatical criterion applies only after this decision has been made. If we here decide that the sentence should be cast into the canonical form, "Speech and Belief blend with not-Being," then we should look to the case of "not-Being" once this transition has been made. This issue has not come up before because I took all the other occurrences of the blending terms to be already in this canonical form, and hence we *could* just look at the grammatical case of the explicit object. But if I am correct, ἅπτω is *not* such a blending term—or more accurately, it is a blending term that needs to be put into canonical form. This being so, we cannot tell what case "not-Being" would have been put in by Plato. Therefore this passage should not be taken as evidence against the adequacy of the grammatical criterion.

Some Remarks on DK-, UNIO-, and ENIO-Participation in Plato

As remarked above, some previous scholars have noted the dative/genitive constructions employed by Plato here. Perhaps most follow Ross (1951, p. 111) in thinking that there is nothing significant here, but Sayre (1969) seems to be the only one to argue the point vigorously (although as mentioned above one might also be able to construct a "grammatical" argument for the conclusion that the distinction is only an illusion). These arguments against the distinction will be considered in the next section. The authors who find something of import in the distinction (Ackrill, Lorenz and Mittelstrass, Vlastos) each give a different explanation, so the first task here is to see why they have distinct explanations and how their explanations are subsumed by the present one.[13] The flaw in all these commentators is to find only two types of participation. Vlastos (1973) draws the distinction between (what I am calling) DK- and UNIO-participation,[14] and it is apparently claimed that the genitive construction is used exclusively.[15] Vlastos also argues that all participation is nonsymmetric (see pp. 298–99, n. 66), thus apparently disallowing my symmetric ENIO-participation as an understanding of any simple Platonic statement of the blending of two forms. I also disagree with Vlastos on his calling certain cases (such as 256A1) UNIO-participations rather than DK-participations.

If Vlastos errs in not finding a place for the dative, hence ignoring ENIO-participation, and in finding too many UNIO-participations, Ackrill (1957) errs in the other direction. According to him, the genitive construction marks off DK-participation:

> All the real work, . . . all the exposition of actual connections between particular εἴδη, is done by the terms μετέχειν, μεταλαμβάνειν, and κοινωνεῖν (with genitive), that is, by the non-symmetrical metaphor 'partakes of' which Cornford is so determined to exclude. And the role of 'partakes of' in Plato's terminology is clear: 'partakes of' followed by an abstract noun, the name of a concept, is equivalent to the ordinary language expression consisting of 'is' (copula) followed by the adjective corresponding to that abstract noun. (P. 221)

13. The following discussion owes a lot to F. Lewis (1974).

14. Called by him "ordinary predication" and "Pauline predication," and indicated by 'op' and 'pp' (often as subscripts on 'is') respectively.

15. See Vlastos (1973), p. 273 n. 12, where it is claimed that Plato expresses "inter-Form entailment" by "μετέχειν, μεταλαμβάνειν and [προσ-] κοινωνεῖν with genitive construction," and p. 289n. 44, where "κοινωνεῖν with genitive has the same force as μετέχειν, μεταλαμβάνειν." He furthermore insists that Plato did not see the difference between DK- and UNIO-participation. Also, in some of the examples discussed by him—e.g., 252D7, 254D7—it is not remarked that the dual is used, and that it could as well be a dative. He places considerable weight on these two, however (see pp. 293 n. 49, 308). Immediately prior to 259A6, which Vlastos claims is a DK-predication (p. 306 n. 91), occurs the dative ENIO-predication. However, Vlastos is surely aware of the dative construction. (See my n.6 of this chapter).

On the other hand,

> The dative construction . . . occurs in highly general re-
> marks about the connectedness of εἴδη, where no definite fact
> as to any particular of εἴδη is being stated. . . . It stands for
> the general symmetrical notion of 'connectedness' (P. 220)

With his desire to refute Cornford's claim that there is only "symmetric" blending of the forms, Ackrill has cast the genitive versus dative
distinction incorrectly. I have already indicated that the dative blending
is not characterized properly as there being "no definite fact as to any
particular pair of εἴδη stated." It is rather the determinate fact of necessity of co-instantiation. He further misrepresents the genitive blending
by finding only one "determinate non-symmetrical notion, 'sharing
in'"—the DK-participation relation. There is, in fact, also the determinate, nonsymmetrical notion of UNIO-participation; and this is the relation which is more properly compared to the dative construction than
is DK-participation. With UNIO- and ENIO-participation, the one is
"stronger" the other "weaker"; the one "more widely applicable" the
other "more narrowly applicable"; the one more often ascribed to particular pairs of εἴδη, the other more often (but not always) ascribed to forms
in general. Ackrill, like Vlastos, does not consider all the occurrences of
the blending metaphors and their cases. For one thing, he explicitly
(1957, p. 221) excludes 255D4 from consideration, because it seems
clearly to be a case of ENIO-participation, yet (he thinks) it is a use of
μετέχειν with the genitive. But this is incorrect; it is dual, and therefore
the case cannot be determined by the object. (In a footnote to this [1957,
p. 221 n. 9], Ackrill suggests that a solution would be to read the apparent ENIO-participation as "really" DK-participation. A simpler solution
is to recognize the dual and allow μετέχειν to have dative objects.) Ackrill
also questionably leaves 250B9, 260E2, 260E5 out of the account because
they "are not in the main section on κοινωνία γενῶν."

Unlike Vlastos and Ackrill, Lorenz and Mittelstrass offer no justification for their claims as to what the genitive and dative constructions
amount to.[16] Their sole remark on the matter (p. 131) is merely:

> Plato distinguished two different meanings in κοινωνία (i.e.,
> in ἐπικοινωνεῖν, ἐπικοινωνία, προσκοινωνεῖν) which are exhib-
> ited by different grammatical constructions. Ross had already
> made the remark that the construction with the genitive . . .

---

16. Their usage of A-relation and I-relation reflects Aristotelian A- and I-statements.

represents a 'participation' phrase, or as we want to say, represents an A-relation (e.g., when the Idea Man A-participates in the Idea Mortal, all men are mortal); while the construction with the dative . . . represents a 'compatibility' relation, or as we want to say, are in an I-relation (e.g., when the Idea Man I-participates in the Idea Laughter, some man laughs).

Their footnote to this remarkable few sentences continues

See Ross p. 111, n. 6; Ackrill (1957). Ackrill stressed that Plato made known use of this distinction, which in any case would in no way be disputed. For other reasons Ackrill turned his search to the concept συμπλοκή in the *Sophist*, here justifiably against Cornford, who wanted to read κοινωνία, etc., simply as a symmetrical relation between Ideas; whereas we can already distinguish an unsymmetrical from a symmetrical meaning within the word alone. . . . The distinction in [κοινωνία] can also be found in use in [the other blending metaphors] including μεικτόν.

Lorenz and Mittelstrass do not note that Ross denied any importance to Plato's use of the different cases, nor do they note that Ackrill's genitive was DK-participation rather than A-participation (or my UNIO-participation), nor do they note that Ackrill's dative was "indeterminate" rather than their "strict" I-participation (or my ENIO-participation).

Further, the fact that Lorenz and Mittelstrass have no room for DK-participation in their scheme implies that they can find no "categorial statements about the forms" in the *Sophist:* not even about the distinctness of the forms! In addition to this astonishing consequence, it should be noted that they do not remark on the use of the dual at such crucial places at 255D4—about which they say (n. 61) "Ackrill questionably excludes μετέχειν in 255D4 from the sense of the copula—which is read by us as A-participation."

The reason Ackrill has excluded 255D4 is that he thought that the sentence expressed "an indeterminate relation amongst forms." Here we find Lorenz and Mittelstrass assuming it to express a definite relationship without argument. As argued in my "plausible story," it seems most unlikely that this passage can be read as UNIO-participation.

Some Arguments Against the Distinction

The only critique in the literature about the importance of DK-, UNIO-, and ENIO-participation seems to be Sayre (1969, pp. 196–97, n. 69, 199–

200 n. 74). However, his rebuttal is flawed by (a) not realizing that there are *three* types of participation at work here, and (b) treating the Ackrill dichotomy as if it were identical to the Lorenz and Mittelstrass dichotomy.[17]

Regarding the genitive construction, Sayre first claims that Lorenz and Mittelstrass (following Ross) list 251E9, and that this is a "nonexistent instance" of the genitive (1969, 196 n. 69). I have no idea why he says this. Of the remaining six (Sayre only discusses the ones on Ross's partial list) he says "only two (250B9, 256B2) clearly suggest a relation of 'falling under', or A-predication, and one of these Ackrill disclaims from relevance [250B9]. . . . The others either suggest no particular relationship beyond mere compatibility, or suggest *both* A- and I-predication" (pp. 196–97 n. 69).

The terminology of 'falling under' is Ackrill's, who uses it for what I have called DK-participation. The terminology 'A-predication' and 'I-predication' is Lorenz and Mittelstrass's, who use it for what I have called 'UNIO-participation' and 'ENIO-participation' respectively. Sayre's objection in the last-quoted clause is doubtlessly explained by his not noticing that these are dramatically different views of what the genitive construction indicates. Naturally, if a certain genitive construction is in reality a UNIO-participation, there will be an implied ENIO-participation (= 'I-predication'), so there will be the "suggestion" of ENIO-participation. And if one thinks that the only alternative to ENIO-participation is DK-participation (as Sayre seems to think), one would think there to be a sense in which such a genitive "suggests both." The particular passage Sayre has in mind here is 254C5 ("Consider the capacity some forms have for combining with each other"), and it "suggests symmetry" because (n. 74) "the Forms are considered with respect to how they combine with one another." But all this shows is that 254C5 is not DK-participation—rather, it is UNIO-participation. The remainder of Sayre's argument against assigning any significance to the genitive construction is subject to the same objection: he can find nothing significant merely because he conflates DK- and UNIO-participation. Thus he continues his footnote 74:

> the "predicate" in two of the examples (250B9, 252A2) . . . is existence (οὐσίας . . .), which indicates the 'is' of existence rather than predication. In two other cases the "predicates" are 'difference' (θατέρου, 256B2) . . . and 'not being' (μὴ ὄντος,

17. Some of the arguments here against Sayre are similar to those of Lewis (1974).

260E2), which again are scarcely copulative predicates. In another (252B9) *no* Form is mentioned specifically, so no particular grammatical relation is indicated. . . . And in the final (254C5) the language actually *suggests* symmetry. . . . Three uses of μετέχειν are with ὄντος, (Existence, Being) and two are with ταὐτοῦ (the Same . . .) All uses are to indicate combination, which as we have seen is a symmetrical relation quite distinct from predication.

Sayre's reasoning here is that since we cannot identify all occurrences of the genitive construction with "copulative predication" [= DK-predication], these others must be "combination" [which he identifies with ENIO-predication]. But it then follows, he would say, that there is no differential importance to the use of the genitive construction. Again though, this overlooks the possibility that these non-DK-predication genitives might be UNIO-predications.

Sayre's arguments against finding any significance to the dative construction are worse than those against the genitive construction. Here is his entire argument (n. 69):

Of the eight instances of use with the dative, . . . one suggests both A- and I-predication (concerning whether Existence, Motion, and Rest are capable of association with one another) (251D9), one suggests A-predication (concerning whether some Kinds combine with all other Kinds) (254C1), and six suggest no particular relationship beyond compatibility.

Again, Sayre is using Ross's partial list of illustrations and therefore thinks there are but eight occurrences of the dative construction. He is furthermore using the Lorenz and Mittelstrass terminology of A- and I-predication, although as always it is not clear whether by 'A-predication' he means Lorenz and Mittelstrass's 'A-predication' (= our UNIO-participation) or Ackrill's 'falling under' (= our DK-participation). Since Ackrill's dative construction of "connectedness" probably amounts to "compatibility," and since the account of Lorenz and Mittelstrass explicitly entails that the dative construction will be used for compatibility, it is most unclear why Sayre thinks the last-quoted clause counts *against* either Ackrill or Lorenz and Mittelstrass, rather than in their favor. With respect to 251D9, it is first quite definite that it cannot be interpreted as DK-participation, and second it is also clear that it cannot be interpreted as UNIO-participation if the position of the "all forms blend" schools is to be stated intelligibly. For, their position *cannot* be that for every form, anything instantiating it also instantiates every other form. If that were their position, the "late learners" would not be in contrast to them. The "all forms blend" position must instead be that, for every two forms, they are compatible; that is, every pair of forms stands in the ENIO-participation relation. And in any case, even if their position could be stated as an UNIO-participation thesis, the use of ENIO-participation here does not by itself count against the distinction, since every UNIO-participation entails a corresponding ENIO-participation. Finally, Sayre's remark on 254C1 apparently confuses UNIO-participation between two forms with all-pervasiveness (διὰ πάντων) between a form and a set of forms.

I conclude, therefore, that the arguments in print which have been mounted against finding some significance in the genitive/dative construction are ill-founded and at best inconclusive. I have, however, heard another, "grammatical," argument against finding any importance in the distribution of genitive and dative cases.[18] The conclusion to the argument is that Plato used all the blending metaphors in the same way with the same force; the differences in case are due merely to standard grammatical considerations concerning what cases would normally follow μετα-prefixes, infinitives, and so forth. The specific considerations mentioned are:

(1)   μετα as preposition and verbal prefix (e.g.,
        μετέχειν, μεικτόν, etc.) commonly takes genitive.
(2)   κοινωνία (noun) takes genitive.
(3)   προσ-, ἐπι-, συν- compounds regularly take dative.
(4)   κοινωνεῖν (verb) commonly takes dative.

One putting forth this "grammatical" argument needn't go so far as to say that (1)–(4) are hard-and-fast rules. Indeed Liddel-Scott-Jones will cite many violations of each. Rather, the claim is that this is ordinary, and if all the occurrences comply with (1)–(4), there is no anomaly in Plato's use of cases which needs explaining.

What is to be said about this argument? Well, first, it is not clear that (1)–(4) *are* really the "standard cases." But bypassing this line of attack, I would also note that even if they were, one would still like to know why Plato used a dative-inducing construction here, and a genitive-inducing construction there. Could it be that he wanted to convey different types

18. This argument was presented to me independently by Roger Shiner and Alex Mourelatos.

of participation? This is a line of argument taken up in Ackrill (1957), who points out that the distribution of genitive and dative cases in the text is so skewed as to require some explanation. The general introduction about blending of forms (249D9–254C2) makes heavy use of the dative construction (Ackrill's "general notion of relatedness"), while the central discussion of the greatest kinds (254C3–259B1)[19] makes heavy use of the genitive construction. Thus, even if the choice of case is determined by the choice of blending metaphor, we still want an explanation of why Plato chose that particular metaphor.

It should also be noted that the distinction seems constant across a change in vocabulary, as indicated in the interpretations given above of the passages. And finally, there is occasional difference in construction with the identical vocabulary item, thus showing that (1)–(4) do not entirely exhaust Plato's usage. (Although this is only occasional, it does appear in about 25 percent of the entries in group (d).) For example, 256B9, 260A3, 260B1, 260B11, 260C1, 260C2 violate (1); 251E8, 254C5, 257A9, 260E5 violate (2); 252A2 violates (3), as would 259E6 if it is a true genitive—I argued above that the genitive was due to an adjacent genitive; and 260E2 violates (4).

I do not take the considerations of the last two paragraphs to be a refutation of the grammatical argument. Among other things, a proponent of a grammatical argument might put forth other principles to show that the apparent exceptions are not true violations. Instead I view these considerations as a reason to believe that the interpretation given above of DK-, UNIO-, ENIO-participation is to be taken seriously and is not quickly overthrown by these kinds of arguments.

ALTERNATIVES TO THE DISTINCTION

If one believes that Plato wanted to distinguish, in the philosopher's language, these different kinds of participation statements, say for instance to distinguish the sense of "Motion rests" in which it expresses a truth from (one of) the sense(s) in which it expresses a falsehood, another way besides the one outlined above comes to mind. He could have introduced a new form—say, Immutability—in addition to Rest.[20] That is (for this type of example), an ambiguity in the ordinary-language "Motion rests" is found to reside in the predicate, and this ambiguity is resolved in the philosopher's language by saying that "rest" (of ordinary lan-

19. Ackrill only counts from 255E8–257A11, but the same point could be made about the entire section.
20. This alternative is mentioned by F. Lewis (1974).

guage) names two (or more) different forms. It seems clear that Plato nowhere suggests this sort of resolution of the ambiguity.

A further place to locate the ambiguity would be in the subject term: sometimes it functions as a singular term naming a form, other times it functions as general term. As Bostock (1984, p. 104) puts this option,

> The ambiguity of the Greek idiom which allows us to form a subject-expression out of the definite article and a neuter adjective (or participle) is well-known. In one use, a phrase such as 'τὸ καλὸν' or 'τὸ ὄν' is a generalizing phrase, used to generalize over the things which the adjective is true of ('whatever is beautiful', 'whatever is'). In another it is used as a singular referring expression to refer to the abstract property, characteristic, kind, etc., which the adjective predicates of those things ('beauty', 'being'); in other words it refers to what Plato calls a form (or, in the *Sophist,* a kind). I shall refer to this as its naming use.

Bostock then turns to the question of which use Plato made of this "idiom" in the central part of the *Sophist,* concluding that Plato was confused:

> at the start of this central section of the *Sophist* Plato's abstract nouns are used to generalize, until we come to 255B3 which is crucially ambiguous. From then on they are used to name, until at 257B1 attention switches to what is actually a use of 'is not' where the 'is' is an 'is' of predication. To make sense of what Plato says of this we must then revert to the generalizing interpretation, which continues to predominate to the end of the section, but not quite consistently.

Bostock believes that Plato was quite unaware of this ambiguity—something rather difficult to reconcile with the insistence on such a distinction in the early Socratic dialogues. There, it will be recalled, Socrates is always at great pains to distinguish "individual examples of piety, beauty, courage, justice (etc.)" from "the one εἶδος which makes them all pious (or beautiful, or courageous, or just, etc.)." It seems to me that we should fully expect Plato to be sensitive to just this difference in the *Sophist.* Bostock believes that Plato's shifts are arbitrary and unmarked in the text—that he uses now "the generalizing role," now "the naming role," with only the context to guide one as to which role is in play. But if the grammatical criterion is correct, he *does* announce which role is relevant; and if the account given above is correct regarding how these fit into the overall scheme of the argument, then there is no "arbitrariness" or "randomness" in Plato's usage. Bostock's central argument that 255B3 is crucially ambiguous—under one reading the premises are true but the argument invalid, under the other reading the argument is valid but the premises are false—is incorrect. As I remarked in chapter 3 when discussing the argument, all that is required to show X and Y to be distinct is that X have some property that Y doesn't. And this property can as well be a property of individual X's as anything else; after all, a UNIO-property of X is nonetheless one of its properties, and if Y does not also have this property then X and Y are distinct.

Vlastos (1973) distinguishes also these two uses, but (like me) attributes them to the sentence as a whole rather than to the noun phrases, as Bostock does. In discussing the possibility of representing this distinction by different sorts of subjects in the philosopher's language, Vlastos (1973, p. 321 n. 9) says:

> I rejected this option . . . on a substantive ground: while advertising the shift in function, from singular to general, in the subject term, this alternative notation would have obscured the still more important fact that for Plato it is exactly the same entity whose dual role commissions it to do both jobs in his ontology: the same metaphysical entity which instantiates the [apparent] singular-term in ["Man is$_{op}$ eternal"—which corresponds to our "Man DK-participates in Eternal"] is itself instantiable, exactly like the [apparent] predicate-term in ["Man is$_{pp}$ mortal"—which corresponds to our "Man UNIO-participates in Mortal"]. Plato's ontology violates on principle the Fregean doctrine that no concept-naming expression may ever be used predicatively (a doctrine which is itself not free from difficulty, entailing, as Frege saw, the paradoxical conclusion that "the concept *horse* is not a concept"). . . . For Plato every concept-naming word is systematically ambivalent: it always names a unique metaphysical existent, and yet its principal use is predicative, serving in this capacity not only manifestly, when it occurs in predicate position, but frequently also when its apparent function is only nominative, as, e.g., when it is the subject term of a Pauline predication [= our UNIO-participation].

It thus seems clear that the sort of "ambivalence" Vlastos discusses here amounts precisely to our different kinds of participation, and that it would be decidedly anti-Platonic (although perhaps it would be Fregean) to trace it to an ambiguity in either the subject or the predicate of the sentence under consideration. In contrast, the present interpretation finds the ordinary-language statement ambiguous, but traces the ambiguity to three types of participation when it is cast into the philosopher's language. Not only is this "adequate" (in the sense to be discussed in the next section), but it is most clearly Platonic.

THE PHILOSOPHER'S LANGUAGE

In chapter 4, I urged that "mixed theories" would be necessary if one is to account simultaneously for (1) the 259E5–6 requirement that discourse owes its existence to the interweaving of forms with one another, and (2) explain what specific "part of reality" gives determinate meaning to, and enters into the truth conditions of, individual sentences. I furthermore there urged that schema X (followed by schemata XI and XII) give the most acceptable account of (2). (Schema X, it will be recalled, invoked the notion of "incompatibility ranges" for predicates, and analyzed negative predication as "partaking of some other form in the same incompatibility range.") This was primarily due to its solution of the overarching question of how to overcome Parmenides' Problem in a philosophically respectable and textually responsible way. I recommended it in spite of its inability to explain the issue raised by (1), since the analysis of positive predication did not mention any blending of forms (although I did mention that this portion of the account would be resolved by an account of the "background" of a mixed theory). We are now in a position to explain this issue, and to see how the συμπλοκή requirement is met. I will make use of schema X here because, in addition to its advantages recounted in chapter 4, I find that it fits most naturally into this "background" portion of the Platonic framework; but it should be mentioned that various other schemata could also adopt this "background" with only minor modifications—for example, schemata IX, XI, XII.

I claim that the συμπλοκή of 259E6 is not only the specific blendings indicated by looking for the part of reality that corresponds to the individual sentences under consideration (as the pure correspondence schemata of chapter 4 would have it), but also includes, as an even more important aspect, the notions of DK-, UNIO-, and ENIO-participation. It is the role of these different types of participation, as they are manifested among the forms, that accounts for all the "inter-form relations" (to use Vlastos's phrase) that make speech possible.[21]

---

21. I will not pursue the issue of finding other places where Plato uses these relations, but am confident it can be done. One obvious place to start is the method of division as explained in the *Sophist.* Another is the "clever αἰτία" of the *Phaedo.* I think (following

We have already seen that in the philosopher's language, Plato can talk "directly" about the forms qua immutable objects by using the same sort of participation language he used in his earlier theory, namely DK-participation. Any god-school (of the sort described in chapter 3) is committed to being able to do at least this much: just as we express $\ulcorner \alpha$ is $\Phi \urcorner$, where Ref(α) is a physical object, by the translation $\ulcorner \alpha$ DK-participates in $\Phi \urcorner$ (where Ref(Φ) is a form)—and this yields an explanation of why Ref(α) is a physical object which is Φ; so too $\ulcorner \Psi$ is $\Phi \urcorner$, where this time Ref(Ψ) is a form, is also to be expressed as $\ulcorner \Psi$ DK-participates in $\Phi \urcorner$. And this, too, is to yield an explanation of why Ref(Ψ) qua form is Φ. Different god-schools might give the "explanation" in different ways; that is not at issue here—the present discussion insists only that the god-schools are committed to being able to express such sentences, and committed to producing some such "explanation."

The innovation in the *Sophist* is to pick out two further types of participation to which any god-school must be committed in addition to DK-participation. And along with this goes a commitment to an "explanation clause" for them. Finally, the *Sophist* will show us how to use the form Difference to account for various kinds of negative statements we might make. (It seems to have gone unnoticed by the commentators discussed in chapter 4 that even if they can explain the truth conditions of a sentence like 'Theaetetus is not flying', they will not thereby have an account of the truth conditions for 'No man flies'. Their preoccupation with the specific example mentioned by Plato in his discussion of the issue of falsity seems to have diverted their attention from giving a general account of all negation—something Plato clearly thinks he has offered.[22]

So, what kinds of sentences has Plato offered us an account of? The backdrop portion of the mixed theory is what was mentioned in the preceding few paragraphs—namely, the various DK-, UNIO-, and ENIO-participations which obtain among the forms. Obviously this will completely suffice as an explanation of why the συμπλοκή requirement was

---

Vlastos 1973, p. 321) that the notion of UNIO-participation is especially useful in these places. (He refers to his 1969, p. 102ff.). I limit myself here to explaining what devices are *available* in the philosopher's language.

22. These commentators *should* have noticed another example sentence mentioned by Plato at 262C9: "(A) man learns." Had they tried their account of negation or falsity on this type of sentence, they would have noticed immediately that it couldn't work. What's needed is an account of negation's interaction with *general* sentences.

thought to be so important. Without them there can be no discourse, since (by premise (3)) there would be nothing for them to be about.

I will now offer a correspondence portion of this mixed theory. But first let me remind the reader that the notion of nomic necessity is presupposed by UNIO- and ENIO-sentences. (It is here, I think, that the god-schools will find the requisite "explanation clause" lurking.) As I said above, this means that Plato does not give an account of "strictly accidental generalizations," but only of those generalizations with a nomic, or law-like force. But as I also said above, it is not obvious to me that Plato believes that there really are any truly accidental generalizations. Rather, it seems that part of his point in postulating a world of forms is to show how the truths of the physical world follow from, or are explained by, the necessary or law-like truths that obtain in the world of forms.

I also remind the reader that the "qua" locutions are used merely to disambiguate the ordinary-language sentence under consideration—to indicate that we are talking about "ordinary predication" or of the term "in its naming role." After all, a natural-language sentence like *Reading is interesting* can be seen to mean either that all (most) actual cases of reading something are interesting experiences, or that the concept of reading is an interesting concept. The philosopher's language gives different accounts of these two meanings, so when I wish to emphasize that it is the second meaning we are analyzing, I will say *Reading (qua form) is interesting*. When it is the first meaning we are analyzing, I use *All reading is interesting;* and although in English such a sentence might seem "extensional," admitting of accidental generalizations, the analysis shows that, in the philosopher's language, it is a nomic sentence. It is therefore best to recall that the 'all' is merely added in order to mark which disambiguation we are discussing. We are really giving an analysis of one sense of the original *Reading is interesting*—and according to the philosopher's language this has nomic force. Of course this sentence has yet another meaning, roughly, "among the interesting things, you will find instances of reading." To mark off this sense for separate treatment I will use *Some reading is interesting*. Again, although this looks as if it admits accidental (existential) generalizations, it is best to revert to the original *Reading is interesting* and focus on the sense in which it means "it follows from laws that some instances of reading should be interesting."

The schema here also makes use of the notion: participating in F with respect to G, where F is a "relative form." (The only relative forms considered here are Sameness and Difference). Since we have distinct types of participation at our disposal, we will have distinct types of "relative participation." One way to understand these, the most straightforward way, is to take "F with respect to G" as indicating yet another form. Then "the Same with respect to G" would be the form which indicates the property *being the same as* G (which is not to be confused with the property G). DK-participation in such a form would yield identity-with-G. If we adopt an incompatibility understanding of Different, the phrase "the Different with respect to G" will become "some form which is incompatible with G." DK-participation in this amounts to distinctness, because all forms are necessarily distinct from one another; UNIO-participation in this means "all instances of the subject-form must partake of the Different with respect to G," that is, "all instances of the subject-form partake of some form incompatible with G." I have already mentioned that an incompatibility understanding of the Different is not the only possibility here. We might, for instance, appeal to the schema XII reading of "differs from all instances of the unnegated predicate." In such a case we would give somewhat different accounts of DK- or UNIO-participation in the Different with respect to G. (Of course, the preceding explanations were for *our* benefit. Plato would no doubt wish to have the train of explanation go the other way: we are to understand "is distinct from," "is incompatible with," "is identical to," and the like, *because* we already understand the (ontologically prior) roles of the forms Sameness and Difference and how DK-, UNIO-, and ENIO-participation work. Further discussion of the intuitive content of this schema is in the next footnote.)

Schema XVIIa:

($2a_1$) The meaning of $\ulcorner \Phi$ is identical to $\Psi \urcorner$ is that Ref(Φ) DK-participates in the Same with respect to Ref(Ψ).

($2a_2$) The meaning of $\ulcorner \Phi$ is distinct from $\Psi \urcorner$ is that Ref(Ψ) DK-participates in the Different with respect to Ref(Ψ).

($2a_3$) The meaning of $\ulcorner \alpha$ (qua physical object or qua form) is $\Phi \urcorner$ is that Ref(α) DK-participates in Ref(Φ).

($2a_4$) The meaning of $\ulcorner \alpha$ (qua physical object or qua form) is not $\Phi \urcorner$ is that Ref(α) DK-participates in some form F which UNIO-participates in the Different with respect to Ref(Φ).

($2a_5$) The meaning of $\ulcorner$ All Φ is $\Psi \urcorner$ is that Ref(Φ) UNIO-participates in Ref(Ψ).

($2a_6$) The meaning of ⌜All Φ is not Ψ⌝ is that Ref(Φ) UNIO-participates in the Different with respect to Ref(Ψ).

($2a_7$) The meaning of ⌜Some Φ is Ψ⌝ is that Ref(Φ) ENIO-participates in Ref(Ψ).

($2a_8$) The meaning of ⌜Some Φ is not Ψ⌝ is that Ref(Φ) ENIO-participates in the Different with respect to Ref(Ψ).

The reading of ($2a_4$) will be facilitated if one notices that, according to ($2a_6$), the "F UNIO-participates in the Different with respect to Ref(Φ)" of ($2a_4$) amounts to "necessarily, no F is Φ." Hence the meaning of the ($2a_4$) type of sentence is that the subject DK-participates in some form which prohibits it from DK-participating in the predicate form. This is our way of adopting schema X into the present account. Informally, the DK-participation of two forms in Sameness amounts to their identity; the DK-participation of two forms in Difference amounts to their distinctness; the UNIO-participation of form X in Difference with respect to form Y is necessary distinctness of all instances; the ENIO-participation of form X in Difference with respect to form Y amounts to distinctness of some instances. It should be noted therefore, that negation here amounts to "internal negation": the negation of 'Form X UNIO-participates in form Y', i.e., the negation of 'Necessarily, everything which DK-participates in X also DK-participates in Y', is 'Form X does not UNIO-participate in form Y', i.e., is 'Necessarily, nothing which DK-participates in X also DK-participates in Y', or in other words is 'Necessarily, everything that DK-participates in X also DK-participates in a form incompatible with Y'. It is not the "external negation," which would be 'It is not the case that form X UNIO-participates in form Y', that is, 'It is not necessary that everything that DK-participates in X also DK-participates in Y'. Similar remarks hold for the ENIO-participation: the negation of 'Form X ENIO-participates in' is 'Necessarily, something which DK-participates in X does not DK-participate in Y' rather than 'It is not necessary that something that DK-participates in X also DK-participates in Y'.

Making due allowance for the fact that Plato's general statements are intensional (in having a law-like character) and (perhaps) admit of exceptions, we can see that his philosopher's language has all the expressive power of the Aristotelian syllogistic statements (A, E, I, O statements) and also allows for identity and nonidentity, and for names of individuals (at least as subjects). Viewed from this vantage point, Aristotelian statements are a step backward. (Although viewed as a logical system, with rules of inference, Aristotelian syllogistic is an astonishing advance).

A shortcoming in schema XVIIa is that there is no explicit correspondence given in the philosopher's language for sentences asserting existence and nonexistence of individuals (whether they be physical objects or forms); that is, there is no replacement for premise (2b) of Parmenides' Problem. At the end of chapter 4 I considered some speculations concerning how Plato could have attempted to respond to the challenge posed by negative existentials. Now that we have the various types of participation at our disposal, we are in a position to restate these schemata (XIV and XVI). The schema which restates Owen's XIV is:

Schema XVIIb:

(2b$_1$) The meaning of $\ulcorner$α (qua physical object or qua form) exists$\urcorner$ is that Ref(α) DK-participates in Being.

(2b$_2$) The meaning of $\ulcorner$Φ's exist$\urcorner$ is that Ref(Φ) ENIO-participates in Being.[23]

(2b$_3$) The meaning of $\ulcorner$α (qua physical object) does not exist$\urcorner$ is that Ref(α) DK-participates in some Form F which UNIO-participates in the Difference with respect to Being.

(2b$_4$) The meaning of $\ulcorner$Φ's do not exist$\urcorner$ is that Ref(Φ) UNIO-participates in the Different with respect to Being.

Incorporating schema XIV into schema XVIIb to explain the nonexistence of certain entities (by means of the (2b$_3$) and (2b$_4$) clauses) has both advantages and a disadvantage. The advantages are, first, that it conforms to the account given in schema XVIIa for "ordinary" predication, thus bringing out more clearly the "fused" sense of ἔστιν and how the Eleatic Stranger would think he was truly committing parricide against Father Parmenides. For, so long as the form indicated in sentences containing ἔστιν is taken as Being, the correspondence portion of the theory for (what we would call) existence/nonexistence claims is just what is already in XVIIa, and hence there is no need for a separate XVIIb. That is to say, schema XVIIb is really just schema XVIIa with the understanding that when 'exists' is in a sentence it gets translated into "participates in Being" in the philosopher's language. Thus, if we replace Φ in clause 2a$_3$ of schema XVIIa with 'exist', and make Ref(exist) denote Being, we

---

23. Or, perhaps, UNIO-participates. It is not obvious whether Plato would acknowledge a difference.

generate clause $2b_3$ of schema XVIIb. Similarly, clause $2a_6$ of schema XVIIa would generate clause $2b_4$ of schema XVIIb. The second advantage follows from this, as Owen emphasizes, namely that it shows "not-Being to exist as much as Being." For under the schema XVIIb analysis, (participation in) not-Being (for nonexistence claims) amounts to (UNIO-participation in) the Different with respect to Being. If we believe that "the Different with respect to X" exists as much as X, then it seems that we have given here good sense to the claim that not-Being exists as much as Being. On the other hand, this commits Plato to a decidedly unplatonic, "Meinongian" view that the terms denoting (as we would say) nonexistent objects (e.g., 'Pegasus') or terms denoting (again, as we would say) unsatisfied predicates (e.g., 'centaur') nonetheless pick out a (group of) entities—but these entities don't exist, since they DK-participate in a form that UNIO-participates in Difference with respect to Being. (For example, a form like "Occurs in works of fiction only.") This is the consequence of Owen's remarks cited in discussing schema XIV, at the end of chapter 4.

The Owen schema XIV is not the only possibility for a Plato-like account of claims of existence and nonexistence. Another account, suggested by Furth, was schema XVI in which we introduce another type of participation as well as the notion of a "second-level form"—a form all of whose instances are forms. In such an account we would assign Being to be a second-level form, and we would call our new type of participation (say) X-participation. The second-level form of Being is not akin to the first-level notion presupposed up to now in the account of Being. For, a first-level form of Being has individuals (physical objects or forms) participating in it in a DK manner. And so, these individuals directly manifest the property Being. Here, we want to say instead that, when a form F participates in Being in the X manner, then there are instances of F. Along with the proposal to make Being a second-level form is the proposal that there is another second-level form such that when form F participates in it in the X manner, this amounts to saying that there are no F's. In trying to maintain the dictum that "not-Being exists as much as Being," we might call this new second-level form "not-Being." Again, this is a second-level form, not a first-level form. If it were first level, then the sort of things DK-participating in it would be Meinongian nonexistents. Here the goal is not to countenance such Meinongian objects. So, under this proposal, Being and not-Being are second-level forms, and X-participation of a form Φ in one of them is defined as:

⌜Φ X-participates in Being⌝ is true iff there is something which DK-participates in Ref(Φ).
⌜Φ X-participates in not-Being⌝ is true iff there is nothing which DK-participates in Ref(Φ).

Under this proposal, in place of schema XVIIb we would have:

Schema XVIIIb:

(2b$_1$) The meaning of ⌜α (qua physical object or qua Form) exists⌝ is that Ref(α) DK-participates in some Form F which X-participates in Being.
(2b$_2$) The meaning of ⌜Φ's exist⌝ is that Ref(Φ) X-participates in Being.
(2b$_3$) The meaning of ⌜Φ's do not exist⌝ is that Ref(Φ) X-participates in not-Being.

Perhaps a few things should be said about this schema XVIIIb. First, it is the aim of this schema not to countenance nonexisting objects; therefore, there can be no paraphrase of sentences like ⌜α (qua physical object) does not exist⌝. For, if we were to allow any translation at all of such sentences, we would be admitting some entity into the ontology, claiming that it partakes of some form F, but then adding that F X-participates in not-Being. (Thus the alleged entity is "a mere possibilia.") But it is precisely this sort of move that schema XVIIIb is designed to block, and what sets it apart from schema XVIIb. The consequence is that we have a residual type of sentence for which there is no translation into the philosopher's language.

Secondly, although it might appear as if schema XVIIIb is subject to a Russell-type paradox about whether not-Being participates in itself, it in fact isn't, because X-participation is defined in terms of DK-participation. Specifically, letting 'b' and 'n' stand for the forms Being and not-Being respectively, and letting DK(x,y) and X(x,y) stand for "x DK-participates in y" and "x X-participates in y" respectively, we have the following two principles from schema XVIIIb:

$$(\forall y) \, [(\exists x) \, DK(x,y) \leftrightarrow X(y,b)]$$
$$(\forall y) \, [\sim(\exists x) \, DK(x,y) \leftrightarrow X(y,n)]$$

Instantiating 'y' to each of 'b' and 'n' in both of these principles, we get

$$[(\exists x) \, DK(x,b) \leftrightarrow X(b,b)]$$
$$[(\exists x) \, DK(x,n) \leftrightarrow X(n,b)]$$

$$[\sim(\exists x)\ DK(x,b) \leftrightarrow X(b,n)]$$
$$[\sim(\exists x)\ DK(x,n) \leftrightarrow X(n,n)]$$

which are not contradictory. If we add the plausible assumptions that some form exists, and no form does not exist, which can be represented as (restricting our quantifiers to range over forms):

$$(\exists x)DK(x,b)$$
$$\sim(\exists x)DK(x,n)$$

then we can apply simple truth functional logic to derive

$$X(b,b)$$
$$X(n,n)$$
$$\sim X(b,n)$$
$$\sim X(n,b)$$

that is, Being and not-Being each X-participate in themselves and neither X-participates in the other. Of course, given that they are each forms, then the formulas imply that they each DK-participate in Being:

$$DK(b,b)$$
$$DK(n,b).$$

But this is not paradoxical—there is no Russell-like contradiction here.

Which of schemata XVIIb and XVIIIb would Plato choose, if we were to point out the issues involved? It seems to me that he would want schema XVIIIb in preference to XVIIb, mostly because of the "Meinongian" consequences of the latter, and in spite of the former's inability to account for particular statements of nonexistence. (He might claim, for instance, that sentences like 'Pegasus does not exist' and the like are always shorthand—even in natural language—for statements like 'Winged horses do not exist', and then ($2b_3$) of schema XVIIIb can be put to work on this). However, if we are more faithful to what Plato says, it seems clear that we should say that XVIIb is "closer to the text" in that, by not considering the problem at all, schema XVIIIb is what is entailed by the schema XVIIIa that *can* be found in the text.

In either case, we can see why Plato is truly said to have "shown that not-Being is, in the same sense that Being is," and therefore to have disposed of Parmenides' Problem.

Ackrill, J., 1955. "συμπλοκὴ ἐιδῶν." *Bulletin of the Institute of Classical Studies of the University of London* 2:31–35. Reprinted in G. Vlastos, *Plato I: Metaphysics and Epistemology,* pp. 201–9. Garden City, N.Y.: Anchor Books, 1970. Page references are to reprint.

————. 1957. "Plato and the Copula. *Sophist* 251–259." *Journal of Hellenic Studies* 77:1–6. Reprinted in G. Vlastos, *Plato I: Metaphysics and Epistemology,* pp. 210–22. Garden City, N.Y.: Anchor Books, 1970. Page references are to reprint.

Allan, D. 1954. "The Problem of the *Cratylus.*" *American Journal of Philology* 75:271–87.

Anscombe, G. E. M. 1966. "The New Theory of Forms." *Monist* 50:403–20.

Ayers, M. 1975. "Locke's Doctrine of Substance and Essence." *Philosophical Quarterly* 25:1–27.

Barnes, J. 1982. *The Presocratic Philosophers,* rev. ed. London: Routledge & Kegan Paul.

Barwise, J., and J. Perry. 1983. *Situations and Attitudes.* Cambridge, Mass., MIT Press.

Bluck, R. 1957. "False Statement in the *Sophist.*" *Journal of Hellenic Studies* 77:181–87.

Bostock, D. 1984. "Plato on 'is not.' " *Oxford Studies in Ancient Philosophy* 2:89–119.

Brown, L. 1986. "Being in the *Sophist:* A Syntactical Enquiry." *Oxford Studies in Ancient Philosophy* 4:49–70.

Carlson, G. 1980. *Reference to Kinds in English.* New York: Garland Press.

Cartwright, R. 1960. "Negative Existentials." *Journal of Philosophy* 57:629–39.

Cherniss, H. 1957. "The Relation of the *Timaeus* to Plato's Later Dialogues." *American Journal of Philology* 78:225–66. Reprinted in R. E. Allen, *Studies in Plato's Metaphysics,* pp. 339–78. London: Routledge & Kegan Paul, 1968. Page references are to reprint.

Cornford, F. 1935. *Plato's Theory of Knowledge.* London: Routledge & Kegan Paul.

Dahl, Ö. 1985. *Tense and Aspect Systems*. Oxford: Blackwell.

Demos, R. 1939. *The Philosophy of Plato*. New York: Scribner's.

Donnellan, K. 1974. "Speaking of Nothing." *Philosophical Review* 83:3–31.

Dunn, J. 1971. *The Political Philosophy of John Locke*. Cambridge: Cambridge University Press.

Fauconnier, G. 1985. *Mental Spaces*. Cambridge, Mass.: MIT Press.

Ferg, S. 1976. "Plato on False Statement: Relative Being, A Part of Being, and Not-Being in the *Sophist*." *Journal of the History of Philosophy* 14:336–42.

Fitch, F. 1960. "Some Logical Aspects of Reference and Existence." *Journal of Philosophy* 57:640–47.

Fodor, J. A. 1983. *The Modularity of Mind*. Cambridge, Mass.: MIT Press.

———. 1987. *Psychosemantics*. Cambridge, Mass.: MIT Press.

Fodor, J. D. 1985. "Situations and Representations." *Linguistics and Philosophy* 8:13–22.

Frede, M. 1967. *Prädikation und Existenzaussage. Hyponmemata* 18. Göttingen.

———. 1987. "Introduction: The Study of Ancient Philosophy." *Essays in Ancient Philosophy*, pp. ix–xxvii. Minneapolis: University of Minnesota Press.

Furth, M. 1968. "Elements of Eleatic Ontology." *Journal of the History of Philosophy* 6:111–32. Reprinted in A. Mourelatos, *The Presocratics*. New York: Anchor Books, 1974, pp. 241–70. Page references are to reprint.

Gale, R. 1975. *Negation and Not-Being*. American Philosophical Quarterly Monograph Series 10. Oxford: Blackwell.

Gödel, K. 1944. "Russell's Mathematical Logic." Pp. 125–53 *in* P. A. Schilpp, *The Philosophy of Bertrand Russell*. LaSalle, Ill.: Library of Living Philosophers.

Guthrie, W. 1978. *A History of Greek Philosophy*. Vol. 5: *The Later Plato and the Academy*. Cambridge: Cambridge University Press.

Hackforth, R. 1945. "False Statement in the *Sophist*." *Classical Quarterly* 39:56–58.

Hamlyn, D. 1955. "The Communion of Forms and the Development of Plato's Logic." *Philosophical Quarterly* 5:289–302.

Heinaman, R. 1983. "Being in the *Sophist*." *Archiv für Geschichte der Philosophie* 65:1–17.

Hintikka, K. J. J. 1966. "Studies in the Logic of Existence." *Monist* 50:55–76.

Jackendoff, R. 1983. *Semantics and Cognition*. Cambridge, Mass.: MIT Press.

———. 1987. *Consciousness and the Computational Mind*. Cambridge, Mass.: MIT Press.

Johnson-Laird, P. 1983. *Mental Models: Towards a Cognitive Science of Language, Inference and Consciousness.* Cambridge: Cambridge University Press.

Kahn, C. 1970. "More on Parmenides." *Review of Metaphysics* 23:333–40.

———. 1973. *The Verb 'to be' in Ancient Greek.* Dordrecht: Reidel.

Kaplan, D. 1972. "What is Russell's Theory of Descriptions?" Pp. 227–44 *in* D. F. Pears, *Bertrand Russell.* New York: Doubleday.

Ketchum, R. 1978. "Participation and Predication in *Sophist* 251–260." *Phronesis* 23:42–63.

Keyt, D. 1973. "The Falsity of 'Theaetetus Flies' (*Sophist* 263B)." Pp. 285–305 in *Exegesis and Argument,* ed. E. Lee, A. Mourelatos and R. Rorty. *Phronesis* Supplementary Volume 1.

Kinsch, W. 1974. *The Representation of Meaning in Memory.* Hillsdale, N.J.: Erlbaum Press.

Kirk, G., and J. Raven. 1957. *The Presocratic Philosophers.* Cambridge: Cambridge University Press.

Kirk, G., J. Raven, and M. Schofield. 1983. *The Presocratic Philosophers.* 2d ed. Cambridge: Cambridge University Press.

Kostman, J. 1973. "False Logos and Not-Being in Plato's *Sophist.*" Pp. 192–212 *in* J. M. E. Moravcsik, *Patterns in Plato's Thought.* Dordrecht: Reidel.

Krifka, M. 1987. *An Outline of Genericity.* Technical Report SNS-Bericht 87–25. Seminar für natürlich-sprachliche Systeme: Universität Tübingen.

Lakoff, G. 1987. *Women, Fire, and Dangerous Things: What Categories Reveal About the Mind.* Chicago: University of Chicago Press.

Lawler, J. 1973. *Studies in English Generics.* University of Michigan Papers in Linguistics 1. Ann Arbor, Mich.

Lee, E. 1972. "Plato on Negation and Not-Being in the *Sophist.*" *Philosophical Review* 81:267–304.

Lewis, D. 1972. "General Semantics." Pp 169–218 in *Semantics of Natural Language,* ed. D. Davidson and G. Harman. Dordrecht: Reidel.

Lewis, F. 1974. "Plato's Paradox of Being: *Sophist* 249e ff." Unpublished.

———. 1975. "Did Plato Discover an ἔστιν of Identity?" *California Studies in Classical Antiquity* 8:113–43.

———. 1976. "Plato on 'Not'." *California Studies in Classical Antiquity* 9:89–115.

Lorenz, K., and J. Mittelstrass. 1966a. "Theaitetos Fleigt." *Archiv für Geschichte der Philosophie* 48:113–52.

———. 1966b. "On Rational Philosophy of Language: The Programme in Plato's *Cratylus* Reconsidered." *Mind* 75:1–29.

McDowell, J. 1982. "Falsehood and Not-Being in Plato's *Sophist.*" Pp.

115–34 *in* M. Schofield and M. Nussbaum, *Language and Logos*. Cambridge: Cambridge University Press.

Malcolm, H. 1967. "Plato's Analysis of τὸ ὄν and τὸ μὴ ὄν in the *Sophist*." *Phronesis* 12:130–146.

———. 1985. "Remarks on an Incomplete Rendering of Being in the *Sophist*." *Archiv für Geschichte der Philosophie* 67:162–65.

Matthen, M. 1983. "Greek Ontology and the 'is' of Truth." *Phronesis* 28:113–35.

Moravcsik, J. 1960. "συμπλοκὴ εἰδῶν and the Genesis of λόγος." *Archiv für Geschichte der Philosophie* 42:117–29.

———. 1962. "Being and Meaning in the *Sophist*." *Acta Filosophica Fennica* 14:23–78.

———. 1976. "Critical Notice of P. Seligman, *Being and Not-Being*." *Canadian Journal of Philosophy* 4:737–44.

Mourelatos, A. 1974. *The Presocratics*. New York: Anchor Books.

———. 1979. "Some Alternatives in Interpreting Parmenides." *Monist* 62:3–14.

Neal, G. 1975. "Editor's Introduction." Pp. 9–29 *in* R. Bluck, *Plato's Sophist*. Manchester: Manchester University Press.

Nehamas, A. 1979. "Self-Predication and Plato's Theory of Forms." *American Philosophical Quarterly* 16:93–103.

———. 1982. "Participation and Predication in Plato's Later Thought." *Revue Metaphysics* 36:343–74.

Nunberg, G. 1977. *The Pragmatics of Reference*. Ph.D. diss., CUNY; distributed by Indiana University Linguistics Club, 1978.

Owen, G. E. L. 1968. "Dialectic and Eristic in the Treatment of Forms." Pp. 103–25 in *Papers of the Third Symposium Aristotelicum*, ed. G. E. L. Owen. Oxford: Oxford University Press. Reprinted in G. E. L. Owen, *Logic, Science, and Dialectic*. Ithaca, N.Y.: Cornell University Press, 1986, pp. 221–38. Page references are to reprint.

———. 1970. "Plato on Not-Being." Pp. 223–67 *in* G. Vlastos, *Plato I: Metaphysics and Epistemology*. Garden City, N.Y.: Anchor Books.

Parsons, T. 1980. *Non-Existent Objects*. New Haven: Yale University Press.

Peck, A. 1952. "Plato and the μεγίστα γένη of the *Sophist*." *Classical Quarterly* 2:32–56.

———. 1962. "Plato's *Sophist*: the συμπλοκὴ τῶν εἰδῶν." *Phronesis* 7:46–66.

———. 1962a. "Plato versus Parmenides." *Philosophical Review* 71:159–84.

Pelletier, F. J. 1975. "On Reading 'Incompatibility' in Plato's *Sophist*." *Dialogue* 14:143–46.

———. 1983. "Plato on Not-Being: Some Interpretations of the συμπλοκὴ εἰδῶν (259e) and Their Relation to Parmenides' Problem." *Midwest Studies in Philosophy* 8:35–65.

Peterson, S. 1973. "A Reasonable Self-Predication Premise for the Third Man Argument." *Philosophical Review* 82:451–70.

Pfeiffer, W. 1972. "True and False Speech in Plato's *Cratylus.*" *Canadian Journal of Philosophy* 2:87–104.

Philip, J. 1968. "False Statement in the *Sophistes.*" *Transactions and Proceedings of the American Philological Society* 99:315–27.

Pippin, R. 1979. "Negation and Not Being in Wittgenstein's *Tractatus* and Plato's *Sophist.*" *Kantstudien* 70:179–96.

Prior, W. 1980. "Plato's Analysis of Being and Not-Being in the *Sophist.*" *Southern Journal of Philosophy* 18:199–211.

Quine, W. V. 1951. *Mathematical Logic.* Cambridge, Mass.: Harvard University Press.

Ray, A. 1984. *For Images: An Interpretation of Plato's Sophist.* Lanham, Md.: University Press of America.

Redman, R. 1973. "Exists." *Mind* 82:56–72.

Richardson, M. 1976. "True and False Names in the *Cratylus.*" *Phronesis* 21:135–45.

Robinson, R. 1950. "Forms and Error in Plato's *Theaetetus.*" *Philosophical Review* 59:3–30.

Rorty, R. 1967. *The Linguistic Turn.* Chicago: University of Chicago Press.

Rosen, S. 1983. *Plato's Sophist: The Drama of Original and Image.* New Haven: Yale University Press.

Ross, D. 1951. *Plato's Theory of Forms.* Oxford: Oxford University Press.

Routley, R. 1980. *Exploring Meinong's Jungle and Beyond.* Philosophy Department, Australia National University, Departmental Monograph 3.

Runciman, W. 1965. *Plato's Later Epistemology.* Cambridge: Cambridge University Press.

Sayre, K. 1969. *Plato's Analytic Method.* Chicago: University of Chicago Press.

———. 1970. "Falsehood, Forms and Participation in the *Sophist.*" *Noûs* 4:81–91.

———. 1976. "*Sophist* 263B Revisited." *Mind* 85:581–86.

———. 1983. *Plato's Late Ontology: A Riddle Resolved.* Princeton: Princeton University Press.

Schank, R. 1975. *Conceptual Information Processing.* Amsterdam: North Holland.

Schipper, E. 1964. "The Meaning of Existence in Plato's *Sophist.*" *Phronesis* 9:38–44.

―――. 1965. *Forms in Plato's Later Dialogues.* The Hague: Nijhoff.

Schubert, L., and F. J. Pelletier. 1987. "Problems in the Representation of the Logical Form of Generics, Bare Plurals, and Mass Terms." Pp. 385–451 *in* E. LePore, *New Directions in Semantics.* London: Academic Press.

Seligman, P. 1974. *Being and Not-Being: An Introduction to Plato's Sophist.* The Hague: Nijhoff.

Stough, C. 1976. "Explanation and the *Parmenides.*" *Canadian Journal of Philosophy* 6:379–401.

Swindler, J. 1980. "*Parmenides'* Paradox: Negative Reference and Negative Existentials." *Review of Metaphysics* 33:726–44.

Taylor, A. 1926. *Plato, The Man and his Work,* London: Methuen.

Teloh, H. 1981. *The Development of Plato's Metaphysics.* University Park: Pennsylvania State University Press.

Turnbull, R. 1964. "The Argument of the *Sophist.*" *Philosophical Quarterly* 14:23–34.

van Fraassen, B. 1969. "Logical Structure in Plato's *Sophist.*" *Review of Metaphysics* 22:482–98.

Vlastos, G. 1954. "The Third Man Argument in the *Parmenides.*" *Philosophical Review* 56:319–44.

―――. 1969. "Reasons and Causes in the *Phaedo.*" *Philosophical Review* 78:291–325. Reprinted in G. Vlastos, *Platonic Studies* pp. 76–110. Princeton: Princeton University Press, 1973. Page references are to reprint.

―――. 1970. *Plato I: Metaphysics and Epistemology.* Garden City, N.Y.: Anchor Books.

―――. 1972. "The Unity of the Virtues in the *Protagoras.*" *Review of Metaphysics* 25:415–58. Reprinted with corrections in G. Vlastos, *Platonic Studies,* pp. 221–69. Princeton: Princeton University Press, 1973. Page references are to reprint.

―――. 1973. "An Ambiguity in the *Sophist.*" Pp. 270–322 in *Platonic Studies,* ed. G. Vlastos. Princeton: Princeton University Press.

Weingartner, R. 1970. "Making Sense of the *Cratylus.*" *Phronesis* 15:5–25.

Wekler, D. 1970. "Existential Statements." *Journal of Philosophy* 67:376–88.

Wiggins, D. 1970. "Sentence Meaning, Negation, and Plato's Problem of Not-Being." Pp. 268–303 *in* G. Vlastos, *Plato I: Metaphysics and Epistemology.* Garden City, N.Y.: Anchor Books.

Woozley, A. 1964. "Editorial Introduction." *In* Locke, J., *An Essay Concerning Human Understanding.* London: Collins Books.

Xenakis, J. 1959. "Plato's *Sophist:* A Defense of Negative Expressions and a Doctrine of Sense and of Truth." *Phronesis* 4:29–43.

Index Locorum ☐

Name Index ☐

Subject Index ☐